THE MYSTERIOUS
PRIVATE
THOMPSON

The Double Life of
Sarah Emma Edmonds,
Civil War Soldier

Laura Leedy Gansler

Free Press

New York   London   Toronto   Sydney

FREE PRESS
A Division of Simon & Schuster, Inc.
1230 Avenue of the Americas
New York, NY 10020

Free Press and colophon are trademarks of Simon & Schuster, Inc.

For information regarding special discounts for bulk purchases,
please contact Simon & Schuster Special Sales
at 1-800-456-6798 or business@simonandschuster.com

Frontispiece: *Sarah Emma Edmonds as Frank Thompson,*
State Archives of Michigan

Designed by Jeanette Olender
Manufactured in the United States of America

1   3   5   7   9   10   8   6   4   2

Library of Congress Cataloging-in-Publication Data is available

ISBN-13: 978-0-7432-4280-6
ISBN-10: 0-7432-4280-7

To Jean and Bill Leedy

my beloved parents and dearest friends

CONTENTS

Preface   xi

ONE   New Brunswick, Canada, December 1841, 1

TWO   December 1860, 17

THREE   June 1861, 33

FOUR   July 1861, 51

FIVE   March 1862, 75

SIX   May 1862, 95

SEVEN   June 1862, 119

EIGHT   November 1862, 145

NINE   December 1862, 163

TEN   Flint, Michigan, March 1882, 179

ELEVEN   March 1882, 197

Afterword   221
Notes   223
Bibliography   239
Acknowledgments   243
Index   245

PREFACE

If you Google Emma Edmonds, you will be directed to any number of Web sites that recount her story: how, as a young farm girl, she adopted a male alias to escape an unwanted marriage, became a successful traveling salesman, enlisted under her alias in the Second Michigan Infantry at the outbreak of the Civil War, and served, undetected, for more than two years. But the focus of these sites, and of much that has been written about her, is her claim, made shortly after she left the army, that she also served as Union spy, repeatedly going behind enemy lines dressed as a slave boy, an Irish peddler woman, and even a Confederate soldier. These claims have been widely and uncritically accepted as fact by popular culture, despite the fact that Emma herself would neither confirm nor deny them in later years. Among some academics and historians, however, her espionage claims are a matter of dispute.

The more time I spent with Emma, however, the less interested I became in whether or not she ever actually did slip behind enemy lines. Instead, I became more and more fascinated with the actual woman behind the mythological denizen of pop history. I was curious about why a young girl in 1858 would choose to abandon everything she knew—her family, her home, even her own identity—for the chance to live as a man, a transformation that had much to say about both what kind of person she was, and what kind of society she lived in. I was curious about how she did it, and was amazed by both her ingenuity and fearlessness. I was also curious about how the experience of living such a monumental lie for so long affected her, and awed by the high personal price Emma had to pay for the audacity to seize for herself the privileges, independence, and opportunities that her world offered only to men. It was Emma's journey from Emma Edmonds to Frank Thompson, and back, and her struggle ever afterward to reconcile the girl and the soldier into a cohesive sense of self that ultimately captured my imagination; it is the story of that journey that follows.

THE MYSTERIOUS
PRIVATE THOMPSON

CHAPTER ONE

———————◆◆◆———————

New Brunswick, Canada
December 1841

DECEMBER is bitterly cold on the granite-strewn shores of Maga-guadavic Lake, and the night that Sarah Emma Edmondson was born was no exception. The lake was a three-foot sheet of ice; the rocky ground was covered in hard-packed snow. The vast, dense forest of hemlock and white pine surrounding the lake was dark and foreboding. But as cold and inhospitable as it was outside, a different, icier chill permeated the Edmondsons' small farmhouse the night that Betsy Edmondson gave birth to her sixth child, and fifth girl. Betsy's husband, Isaac, a stern and taciturn Scot, had been hoping for a son, as most farmers in New Brunswick did. It was hard work to carve a farm out of this remote wilderness, harder still to work the unforgiving land and to keep the forest at bay. It was a part of the world attractive only to tough, resourceful, and independent people, most of whom were there because, and only because, it afforded them the chance to work for themselves. What hired help could be found sought out one of the many logging camps along the Saint James or Miramichi rivers, where pay was better than most farmers could afford. The only way to ensure a decent workforce was to raise it yourself.[1]

The four older sisters did what they could to help, but for Isaac, it

1

was never enough. To make matters worse, Emma's only brother, Thomas, was an epileptic, and therefore of no use at all in Isaac's eyes.[2] Any farmer in his position would have been disappointed at the arrival of yet another girl. But Isaac's reaction went well beyond annoyance. Isaac was prone to violent rages, a tendency that had increased with the birth of each child, but always he held out hope that God would grant him healthy sons one day. But this time was different. Betsy was now well into her thirties and not strong to begin with. Years of childbearing had taken their toll, and this baby would likely be—and in fact was—her last. As that realization dawned on Isaac that December night, his periodic rage curdled into a permanent, poisonous anger that would seethe within him for the rest of his life.[3]

Emma, as the baby girl was called, could not immediately understand how unhappy a home she had joined, but years later, she would say that she believed that some of the despair and anger that permeated that house had seeped into her veins through her mother's milk. "I think I was born into this world with some dormant antagonism toward man. I hope I have outgrown it measurably, but my infant soul was impressed with a sense of my mother's wrongs before I ever saw the light, and I probably drew from her breast with my daily food my love of independence and hatred of male tyranny."[4]

Life on the shores of Magaguadavic Lake was never easy, but it was not always bleak; for brief golden moments each year, it was paradise. In the spring and autumn, the ill-humored, ice-covered forests of winter were transformed into an inviting, beautiful, magical realm. The woods were full of game—whitetail deer, moose, and black bear—and riotous color, and valuable hardwoods and other timber. When the ice finally melted, the lake became a playground. The huge granite boulders that laced the shoreline were perfect for climbing and hiding, and here and there tiny spits of sand formed private, pristine beaches. The water was cold even in the summer, but the few hardy children who grew up on its shores became accustomed to it. And fishing—for landlocked salmon, and bass, and trout—was almost always rewarding.

Even at the Edmondson farm, there were some perfect summer days, when the sun was shining, the winds were gentle, and loons sang their eerily beautiful songs to one another. On those rare days, Isaac's hard mood would soften. If it happened to be washing day, Betsy would make a picnic for the family to eat on the edge of the lake, and the children would laugh and swim and play while the clothes dried on lines strung between the trees. But such days were few and far between. Mostly, there was constant work. There were potatoes to plant and harvest, livestock to be cared for, cows to be milked, washing and cooking and cleaning to be done, repairs to be made on the barn and house and fences.[5]

The one thing in which Betsy had her way was her insistence that her children all receive an education. When she was old enough, Emma accompanied her siblings to the one-room parish school-house a few miles east on the road to Harvey. Emma loved it. She was a bright and eager student, with a phenomenal memory, and an avid reader all her life. At home, she read the Bible, for want of other material, and early on she committed large passages to memory. Her mother was deeply religious, and the family passed many of the long winter nights around the fire reading aloud from the Bible.[6]

When there was time to play, there were few friends to play with, and her sisters were too much older to be interested in the same games that Emma was. She loved the outdoors, and sometimes played with Thomas, but his physical limitations meant that much of the time she played by herself. By the time she was ten, she could ride a horse better than most boys, and hunted and fished with great skill. She could handle a canoe beautifully, and when time and weather permitted, she was often out on the lake, watching the bald eagles build their nests and the beavers prepare their lodges for the coming winter.[7]

As Emma grew older, she developed a wild, reckless streak; she was the one who broke the wild colts, or volunteered to climb to the highest point on the barn roof when it needed fixing. Family legend has it that she was so heedless of her own safety that one Sunday, Betsy told the parish priest, an old Scot, that she was afraid her daughter would meet an untimely end. But the old priest was sanguine. Emma often recalled hearing Betsy repeat his reply, "It is an auld saying, an' I believe a true one. A wean that's born to be hung 'll never be drooned."[8]

Despite her toughness, Emma was strikingly compassionate and gentle with anything, or anyone, weaker than she was. Above all, she was intensely protective of Thomas, who, although several years older, was frail, and often teased and bullied by other boys, as well as by his father. Thomas apparently accepted his fate with almost beatific tolerance, but Emma seethed with anger, and would frequently come fiercely to his defense.[9] She also tried to protect her mother from her father's frequent rages, but to little avail, other than to leave Emma with a deep anger that spilled over, in her young mind, to his entire gender. Looking back, Emma recalled that "in our family the women were not sheltered but enslaved; hence I naturally grew up to think of man as the implacable enemy for my sex. I had not an atom of faith in any one of them," except of course her dear Thomas. "If occasionally I met one who seemed a little better than others, I set him down in my mind as a wolf in sheep's clothing, and probably less worthy of trust than the rest."[10]

On the whole, life on the Edmondson farm was fairly routine. Days often followed days spent much like the ones before, and nights were even more similar. So Emma would always remember one evening, when she was about thirteen, that a peddler knocked on the door. Peddlers were not uncommon; stores were few and far between, and peddlers were the only source of many goods that the family could not make or grow themselves. But it was unusually late—the sky was nearly dark—and the woods were not safe at night. Betsy, ever hospitable, offered the man a bed for the night. To repay the kindness, as he was leaving the next morning, the man rummaged about in his wagon, and emerged with a small book, which he handed to Emma as a gift. It was a novel, the first novel Emma had ever seen; even if the family had a way to buy such luxuries, Isaac would never have allowed it.[11]

Emma was stunned, and thrilled. She had not received many gifts in her life, certainly none from a stranger. Unable to wait until the evening to examine it, she slipped it into the pocket of her skirt before she and her sisters headed out for a full day of planting potatoes. When they were far enough away from the house to avoid being seen, Emma triumphantly produced the book, to her sisters' amazement and delight. At first, they took turns reading it aloud to take their minds off their work. But soon they were so mesmerized by the story that all four of them flopped down in the warm dirt, and listened intently to the story. Few potatoes were planted that day.[12]

The book was called *Fanny Campbell, the Female Pirate Captain*, by Maturin Ballou, a well-known writer of popular fiction. It was the melodramatic story of a young New England girl in the eighteenth century, whose lover, William Lovell, was a sea captain. One day, he was the victim of a mutiny, and taken prisoner in the Caribbean. To rescue him, young Fanny cut off her curls, put on breeches, and went to sea. Eventually, after a series of exciting adventures, in which young Fanny became a feared pirate, she rescued her lover and lived happily ever after.[13]

For Emma's sisters the story was a welcome diversion from a dull task. But for Emma, it was something else entirely. Emma saw herself in Fanny, whom the author described as "a noble looking girl" but not a delicate "belle . . . ready to faint at the first sight of a reptile." Instead, just like Emma, Fanny could ride horses, shoot straight, and "do almost any brave and useful act." It was a revelation to Emma, almost as if the author knew her and was speaking directly to her. Later, Emma would remember that day as "the most wonderful day" in her life. "I felt as if an angel had touched me with a live coal from off the altar. All the latent energy of my nature was aroused, and each exploit of the heroine thrilled me to my finger tips. I went home that night with the problem of my life solved. I felt equal to any emergency. I was emancipated! And I could never again be a slave. When I read where Fanny cut off her brown curls, and donned the blue jacket, and stepped into the freedom and glorious independence of masculinity, I threw up my old straw hat and shouted." But her heroine did have one flaw. "The only drawback in my mind," Emma would recall later, "was this: She went to rescue an imprisoned lover, and I pitied her that she was only a poor love-sick girl, after all, like too many I had known, and I regretted that she had no higher ambition than running after a man. Perhaps later on in life, I had more charity, and gave her a credit mark for rescuing anybody—even a lover." Still, the story of Fanny Campbell gave Emma something to dream about. "From that time forth I never ceased planning escape, although it was years before I accomplished it." [14]

When Emma was seventeen, her father announced that she was to be married to an elderly, newly widowed neighbor. Emma initially agreed to the marriage, but only reluctantly, and the more she thought about the dreary life that stretched in front of her—a life like her mother's and that of her two oldest sisters, who had by then married and were now mothers themselves—the more she realized that she could not go through with it. Years later, she would explain that "very early in life I was forced to the conclusion, from close observation and bitter experience, that matrimony was not a safe investment for me." [15] The time had come, she concluded, to put into action the plan that Fanny Campbell had first planted in her reckless, restless mind.

There are several family versions of how Emma finally put her plan into action, but all that is known for certain is that at some point in her seventeenth year, she left home, as she put it, "unceremoniously, for parts unknown." [16] The most widely credited story is that she escaped home with the help of Betsy and Betsy's friend Annie Moffit, who lived in Salisbury, in Westmorland County. According to this version, Annie came to visit relatives in the neighboring village of Harvey, and stopped in to see her friend soon after Betsy learned that Isaac had decided to marry Emma off. Betsy, hoping to spare her youngest child the kind of life she had known herself, prevailed upon Annie to take the girl back to Salisbury with her. And so, one day, presumably while Isaac was working in the fields, Emma stowed away in the back of Annie's carriage.[17]

Betsy probably paid dearly for her role in her daughter's escape. The most credible version of what Emma did when she arrived in Salisbury, passed down from one generation to the next, is that Emma worked for a time in Annie's millinery shop, and then later moved to the even larger town of Moncton with Henriette Perrigo, the daughter of one of Annie's friends, to open her own hat shop. Emma lived and worked in Moncton for several months, possibly as long as a year, but was always fearful that her father would track her down and bring her back to Magaguadavic.[18]

All of her life, she had dreamed of becoming a foreign missionary, a career that appealed to both her deep faith and her sense of adventure. But before she could pursue that idea, something else caught her eye: an advertisement from a publishing house seeking traveling book salesmen for subscription publications. Subscription publishing, a growing industry in cities like Boston and Hartford, Connecticut, was a kind of bastard child of the proper publishing trade in New York. Instead of publishing a predetermined number of books, and selling them in bookstores in larger cities, subscription publishers sent salesmen out to smaller towns and rural areas to take orders based on samples, and printed copies to fill the orders. Most prestigious authors still favored the New York trade, which looked down its nose at subscription publishers for generally offering sentimental fiction on cheap paper with gaudy covers. But as American demographics shifted away from the high population areas on the East Coast, subscription publishing satisfied the growing demands of a highly literate and widely dispersed population.[19]

As the subscription publishing industry boomed, more and more salesmen were needed to cover an ever-widening territory, and publishers began running advertisements in local newspapers. One illustrative advertisement ran in a variety of New Brunswick periodicals at the time Emma was most likely living in Moncton.

Book agents wanted in New Brunswick to canvas for New Pictoral, Standard, and Historical, and Religious works. . . . The subscriber publishes a large number of most valuable books, very popular and of such a moral and religious influence that while good men may safely engage in their circulation they will confer a public BENEFIT and receive a FAIR COMPENSATION for their labour. To persons of enterprise and tact this business offers an opportunity for profitable enjoyment seldom to be met with. There is not a town in British North America where a right, honest and well-disposed person can fail selling from 50 to 200 volumes according to the population. Persons wishing to engage in their sale will receive promptly by mail a circular containing full particulars, with Directions to persons disposed to act as Agents, together with the terms on which they will be furnished by addressing the subscriber postpaid.[20]

This was just the kind of opportunity she had been hoping for. It would allow her to travel frequently, making it harder for Isaac to track her down, and it promised adventure, of a sort. It required no family connections or investment of capital, and, above all, it offered the chance to make more money than she had ever dreamed of. The one drawback, of course, was that traveling book salesmen had to be men. For some women, this would have been too high a hurdle to clear, but to Emma, always carrying the image of Fanny Campbell in her mind, the problem was easily solved. She simply wrote to a company in Hartford under the name of Franklin Thompson, and, while she was waiting for the materials to arrive, she gathered together a suitable disguise. Before "going over to the enemy,"[21] she procured a suit of men's clothing, and, once the canvassing materials arrived, she set about to transform herself, as her heroine, Fanny Campbell, had done. She cut her long thick hair in a classic man's haircut that accentuated her dark, intelligent eyes, her high cheekbones, and her rather squarish jaw. Emma's features, which were slightly too strong to be classically beautiful—as a woman she was more what was then called "handsome" than delicate—were well suited to her disguise. Her mouth was the most feminine feature of her face, with lips that were a bit softer and fuller than the average man's. Her body type— slim, muscular, and, at five feet, six inches, well within the average male height range at the time—also served her well. In all probability she did not have to bind her bosom—she was only seventeen, and had a naturally boyish, narrow-hipped figure. When she turned to look at herself in the mirror, she would have been pleased with the success of her transformation.

But changing her appearance was the easy part. The trick would be to act the part as well. Still, even this was easier for Emma than it would have been for many young women. Growing up as a farm girl in remote Magaguadavic meant that she had not been as bothered about learning the elaborate ins and outs of how ladies move and sit as most city girls would have been. She was used to walking through the forests and across the fields in long, loping athletic strides, and to riding astride rather than sidesaddle, which would have been viewed as a silly affectation on a working farm. And Emma had an unusual gift for mimicry. Once she put her mind to it, it would not have taken her long to pick up the tiny but telltale mannerisms she needed to convince the world she was male.

However, it was, technically, illegal to impersonate a man under British law at the time; it was viewed as an infringement on the rights of the "Lords of Creation." Such laws were rarely, if ever, enforced, and there was little danger of being sent to prison if she was discovered. The worst that could happen would be that she would be sent home to Isaac in disgrace, which, in Emma's mind, was probably worse than jail. But abandoning her identity also meant plunging herself into a world of isolation, where the truth could never be revealed, and even friends were, by necessity, kept at arm's length. It demanded an enormously high level of self-reliance, an ability to keep one's own counsel, and a willingness to forgo the intimacy with another person that only honesty can produce. It meant being willing to live a lie, with all the attendant moral and practical burdens that would entail. Above all, it meant being alone, even when she was not. But being alone was something Emma was used to, from the many solitary hours in the woods and on the lake as a child. In her excitement and nervousness, she was likely more focused on the challenge of pulling off her masquerade than on the consequences.

As Emma walked out into the streets for the first time in her new guise, carrying her valise filled with sample books and order forms, she must have been overcome with a sense of physical freedom. She undoubtedly had worn pants on the farm, at least occasionally, but never in public, and certainly not since living in town. At the time, a well-dressed woman's ensemble could weigh as much as fifteen pounds, including petticoats, a corset stiffened with thin strips of whalebone, wire hoops, and yards and yards of fabric. Maneuvering in such dresses was so complicated that instructions had to be given. The best-selling *Ladies' Guide to Perfect Gentility in Manners, Dress, and Conversation,* published in 1854, included admonitions against bad breath ("The purity of the breath is of the greatest consequence; what, indeed, could be so afflicting to one of the gentle sex as impurity in this respect?"), tips for avoiding freckles ("Green is the only color which should be worn as a summer veil"), and guidelines on how to manage long skirts ("When tripping over the pavement, a lady should gracefully raise her dress a little above her ankle. With the right hand, she should hold together the folds of her gown, and draw them towards the right side. To raise the dress on both sides, and with both hands, is vulgar. This ungraceful practice can only be tolerated for a moment, when the mud is very deep").[22] Emma may not have worn costumes as elaborate as those worn by the most fashion-able women of her time, but she still would have been accustomed to tight bodices, and heavy full skirts that trailed on the ground and were prone to catching on all sorts of impediments.

Worse, the physical limitations imposed by the favored style of women's clothing reflected the limitations imposed on their behav-ior, and how society expected them to act. What women could do, what they were in fact expected to do, was to devote themselves to their families. An editorial in *Harper's New Monthly,* published in 1854, captured the popular concept of the ideal woman:

> The true Woman, for whose ambition a husband's love and her chil-dren's adoration are sufficient, who applies her military instincts to the discipline of her household, and whose legislative faculties exer-cise themselves in making laws for her nursery; whose intellect has field enough in communion with her husband, and whose heart asks no other honors than his love and admiration; a woman who does not think it a weakness to attend to her toilette, and who does not disdain to be beautiful; who believes in the virtue of glossy hair and well-fitting gowns, and who eschews rents and raveled edges, slip-shod shoes, and audacious make-ups; a woman who speaks low and who does not speak much; who is patient and gentle and intellectual and industrious; who loves more than she reasons, and yet does not love blindly; who never scolds, and rarely argues, but who rebukes with a caress, and adjusts with a smile: a woman who is the wife we all have dreamt of once in our lives, and who is the mother we still wor-ship in the backward distance of the past: such a woman as this does more for human nature, and more for woman's cause, than all the sea-captains, judges, barristers, and members of parliament put to-gether—God-given and God-blessed as she is! [23]

This version of the feminine ideal was of no interest to Emma. "Although I was favored with more than one touching declaration of undying love, I greatly preferred the privilege of earning my own bread and butter," she later explained.[24] But Emma was probably too nervous to savor her newfound freedom for long. She was terrified that she would be recognized immediately as a girl. Not at all sure that her disguise would work at close range, she left the city as quickly as she could, and took to the woods lining the road. All day, she stayed out of sight, certain that the first person she met would see through her fraud. Finally, at twilight, when the light was kinder, she ventured out of the protection of the forest and approached a nearby farmhouse. Summoning all her nerve, she knocked tentatively on the door. With much relief, Emma was greeted with "so much respect and kindness that I concluded I must be quite a gentleman."[25]

From that night on, Emma discovered that not only could she pass herself off as a young man, but that she was happy doing it. Life as the "enemy" was not too bad. She relished the freedom it gave her to go where she wanted, do what she wanted, earn what she could, without the nagging restraints society placed on unattached women.

Emma proved to be a born salesman. For the next year, she traveled throughout New Brunswick and New England, taking orders for Bibles and other books, relaying them to the publishing company, and then delivering the books when they were ready. "Such success as I met with deserves to be recorded in history. . . . The publishing company told me that they had employed agents for thirty years, and they never had employed one that could outsell me. I made money, dressed well, owned and drove a fine horse and buggy—silver mounted harness and all the paraphernalia of a nice turnout."[26]

At some point during that year, she went home to see her mother. Although the story might have been one of her many embellishments, it survived as family lore for generations. According to Emma, she went home one day in the fall of 1859, when her father was out. Her mother did not recognize her at first, although her sister Frances instantly did. Thomas eventually did, too, tipped off by the fact that the family animals seemed strangely calm despite the presence of a "stranger." Emma was finally able to convince her mother that she was her youngest child, and the four of them spent a happy hour or so before Emma began to worry that it was coming close to the time that her father might walk through the door. After a last, long hug for her mother, she took her leave. Thomas walked her to the train depot at Magaguadavic Siding, several miles away. On the way, Emma borrowed Thomas's gun, and shot down six partridges for him to bring home for supper, presumably much to the surprise of Isaac; he did not generally think much of Thomas's hunting skills.[27]

Emma returned to her bookselling, and continued to prosper, for several more months. But sometime in the winter of 1859, something that Emma only referred to later as a "disaster" caused her to lose all of her money and possessions, with the exception of one sample Bible and a gold pocket watch. Instead of going home, however, she headed for Hartford, then the subscription publishing capital of America, to start anew. In recalling that trip years later, Emma said:

> I started for the United States, in mid winter, snow three feet deep in New Brunswick. In that way I performed the journey from Fredericton, New Brunswick, with the exceptions of a few miles' ride occasionally. Oh! I could tell you a tale of suffering and hardships and weariness endured on that journey . . . I reached Hartford in a most forlorn condition. A stranger in a strange country—a fit subject for a hospital—without money and without friends.[28]

Whether Emma did in fact walk all the way to Hartford from New Brunswick—a distance of nearly four hundred miles—in the middle of the winter is questionable. All her life, her taste for drama would flavor her recollections. More probable is that she walked part of the way, and went either by ferry, coach, or horseback the rest.[29] One way or another, she did arrive there in the early weeks of 1860, and it was true enough that she had nothing going for her but her own wits, and the address of the publishing house. Before she could present herself there, she needed to recuperate from her trip. "I went to a hotel just as if I had plenty of money, and rested several days before presenting myself to the publishers. My feet were badly frost-bitten and my boots literally worn out, and my last suit of clothes were rather the worse for wear, and my linen—well, it is hardly worth speaking of." After several days, she finally felt well enough to venture out of her room. Taking her gold watch and chain, the one thing of value she still possessed, she walked into the bustling, jangling streets and found a pawnshop. With the money, Emma bought a new suit of clothes, as well as new boots. Feeling more presentable, she made her way to 155 Asylum Street, the office of W. S. Williams & Co.[30]

Inside the narrow row house, three distinguished, prosperous-looking men turned to size up their visitor. Emma steeled her nerves, and, "with as gentlemanly address as I could get up, I introduced myself to the publishers, and almost in the same breath I asked them whether they had any use for a boy who had neither friends nor money, but who was hard to beat at selling books." The men looked at her for a moment, and then, much to Emma's relief, one of them—whom she soon learned was Mr. A. M. Hurlbert—leaned back and laughed a deep, hearty laugh. "I told them they would have to take me on trial, as I had no security to give them." Another of the men, Mr. Scranton, replied, "We'll take your face for it." When the jolly Mr. Hurlbert discovered that Emma was staying in a nearby hotel, he promptly invited him to dinner, an invitation that Emma readily accepted. Mr. Hurlbert led his visitor up the street to a well-appointed row house at 285 Asylum. There he jovially introduced Emma to his family as "a boy who was hard to beat on selling books." Mr. Hurlbert's wife was as welcoming as her husband, and after a warm, satisfying meal, they treated Emma to a leisurely carriage ride around the city. Emma was touched by the warm reception. "The kindness I received that day was worth a thousand dollars to me. I have never forgotten it, and I hope they have never had reason to regret it."[31] It must have felt good to sit and laugh, to be treated as one of the family, for the first time in a long time.

Several days later, with a $50 advance and a valise full of samples, Emma boarded the ferry for Halifax, Nova Scotia—her first assignment for W. S. Williams & Co. As the ferry headed out into the cold vastness of the Atlantic Ocean, Emma stood at the railing, relishing her independence. "Oh, how manly I felt," she recalled, "and what pride I took in proving to them that their confidence in me was not misplaced."[32]

Halifax, Nova Scotia, was in the midst of a growth spurt when Emma arrived in February 1860. Swollen with recent immigrants from Ireland and Scotland, Halifax's economy, already thriving from its trade with New England and its shipbuilding industry, was exploding. Like New Brunswick, the population in Nova Scotia was highly literate and relatively isolated—a perfect place for selling books. Emma did even better in her nine months in Nova Scotia than she had in New Brunswick the year before. It did not take her long to earn back her advance, and much more besides. Soon Emma was staying in the best hotels in Halifax, Yarmouth, and Digby, once again dressing well and traveling in elegant style. But money for its own sake was not something Emma craved, and in a pattern that she would continually repeat, she gave most of her earnings away. That year, Emma "gave away more money to benevolent societies, etc., than in all the rest of my life." She also dated a bit, to keep up appearances, as well as for the companionship. In those Victorian days, dating involved well-chaperoned outings that involved nothing more intimate than witty conversation, something the theatrical and imaginative Emma excelled at. But sometimes these outings led to expectations that "Frank Thompson" could not fulfill. Many years later, she recalled that "I came near marrying a pretty little girl who was bound that I should not leave Nova Scotia without her."[33] If

Emma ever appreciated the irony of someone who once railed against men as, at best, wolves in sheep's clothing blithely leaving broken hearts in her wake, she left no record of it.

Emma stayed in Nova Scotia for nine months. When she finally returned to Hartford in November, she had earned over $900, a staggering sum of money for a farm girl from Magaguadavic. [34]

CHAPTER TWO

December 1860

WHEN EMMA returned to Hartford, she spent several days as a guest of the Hurlberts, who were thrilled with her success in Nova Scotia. Then, in early December, she set out again. This time, following Horace Greeley's famous advice to "go west," she boarded a train bound for Detroit, Michigan.

The country through which Emma's train passed on the way to Detroit was in turmoil. During the nine months that Emma was in Nova Scotia, the regional crisis between the North and the South, so many years in the making, had reached new and seemingly irreversible proportions. Abraham Lincoln had only just been elected president in November, but would not take office until the following March. Although Lincoln himself was considered relatively moderate on the issue of slavery—he was not an abolitionist, but was firmly opposed to the expansion of slavery to the western territories—his victory was the direct result of the politics of slavery. The issue had been simmering for decades, ever since the Missouri Compromise of 1820, under which Missouri was admitted to the Union as a slave state, in exchange for the agreement that all future states north of Missouri's northern boundary would be free. But the issue resurfaced with a vengeance with the sudden acquisition of vast new territories west and south of that line as a result of the Mexican War. The

17

abolitionist movement in the North had been steadily gaining ground in the intervening years, and some politicians vowed that no new slave states would be admitted to the Union. Another compromise was reached in 1850, then another in the form of the Kansas-Nebraska Act in 1854, which would essentially allow the people of each new state to decide for themselves whether to allow or prohibit slavery. On paper, this seemed reasonable to many on both sides of the issue, but in practice, it only worked in places where the populace was in relative agreement on the issue. This was not the case, however, in Kansas, where the people were nearly evenly split on the issue. There the political process deteriorated quickly into sectional violence. The Dred Scott Decision, in 1857, made things worse. By deciding that a slave living with his master in a free territory was nonetheless still a slave, the Supreme Court of the United States cast doubt on the ability of the Federal government, or any state government, to outlaw slavery anywhere.

From there, things got steadily worse. Rhetoric on both sides escalated to a fervent pitch, and politicians everywhere found that their position on slavery was the litmus test by which they would be judged. But it was John Brown's raid of the Federal arsenal at Harpers Ferry in the fall of 1859 that most believe was the point of no return. When the radical abolitionist attacked the arsenal with the stated intent of arming the slaves and inciting a violent rebellion against their masters, he was quickly arrested and almost as quickly hanged by the Federal government as a traitor to the United States. But the damage was done. Many in the South believed that Brown represented a prevailing attitude in the North—that slavery must be ended with violence against them—and that perception was exacerbated by numerous articles and editorials in Northern anti-slavery newspapers heralding John Brown as a martyred hero to a noble cause.

Ironically, the new Republican Party had nominated Lincoln in part because he still believed a political compromise on the question of slavery was possible—that it could be permitted to exist in the

South so long as it did not expand to new states. It was a lukewarm position compared with the strongly abolitionist leanings of the other Republican candidates. But it was not Lincoln's moderate stance that won him the election so much as it was the fact that the Democrats were deeply divided between Stephen Douglas, who was pro-slavery but also believed a compromise was possible, and the virulently pro-slavery and anti-compromise wing of the party in the South. Talk of secession had grown louder during the 1850s, as hope for a lasting compromise faded, but most people probably assumed that it was mere rhetoric. But almost immediately after Lincoln's victory was confirmed, South Carolinians turned it into reality by voting to secede from the Union on December 20, 1860.

This was the crisis embroiling the country through which Emma traveled in the winter of 1860–1861. She was aware of it, of course—it was impossible not to be. As a Canadian, she was naturally disposed to side with the North. Emma was opposed to slavery on religious and humanitarian grounds. But like most people, she hoped that the regional crisis would not devolve into armed conflict, even as that eventuality seemed ever more likely.

Detroit was a busy, thriving city of forty-five thousand people. Like many other areas in the upper Northwest, Michigan at mid-century was expanding and modernizing rapidly. With a literacy rate of more than 90 percent, and a growing populace hungry for information and entertainment, it, like Nova Scotia, presented a ready-made market for book canvassers.

Soon after arriving in Detroit, Emma made her way to the small but thriving town of Flint, sixty miles northwest of Detroit on a bend in the Flint River. Flint's origins were as a lumber town, and a trading post for the northern Michigan fur and trapping trade. Now, with the recent influx of German and Irish settlers looking for land to farm, the heavily forested area around the town was being converted to agricultural purposes. With its proximity to Detroit, it was an ideal home base for Emma's peripatetic business. For a time, she boarded on the farm of Charles Pratt, who, like many farmers at that time, took in tenants to help pay the bills. Pratt's seven-year-old daughter, Lara, became quite fond of their new boarder, and spent many hours with "Frank," listening to his stories of his travels back east. Years later, Lara recalled thinking that Frank had oddly delicate features, and that he pitched hay "like a girl."[1] But these observations were recorded many years after the fact, when Lara had the benefit of knowing the truth about Frank Thompson. If anyone had any serious suspicions about the polite young Bible salesman at the time, he must have kept them to himself.

After several months as a boarder at the Pratt farm, Emma moved into town, where she rented a room from T. J. Joslin, the new pastor of the Court Street Methodist Episcopal Church. The Court Street church was one of the oldest and most prominent in town, and the Reverend Mr. Joslin's new boarder became an active member of the congregation. Emma felt at home with the church's strong anti-slavery and temperance leanings, and welcomed the opportunity to be part of a community again after several years of constantly moving around. Still, the Joslins got used to their boarder being gone for days at a time, as "he" crisscrossed Genesee County, and beyond, to the scores of new settlements that were springing up along the Flint and Saginaw rivers.

Meanwhile, as the new year progressed, the country was inching ever closer to war. By the end of January, Mississippi, Alabama, Georgia, Florida, Texas, and Louisiana followed South Carolina's lead and seceded from the Union. On February 8, 1861, the seceded states joined together to create the Confederate States of America, and elected as its president a Mexican War veteran from Mississippi named Jefferson Davis. Even so, there were still some who hoped for a reconciliation in the form of a political compromise that would allow the errant states to return to the Federal fold, but more and more, it seemed that civil war was inevitable. What was still not clear, however, was where, and when, it would start.

Abraham Lincoln was sworn in as the sixteenth president of the United States on March 4, 1861. Almost immediately, Jefferson Davis sent delegates to Washington to demand that the new president remove all Federal troops from military installations in the Confederacy. Lincoln refused. This might not have escalated to crisis proportions, however—after all, Davis had made the same demand of Lincoln's predecessor, James Buchanan, with the same results—had it not been for the fact that the small Federal garrison at Fort Sumter, in Charleston Harbor, was running out of supplies. This meant that the troops there would have to abandon the fort if it was not resupplied. And resupplying it meant sending the Federal navy into the heart of hostile territory, an act that Davis promised to treat as a declaration of war. To prove it, he surrounded the harbor with all of the force he could muster, and gave command of that force to a promising former West Pointer named Pierre Gustave Toutant Beauregard.

Militarily, South Carolina did not present much of an obstacle to the Federal navy, but Lincoln also had his eye on politics. Virginia, as well as a number of other important border states in the upper South, had not yet seceded, but Lincoln knew that the Virginia legislature was currently convened for the purpose of debating secession, and he feared that, with anti-Union passions running high there, any perceived act of aggression by the Federal government would cause Virginia to cast its lot with the new Confederacy. On the other hand, the Northern populace, and the vociferous Northern press, were adamant that abandoning the fort would be tantamount to conceding defeat, and the permanent dissolution of the Union. So, all eyes turned nervously to the goings-on in Charleston Harbor.

By early April, food at the fort was nearly gone. Lincoln tried to walk a tightrope by announcing that he was going to send in unarmed transports carrying only non-military supplies, to allow the troops there to avoid starvation. This put the ball in Davis's court: He would have to either permit the relief convoy to enter the harbor unmolested or fire on defenseless men. Either way, it was a publicity nightmare for the Confederacy. But Davis was cunning, too, and he saw the trap that Lincoln had set. To avoid it, Davis decided that he had no choice but to fire on the fort before the unarmed relief convoy arrived. On April 9, Davis ordered Beauregard to take the fort.

Before he did so, Beauregard gave the fort's commander, Major Robert Anderson, the chance to surrender without a fight. The two men knew each other—Anderson had been one of Beauregard's instructors at West Point—and Beauregard knew that Anderson, who was from Kentucky, was hoping that war could be avoided. But Anderson politely replied that his sense of duty precluded him from surrendering. So Beauregard allowed his eager South Carolinians to begin shelling the fort in the early morning of April 12. Within hours, it seemed as though all of Charleston had come down to the Battery to watch the fireworks.

The fort was poorly prepared to defend itself. It was not fully completed, and had only 15 of the 135 cannon it was supposed to have mounted and ready for use. The hundred-odd soldiers inside were seriously hungry and weak. Anderson and his men mounted what defense they could, firing the few guns available as their stronghold was torn to pieces around them. By the next day, large portions of the fort were on fire. Beauregard, not wanting to incinerate his old teacher, ordered a cease-fire and sent a party to the fort to negotiate a surrender. This time, Anderson reluctantly agreed, and, with no more shots fired, turned over the fort the following day.

The news that Fort Sumter had fallen spread across the country like a raging wildfire, fueled by years of pent-up emotion. Everywhere, people stopped what they were doing, and rushed to get every detail they could. Flint, Michigan, was no exception. Emma was waiting for a train to take her back to Hartford for more book samples when she suddenly heard the voice of a newspaper boy in the street crying out, "New York Herald. Fall of Fort Sumter. President's proclamation. Call for seventy-five thousand men!"

Lincoln's call to arms showed that, despite the fact that war had been looming for several years, the U.S. government was ill-prepared when it finally came. At the beginning of 1861, there were fewer than seventeen thousand soldiers in the entire U.S. Army. Of those, less than a quarter were on the East Coast. The remainder were scattered in remote outposts on the western frontier. To make matters worse, a sizable number, including a third of the officers, resigned to join with the Confederacy.

Years later, Emma recalled her reaction to the news of the fall of Fort Sumter. "War, civil war, with all its horrors seemed inevitable, and even then was ready to bust like a volcano upon the most happy and prosperous nation the sun ever shone upon. The contemplation of this sad picture filled my eyes with tears and my heart with sorrow. . . . But the great question to be decided, was, what can I do? What part am I to act in this great drama?"[2] But it would be several weeks before she knew the answer to her own question.

For most young men in America, the question was not a hard one: They would join up. For many, it was an opportunity for adventure and glory; the chance of a lifetime. Almost all, on both sides, believed that the war would be a rout, and that if they did not get into the fight right away, they might miss it altogether. In most places, joining up meant enlisting in a local militia, if you were not a member already. Almost every town across both the North and South maintained local militia companies that could be called up by the state governors as necessary. Such volunteer militias had played a large role in the Mexican War, but their services had not been needed since that conflict ended in 1848, and most local militias were now primarily social organizations. In bigger towns, membership in the local militia was a sign of status, and competition to join was fierce. Officers were elected by the members, and many militias had far more officers than were necessary from a military point of view. The members wore homemade uniforms, usually sewn by their wives or mothers, that were often gaudy and colorful, and completely different from those of neighboring towns. Occasionally, some militias would actually drill, but for the most part, they marched in parades, held dances or picnics, and generally gave their members an opportunity to play at being soldiers without having to submit to the hardships of actually serving in the U.S. Army.[3] Now, though, these part-time companies of amateur soldiers would be the bricks and mortar with which Lincoln's new army was built.

To fulfill Lincoln's call for 75,000 volunteers, the War Department gave each state a quota based on its population. Michigan, with a population of nearly 750,000, was originally asked to send one regiment of 1,000 men, but Michigan's governor, Austin Blair, thought, presciently, that more would eventually be needed. Blair issued his own proclamation calling for the formation of two infantry regiments, each to be composed of ten 100-member militias. The first regiment would be sent to Washington immediately; the second would be made ready should the need arise.[4]

In April 1861, Michigan boasted twenty-eight local militias, including the Flint Union Grays—gray not yet being a color associated with the Confederacy. As an organization, the Grays were only three years old, and, though relatively active, had far fewer than a hundred members. Emma was acquainted with many of the Grays who were members in the Court Street Methodist Church, including the Grays' popular captain, William Morse. Eager to be part of the First Michigan Infantry Regiment, the Grays' officers staged a recruiting meeting on the steps of the Flint courthouse on April 18. As what seemed like the entire town gathered in the courthouse square, rousing patriotic speeches were made, various committees were formed, and soon the Grays had enough recruits to fill their hundred-man quota. Emma, who was in the crowd that day, watched the proceedings intently.

Captain Morse sent word to Governor Blair that the Flint Union Grays were at full strength, but competition to be part of the First Michigan Infantry was fierce, and the honor went primarily to militias from the larger cities, with Detroit alone contributing two. The eager Grays were bitterly disappointed to learn that they were not among them. But a week later, Captain Morse received word from the Governor's Office that they would be part of the second, reserve regiment, and were ordered to report as soon as possible to the rendezvous point in Detroit.[5]

The disappointment over not being chosen for the First Michigan quickly faded, replaced with sheer excitement. On April 29, the night before the Grays' departure, Emma was again in the large crowd that turned out for a parade and more speeches in their honor. Judge Fenton, their honorary colonel, who was too old to go with them, gave a rousing speech on the subject of courage, honor and duty, and administered an oath of loyalty to the Constitution of the United States, and to each other. Women—many dressed in red, white, and blue—pinned rosettes on their chests that read "For Union and for Constitution." Bands played patriotic marches, and girls waved handkerchiefs. The Reverend Mr. Joslin said the closing benediction, and gave each volunteer a Bible from the Court Street congregation inscribed with the words "Put your trust in God, and keep your powder dry." The festivities lasted well into the night. The next morning, the Grays were escorted amid much fanfare to the railroad depot, where, after the town band played one final rendition of "The Star-Spangled Banner," the new soldiers boarded trains for Detroit.[6]

The sight of her friends going off to war moved Emma deeply. "It was while witnessing the anguish of that first parting that I became convinced that I, too, had a duty to perform," she recalled later. After the Grays' departure, "I spent days and nights in anxious thought in deciding in what capacity I should try to serve the Union cause." Emma may have been tough, but she had no lust to fight. Yet she knew she would not be content to help from the sidelines. Eventually, she concluded to enlist under her alias, believing that "I could best serve the interest of the Union cause in male attire—could better perform the necessary duties for sick and wounded men, and with less embarrassment to them and to myself as a man than as a woman."[7]

But how could she enlist, with the Grays already gone? She could go to another town, but with competition to join up so stiff, it was unlikely that any militia would accept a complete stranger. And there was no way to know if Michigan would in fact send another regiment. Later in the war, of course, the enthusiasm for enlisting died down to the point that a draft was instituted, and Michigan ended up organizing more than thirty infantry regiments. But at the moment, it seemed to Emma that the window of opportunity had closed.

It opened again sooner than she expected. President Lincoln's original call had been for three-month regiments, but almost as soon as the Grays reached Detroit, word arrived from the War Department that no more short-term regiments would be accepted. From then on, only those troops who committed to serving for a term of three years would be mustered into Federal service. This longer commitment caused several of the Grays' original recruits to change their minds, leaving the company short-handed. On May 18, Captain Morse returned to Flint to fill the vacancies. This time, Emma did not hesitate; when Morse returned to Detroit, three days later, "Frank Thompson" was with him.

Emma was not the only woman who had a desire to do her part for the war effort. In the spring of 1861, women as well as men were struck with war fervor.[8] For most, participating in the war effort would mean applying their domestic skills in the public realm: sewing uniforms, flags and bandages; knitting wool caps and socks; packaging and sending off baked goods and delicacies for the troops.[9] But a rather surprising number sought more active roles. Some women, like Annie Etheridge and Bridget Divers, both from Michigan, and Katy Brownell of Rhode Island, went to war with their husbands.[10] They did not pretend to disguise themselves as men or be anything other than what they were: women who refused to stay home. In all three cases, their presence in camp was first barely tolerated, but later welcomed, by their regiments. Even when Etheridge's husband deserted early in the war, she stayed on, serving as nurse, seamstress, and general morale booster for the Third Michigan throughout the war. But it would have been a very different thing for a single woman to try to attach herself to a regiment; her motives and morals would have been instantly suspect.

Other women got involved in the war by disguising themselves as men and enlisting under an alias. The exact number of cross-dressing soldiers in the Civil War is not known, but is estimated to be between 250 and 500.[11] Some did it to stay with husbands or lovers, others to escape them. Some did it out of patriotism, or regional pride; others for the money—the $13 monthly salary of a private in the U.S. Army was nearly four times what an average domestic servant could earn. And others enlisted primarily for the thrill of it. Some, like Emma, may have been inspired by fictional examples of female warriors: Fanny Campbell was but one of many such heroines in the popular fiction of the day. Others may have been inspired by real-life examples, such as the well-known story of Deborah Sampson, who served in the Fourth Massachusetts under the alias Robert Shurtleff during the Revolutionary War, or, going even further back, Joan of Arc, who, though not a cross-dresser, was the archetype of a woman going off to war to fight for a noble cause.[12] For women as well as men, war had always offered opportunities—to pursue treasure and glory, see the world, sacrifice for a noble cause—that did not exist in peacetime. To the women who were inclined to pursue them, the fact that they had to dress as men did not necessarily make the opportunities any less attractive, and may, in some cases, have made them more so.

Although most women who enlisted during the Civil War adopted their disguises specifically for that purpose, a handful of female soldiers had, like Emma, been living as men before the war broke out, in order to pursue economic opportunities, avoid the institution of marriage, or simply to participate in civic life more fully. When Jennie Hodgers arrived in the United States from Ireland shortly before the war broke out, she found she could get a better job under the alias of Alfred Cashiers; in August 1862 she enlisted in the Ninety-fifth Illinois. Although Hodgers was petite—just five feet tall—with a delicate complexion and soft blue eyes, she was so successful at her disguise that not only was she not discovered during the war, but she continued to live as Cashiers for the remainder of her life. Her secret was not discovered until she broke her leg in 1911, at the age of sixty-seven. Even then, those closest to her kept her secret until she became a permanent invalid. After a short stint at a retirement home for veterans, her sex became more widely known; ultimately, whether due to her cross-dressing, or to actual impairment, she was deemed mentally unfit, and committed to an insane asylum, where she was forced to wear skirts for the first time in her adult life.[13]

Likewise, Sarah Rosetta Wakeman was working as a domestic servant when she decided, in the summer of 1861, that she, too, would fare better in the job market as a man. Unlike Emma, however, she let her family in on her plan, and had their blessing when, as Lyons Wakeman, she found work as a boatman in upstate New York. The following summer, an army recruiter offered Wakeman and the rest of her crew substantial bounties to enlist—a common practice by the second year of the war after the initial enthusiasm for joining up was gone but before the draft began. As Wakeman explained in a letter to her parents, "They wanted me to enlist, and so I did." The $152 bounty, which she enclosed, played a large part in her decision.[14]

Emma, Jennie Hodgers, and Sarah Wakeman were all from rural or working-class backgrounds. All were raised to work hard, and had developed strong bodies as well as a variety of traditionally male skills that made it easier to fit into the rugged life of an infantry private.[15] Unlike Hodgers and Wakeman, however, Emma was highly educated, and was making more money before the war than she would as a soldier. Nor did she need to escape an unhappy home—she had already done that. Something else, then, must have contributed to her decision. According to Emma, she "had no other motive in enlisting than love to God, and love for suffering humanity. I felt called to go and do what I could for the defense of the right—if I could not fight, I could take the place of someone who could and thus add one more soldier to the ranks."[16]

No doubt this was at least a part of her decision, as was her love of adventure and danger, but it may also have been that for Emma, the war offered a chance to have something quite the opposite of freedom. It may have been that the years of isolation that came with living under an alias, the necessary lack of intimacy, the need to keep everyone at arm's length, played a role in her decision as well. Most of the members of the Flint militia, like most of the members of militias all over the country, and particularly those from the rural states, had grown up together. The militias would become companies in larger regiments, which in turn would become part of brigades and divisions and corps, and ultimately, of armies, but at the company level, the units of boys and men from the same town functioned a lot like families. For Emma, so long without a family of her own, the chance to join in that camaraderie may have been part of the inducement.

When Emma arrived in Detroit with Captain Morse on May 20, the Grays were ensconced at Fort Wayne, a sprawling brick military complex on the banks of the Detroit River. Built in the 1830s, when the memory of the War of 1812 was still fresh and states on the Canadian border viewed their northern neighbor with suspicion, the fort had never been occupied by regular army troops. Now it was the picture of military fanfare. Each of the ten militias that were to form the Second Michigan had been designated as a separate company, identified by a letter. The Scott Guard became Company A, the boys from Hudson became Company B, the Battle Creek Artillery became Company C, and so on. The Grays were Company F. When they first arrived, each militia was easily identifiable in its own unique uniforms, but now they were all clad in navy-blue flannel coats that came down to the mid-thigh, loose flannel pants, and, when the weather demanded it, long gray overcoats. Emma had no trouble with the fit; at five feet, six inches, she was only two and a quarter inches shorter than the average Union army recruit. The boots, however, were a bit too big for her feet. The new regiment also received their muskets—not the newer, rifled versions they would be issued later, but the old-fashioned, unreliable smoothbores that the Michigan Armory had on hand when the war broke out. They did not, however, receive live ammunition for drills, for fear that the unseasoned troops would injure themselves before the rebels got the chance.[17]

At some point in those first few days or weeks, Emma's company was summoned for medical examination. The army regulations governing the examination process were stringent:

> In passing a recruit, the medical officer is to examine him stripped; to see that he has free use of all his limbs; that his chest is ample; that his hearing, vision, and speech are perfect; that he has no tumors, or ulcerated or cicatrized legs; no rupture or chronic cutaneous affection; that he has not received any contusion, or wound of the head, that may impair his faculties; that he is not subject to convulsions; and has no infectious disorder that may unfit him for military service.

Fortunately for Emma, however, the examiners at Fort Wayne were not by-the-book, and, like examiners all across the country, they were under enormous pressure to get troops mustered in and moving east. She did have one moment of danger, when the examiner picked up her suspiciously delicate hand and asked, "Well, what sort of living has this hand earned?" to which Emma calmly replied that she had spent most of her youth in getting an education.[18] But in more instances than not, recruits were simply lined up and reviewed en masse; only those with chronic conditions discernible at first glance—a hacking cough, a disfigured limb—were rejected. Had Emma waited to enlist, she might have been discovered. By August, regulations requiring examination of all recruits were more strictly and thoroughly enforced, leading to the discovery of a number of female would-be soldiers.

Although most of the recruits in the Second Michigan were already skilled marksmen, an advantage that the Western regiments had on many of the urban troops from the East, knowing how to shoot was not all that a soldier needed to know. To become an effective fighting force, they had to know how to move in unison, as a company, as a regiment, and as a brigade. And so they drilled—day in and day out. As one observer to Fort Wayne during this period noted, "In one place, a company, fully armed, may be seen exercising in the manual, in another an awkward squad is receiving its first lessons in the facings, and in another a platoon is being hurried up on the double quick step; yet out of this chaotic element, order is being brought."[19]

Turning a group of headstrong farm boys into a disciplined, well-trained regiment was not easy. The regiment's colonel, Israel B. Richardson, known as Fighting Dick, was a tough, regular army disciplinarian. But each company elected its own line officers, and it was often hard to take orders seriously when issued by childhood friends. One member of the Second remembered, "It was a long time before Captain and Lieutenant are anything other than Sam or John. The private talked back to the non-coms, and the non-coms argued with the captains, and whenever an order was issued, the boys asked their superiors 'what for?' "[20]

The time at Fort Wayne may have been the most perilous time for Emma in terms of being discovered. The recruits were packed tightly into barracks—large rooms with rows and rows of bunks or aboard steamers docked at the fort's wharf. Once they left Detroit, camp life would consist of tent cities that were more conducive to her disguise. The tents offered more privacy than open barracks, and wooded areas provided plenty of opportunities to discretely take care of what were then referred to as "the necessaries." However, the fort did have proper privies—the last time in a very long while that the members of the Second would enjoy such luxury. Fortunately for Emma, the men rarely undressed completely for bedtime, if only to cut down on the time it took to be ready for roll call in the morning.[21] In addition, prevailing Victorian sensibilities about modesty and privacy applied to men as well as to women, and the fact that a man did not strip down to his "linens" in view of the others would not have raised any suspicions.

In between the incessant drills, life at Fort Wayne was far from onerous. The food was good, and plentiful—pork, potatoes, fresh beef, bread, butter, milk, sugar, tea, and coffee—and there was time to get to know their new comrades. They were often allowed to go into downtown Detroit, something many of the boys had never done, despite having grown up in Michigan. Day passes were liberally granted, and even furloughs of several days were fairly common, giving the proud new soldiers a chance to go home to show off their uniforms.[22]

Despite the pleasant conditions, most recruits were eager to head east, where the action was—or would soon be. When news arrived that the First Michigan played a significant role in occupying Alexandria, Virginia, a secessionist town across the Potomac River from Washington, D.C., more than one member of the Second expressed the fear that it would be over before they could even leave the state. Emma was more patient, knowing that their time would come soon enough. In the meantime, she recalled later, "I could only thank God that I was free and could go forward and work, and was not obliged to stay home and weep."[23]

CHAPTER THREE

June 1861

THE ORDER to march on Washington finally arrived on June 2, two weeks after Emma arrived at Fort Wayne. As the news spread, cheers rang out from every corner of the fort. For the next three days, everything and everyone was in an uproar, as last-minute preparations were made. Then, on June 6, the Second Michigan were on their way to war.

The regiment left the fort late that afternoon, bayonets gleaming in the late afternoon sun, and paraded their way to the city's main wharf. There, amid much cheering, jostling, and general confusion, they boarded steamers for the trip to Cleveland, a distance of 150 miles. In the morning, the steamers pulled alongside the wharf at Cleveland, and the Second Michigan once again shouldered their muskets and marched, amid more cheering of excited citizens who had come out to see them off, to the railroad depot, where they boarded trains for the trip to Pittsburgh. All through Ohio and Pennsylvania, they were greeted as heroes by the crowds gathered at each depot they passed. Men waved flags, women waved handkerchiefs, and children ran along the trains shouting and hollering. When they stopped long enough, they were offered pies, and cakes and lemonade, which they gratefully accepted. When they pulled into Pittsburgh just after midnight, an enthusiastic crowd awaited them. By then, most of the soldiers were too tired to take much notice, and, with knapsacks serving as pillows, they concentrated instead on getting comfortable enough in the crowded cars to sleep.[1]

They next morning, they awoke to find themselves in the beautiful green mountains of western Pennsylvania. For many of the boys, it was the farthest from home they had ever been, and they exclaimed over the differences between the dramatic landscape before them and what they were used to back home. The scenery was less exciting for Emma, who had traveled through it before, but she loved every minute of the jovial, masculine company. Disaster nearly struck when one member of Company K climbed onto the roof of the car for a better view, and was knocked off by an overhanging branch. The train screeched to a halt, and the man was rescued. His injuries were determined not to be fatal, and the journey continued, with the Second Michigan having sustained its first casualty while on active duty.[2]

Before nightfall, they came within a mile and half of Harrisburg, Pennsylvania, where they disembarked and marched to Camp Curtis, a Union army training facility. Almost three thousand other soldiers from various states were encamped there while waiting for uniforms. The Second pitched tents—another first—and settled down for the night. The new experience of being in the company of so many other troops, combined with receiving their first allotment of live ammunition before leaving for Washington the next morning, made many of them realize, perhaps for the first time, that this really was no lark they were on.

That realization was further driven home as their train reached the Maryland border. Maryland was deeply divided about the war, and although it had not seceded, there was a fear in the North that it would do so soon. Since Virginia voted to leave the Union after Fort Sumter, as Lincoln had feared, Washington would be completely surrounded by enemy territory if Maryland followed suit. So far, Maryland was being held in check by its pro-Union politicians, but it was still full of Southern sympathizers.

As the Second's train drew within sixteen miles of Baltimore, they were ordered out of the cars, and told to load their guns to be ready for any emergency. They did not have to ask why; they all were well aware of what had happened when the first Federal troops passed through Baltimore several months earlier. On April 19, the Sixth Massachusetts had been met by a hostile crowd who threw bats and bricks, and ultimately fired into their ranks. Unsure how to respond, the green troops had fired back. By the time things were back under control, four soldiers and twelve civilians were dead. Soon afterward, the city was occupied by regular army troops, a move that may have prevented Maryland from seceding, but that had only fueled Confederate sympathy in the state. Emma and her comrades knew that Baltimore remained a dangerous place for newly arriving troops.

The risk was exacerbated when, after the incident with the Sixth Massachusetts, the railroad tracks into the heart of the city were destroyed by Southern sympathizers. They had not yet been rebuilt. The Second would have to march through the city on foot, and board cars for Washington on the far side of town. As they entered the city, their officers ordered them to shoot anyone who "undertakes hostilities" against them. For several miles, the march was tense but uneventful, save for a few derogatory remarks, a far cry from the reception they received in Ohio. As they reached the center of town, one civilian in the gathering crowd threw a rock at the orderly sergeant of Company E, who, following orders, fired at the man. For a moment, it seemed that another full-scale riot would erupt, but the officers shouted at the men to stay in rank and keep moving, which, miraculously for such green troops, they did, and they arrived at the south-side depot without further incident.[3]

The Second Michigan arrived in Washington on June 10, after three long days of travel, to find the city in a state of high martial excitement. Everywhere they looked, soldiers from all over the North were camped on the grounds of the U.S. Capitol, drilling on the Mall, even relaxing in the halls of Congress. Colors flapped in the breeze, bayonets glistened, and the streets shook with the sound of hooves as officers rode through the streets looking very impressive indeed.[4] Emma recalled years later, "The Capitol and White House were common places of resort for soldiers. Arms were stacked in the rotunda of the one and the lobbies of the other, while our 'noble boys in blue' lounged in the cushioned seats of members of Congress, or reclined in easy chairs in the President's Mansion."[5]

Emma and her comrades were exhausted. The Second was initially quartered in the same building where Lincoln's inaugural ball had been held just three months earlier. On the eleventh, they were formally reviewed by President Lincoln and general in chief of the army, General Winfield Scott, who pronounced them "as good a regiment as had visited Washington."[6] The next day, they marched up Pennsylvania Avenue, through the cobbled streets of the quaint old village of Georgetown, and out into the country beyond. It was blisteringly hot, and several of the men fainted during the march. Eventually they arrived at a nice piece of land overlooking the Potomac River. There they formed a brigade with the Third Michigan, First Massachusetts, and Twelfth New York, with command of the brigade given to their own Colonel Richardson.

As soon as they recovered from the march, the regiments set about establishing a proper camp. Tents were pitched in neat long rows on either side of wide "streets," which were often given names indicating where the company that fronted them was from; one might be Flint Avenue, another, Saginaw Street. The wedge, or "A," tents in common use at the beginning of the war consisted of a large piece of canvas stretched over a horizontal pole, which was itself supported by two vertical poles. The area inside the tents was approximately seven square feet, plenty of room for between two and four men. Some enterprising soldiers went to great lengths to make their tents comfortable, building "beds" out of branches or felled timber, even building tables and stools. Most recruits discovered that a dismounted and upturned bayonet made a decent candleholder, and the wooden boxes in which hardtack was stored—the cracker-like substance that became a much-ridiculed but nonetheless useful staple of the army diet—made excellent writing desks.[7]

Life in camp was similar in some respects to life at Fort Wayne. Reveille sounded at 5 a.m., taps at 9 p.m. (That first year, the melody for the lights-out call was different than it is now; the modern version of taps would not be composed until the following summer.) In between, there was fatigue or guard duty, drills, and often dress parades, full of military pomp and stirring music. At night, when the day's work was over, most men from each company would gather by a campfire and socialize. If someone had received a letter that day containing news from his hometown, he might read it aloud for all to hear, or the men would share gossip and stories of past adventures. Sometimes one of the men would produce an instrument, and the evening would be spent singing songs.[8] It was a happy time for Emma, who enjoyed the crisp, routine days, and the jovial camaraderie of the balmy June nights. "I have spent some of the pleasantest, happiest hours of my life in camp," she said, "and I think thousands can give the same testimony."[9]

That first June, Emma had only one tent mate—Damon Stewart, a twenty-six-year-old shopkeeper from Flint whom Emma knew before the war. Stewart assumed that his baby-faced tent mate was one of the many adolescent boys who lied about their age in order to enlist, and took his younger bunk mate under his wing. Many of Emma's comrades assumed the same thing, which explained not only "Frank's" rather delicate features, but also his lack of bad habits such as swearing, drinking, and smoking.

As at Fort Wayne, there was no need for Emma to undress in front of Stewart, or anyone else; it was extremely rare for anyone to change into nightshirts for sleeping, or even undress to their undergarments. At most, they might remove their coats and boots, and sleep in their flannel shirt and pants. On warm nights, many soldiers took their bedrolls outside and slept under the stars.

In place of the privies at Fort Wayne, army regulations called for the construction of latrines, or "sinks," to be dug eight feet deep, and then covered with dirt or leaves after each use. Sometimes the sinks were quite elaborate, partially covered with wooden planks for seats, or screened by boughs of greenery for privacy.[10] Even so, the sinks were so foul and fly-infested that their use was the exception rather than the rule.[11] Most soldiers preferred to slip off into the woods to tend to their personal needs, a practice that gave Emma the privacy she needed to maintain her disguise.

Emma had to take care not to appear overly competent at domestic skills like cooking, washing, and sewing, at least at the beginning of the war. By the end, most veterans were quite adept at all of these things, but early on, agility in any of these areas would be particularly conspicuous. Although companies often designated cooks whenever they were in camp for a long enough interval, there were plenty of times when men who had never so much as made a cup of tea at home had to prepare their own meals, and their inexperience showed. Likewise, washing dishes was something that was, and remained, foreign to most soldiers throughout the war. Standards varied, but few of them were high. While a small number of fastidious soldiers carefully rinsed out their tin plates and cups after every meal, many more simply gave their plates a quick scrape with a knife and shoved them back under their bedrolls or into their knapsacks. Others found that, when available, soft bread dampened with a few drops of coffee made a perfectly good edible sponge.[12]

Approaches to doing laundry also ranged widely, although even those with the worst habits had to wash their clothes sometimes. Boiling was the only thing that would kill the vermin that infested almost everyone's clothes at one time or another throughout the war. And every man had his own "housewife," a small kit of needles and thread, buttons, and thimbles, and was expected to darn his own socks and make any other necessary repairs.[13]

Occasionally, an enterprising soldier would offer to wash or sew for others, for a fairly steep price. Emma, with her years of training at the side of her mother and sisters, could have done quite well had she set up her own business, but it was far too risky. It was often the small but crucial details that gave away many of the other women who enlisted in the army. One woman in an Ohio regiment was suspected early on by the way she would wring a dish towel, as well as by her sewing ability.[14] Another was given away by the way she shrieked when accidentally hit on the head, and yet another by the way she put on her socks and boots.[15] But most of these women had only just assumed their disguises. Having lived as Frank Thompson for years, Emma had perfected the walk, the voice, the mannerisms of a man. And the years of practice gave her one of the most crucial and elusive elements of any disguise: the confidence that she could pull it off. Even when she was teased about her small feet, or her beardless face—even when she was given the nickname "our woman" early in the war, she had the nerve to laugh along with the rest of them.

Perhaps more important than how she looked or behaved, however, was how she was seen. Despite the prevalence of female warriors in popular culture—stories like that of Fanny Campbell, or celebrated historical examples, such as Joan of Arc—nineteenth-century Victorians did not really believe that women could make good soldiers; ergo, good soldiers, they reasoned, could not be women.[16]

As the month of June wore on, the novelty of camp life began to wear off, and Emma and her comrades came face to face for the first time with two of the most treacherous enemies they would encounter during the war. The first was boredom, which, while not lethal, would stalk them almost the entire time they were in the army. In the entire 1,500 days of the war, fewer than 100 were occupied with actual fighting, and even then no soldier saw action in every engagement. Some of the rest of the time included picket duty—posting guard along the front line—which could, and often did, result in an exchange of fire; other days were consumed by long and tiring marches. But the vast majority of a Civil War soldier's days were spent in camp, and even with fatigue and guard duties and the daily drills, there were still hours and hours with nothing to do.

As a whole, nineteenth-century Americans were enterprising people, used to making their own entertainment, and Civil War soldiers, being no exception, found innumerable ways to amuse themselves. Letter writing was a popular diversion, as were reading and playing music. One veteran recalled that soldiers were not picky about their reading material. "[T]here was no novel so dull, trashy, or sensational as not to find someone so bored with nothing to do that he would wade through it."[17] Some men whittled; others played cards or checkers. Sometimes boxing matches were staged. Fishing was very popular when time and geography allowed. And when camped near Washington, passes were liberally granted. The U.S. Patent Office, where George Washington's sword and Benjamin Franklin's printing press were on display, was a popular destination, as was the Smithsonian Castle, with its stuffed animal skins, preserved insects, Egyptian mummies, and curiosities from around the world.[18] Others used their passes to visit alehouses, or to frequent one of the many brothels that popped up in Washington seemingly overnight.

Aside from the occasional sightseeing trip, Emma was not interested in most of the amusements that occupied her friends. She rarely wrote letters, because she had no one to write to. With her deeply religious background, she viewed card playing as a serious vice, if not an outright sin. And she did not dare swim, or sing, or box or play ball, for fear some physical clue might give her away.

Whenever possible, Emma attended prayer meetings or lectures, which were fairly common during the first part of the war. But she found her calling when the regiment confronted its second unexpected enemy: rampant illness. Every morning after roll call, the medical staff held sick call, in which any soldier who felt unwell, or who at least wanted to avoid the day's duties, could present himself for examination. Often a little "medicinal" whiskey was all that was needed to make the sufferer feel better. As Emma recalled, sick call generally involved an "examination of tongues and pulses, and a liberal distribution of quinine and blue pills, and sometimes a little eau- ds-vie, to wash down the bitter drugs."[19] Within weeks of establishing camp, the commanding officers noted, to their growing dismay, that the sick-call lines in the Second Michigan were getting longer every day. The combination of overcrowding, thousands of farm boys never exposed to childhood diseases, unfamiliar foods, and poor sanitation turned the volunteer army into what one historian has aptly called "a gigantic petri dish."[20] Disease was so rampant in both the Union and Confederate armies that two-thirds of all wartime fatalities were due to illness.

By the middle of June, nearly 30 percent of all of the troops in and around Washington were on the sick list, and the Second was no exception.[21] The most common complaint was diarrhea, a problem that plagued soldiers throughout the war so badly that chronic diarrhea alone was responsible for killing more Federal troops than Confederate weapons. Diarrhea was not itself a disease, but a symptom of several. Sometimes it was caused by unbalanced diets, or food poisoning. But other times it was the symptom of a viral or bacterial infection, often caused by polluted water and food supplies. At the time the war broke out, the relationship between hygiene and health was still poorly understood. It had been only two years since Florence Nightingale's influential book, *Notes on Nursing*—one of the first widely read publications that highlighted the relationship between sanitation and disease—was published, and the importance of the link had not yet become common knowledge. There were those who were trying to bring wider attention to the problem, most notably the U.S. Sanitary Commission, a government-backed civilian relief organization, but the commission was only just getting under way.

Of all the diseases spreading through the camps in the spring of 1861, typhoid, which was then fatal more than 25 percent of the time, was one of the worst. Caused by bacteria from contaminated food or water entering the bloodstream, typhoid caused chronic fever, abdominal pain, and, in the most severe cases, pulmonary arrest. An outbreak of typhoid hit the Second Michigan in the middle of June, and, as Emma remembered, "the hospitals were soon crowded with its victims."[22] Each regiment was responsible for establishing its own hospital, which was really a collection of tents—army regulations called for three per regiment—that were specially designed to serve the purpose. They were fourteen feet square, and eleven feet high in the center, each capable of accommodating up to eight patients. Sometimes they were set up end to end, to make one large facility.[23] Each volunteer regiment supplied its own surgeons and assistant surgeons, as well as nurses, stewards, and a ward master. The hospital tents were usually pitched in the shadiest part of camp, and when time permitted, floorboards were cut and laid. If not, the ground was covered with rubber blankets to keep moisture out, and trenches were dug around the perimeter to prevent flooding during heavy rains.

The quality of medical care varied widely among the volunteer regiments. The Second Michigan was particularly lucky, having come east with two distinguished surgeons, Alonzo B. Palmer and Henry B. Lyster. The dignified, elegant Palmer was a professor at the University of Michigan Medical School, and Lyster, a jovial Irishman, was one of his best students. But the nurses and stewards were almost always men with no medical training; they were taken from the rank and file, and for most soldiers, nursing duty was an undesirable detail, to be avoided at all costs. Most men would rather split logs, or dig sinks, or perform just about any other kind of fatigue duty before working in the hospitals.

When the typhoid epidemic broke out, Emma spent all of her free time going "from tent to tent, ministering to the wants of those delirious, helpless men." When Emma's superiors noticed "Frank's" interest in nursing, they assigned him to permanent hospital detail. The work suited Emma perfectly, appealing as it did to the same sense of compassion for the weak and helpless that she had had since childhood. She was convinced that she had inherited a particular gift for nursing from her mother, that there was almost a "magnetic power in my hands to soothe the delirium."[24] The assignment also had practical benefits; it meant that she was often on duty at night, and allowed to sleep during part of the day, giving her time alone in her tent. And it meant that she had an excuse for the bloody clothes and rags that she would have to deal with every month.

Not once did the doctors or patients suspect that the competent, gentle nurse with the oddly small feet was a woman, or, if they did, they did not let on. Had they known, though, it might have struck them as ironic that just then, a fierce debate was raging just a few miles from them in Washington, and indeed, throughout the country, about whether or not women should be allowed to serve as nurses during the war. Medicine in general was still a male profession. There were a handful of female doctors in the United States, including Elizabeth Blackwell and Mary Walker. Blackwell, the first woman in the country to be licensed to practice medicine, received her degree from Geneva Medical College in 1849. Walker followed six years later with a degree from Syracuse Medical College. But they were aberrations, and shortly after Walker received her degree, both medical schools closed their doors to women for the time being. Professional nursing was not yet much of a profession at all. In civilian life, some hospital nurses were nuns, but in general, nursing as such was done in the home, by family members. To the extent that nursing existed, it was in the military, and there, nurses were uniformly men, although, unbeknownst to Emma, that was about to change.

Just weeks after Fort Sumter fell, a dour, straight-backed sixty-year-old reformer and activist named Dorothea Dix arrived in Washington to inspect the preparations being made for caring for wounded Federal troops. Dix, who had run health-care centers for the indigent in New York City, was horrified by what she found. There were only thirty permanent hospital beds in all of Washington, and even fewer supplies. And despite the regimental hospitals, there was a desperate shortage of trained nurses. Dix concluded that the Army Medical Corps was not ready for a massive, prolonged war, which was due in part to the fact that no one expected the conflict to be either. Dix went to see the Secretary of War, Simon Cameron, and demanded that he allow her to organize a volunteer corps of female nurses patterned on the model pioneered by Florence Nightingale for British troops in the Crimean War, a decade earlier. At first, Cameron rejected Dix's proposal out of hand. Military nursing was a male domain, and always had been. But Dix was relentless. She spent several weeks in Washington promoting her cause to anyone who would listen, including President Lincoln. Finally, on April 23, 1861, Cameron, recognizing that the War Department was in fact overwhelmed, relented, and issued a directive appointing Dix as Superintendent of Female Nurses for the Federal army. But Dix's jurisdiction was strictly limited to the general hospitals in and around Washington. Under no circumstances was she to send female nurses to the front. Battlefield nursing was and would remain man's work.[25]

Even this compromise caused an uproar. The idea was ridiculed as impractical, on the theory that women were too emotional and fragile to be of any use. They would faint, cry, become hysterical at the sight of blood. They would create more problems for the doctors than they were worth. At the very least, they would be too physically weak to be of assistance. The idea was also denounced as an affront to both modesty and morality. Either a lady's delicate sensibilities would be offended by such intimate contact with strange men, or, the implication was, she was no lady, in which case, she was surely drawn to the hospitals for immoral reasons. A number of popular but scandalous novels about the Crimean War had centered on the romantic exploits of female British army nurses.[26]

To counteract such criticism, Dix issued stringent requirements for her nurses. Among other things, they must be "plain almost to repulsion in dress, and devoid of personal attractions." They must wear petticoats, not hoopskirts, which would have gotten in the way of the doctors, and they must not decorate themselves in any way. And they must be at least thirty years old. But, as Emma noted, some very non-Dixian nurses managed to get past the superintendent.

We have some sentimental ladies who go down [to the hospital] and expect to find everything in drawing-room style, with nothing to do but sit and fan handsome young mustached heroes in shoulder straps, and read poetry, etc., and finding the real somewhat different from the ideal, which their ardent imaginations had created, they can not endure such work as washing private soldiers' dirty faces and combing tangled, matted hair. So after making considerable fuss, and trailing round in very long silk skirts for several days, until everybody becomes disgusted, they are politely invited by the surgeon in charge to migrate to some more congenial atmosphere.[27]

Emma, not yet twenty, would not have met Dix's qualifications. She had more in common with another woman in Washington who was eager to be directly involved in tending to the sick and wounded. Clara Barton, at thirty-nine, and famously plain in appearance, was exactly the kind of no-nonsense, hard-working woman Dix was looking for. But, like Emma, Barton was also independent and headstrong, and could not bring herself to submit to Dix's high-handed authority. The similarities between Emma and Clara Barton are striking. Both were raised in households dominated by unhappy marriages. Both were excellent students and childhood tomboys; Clara's father described her as "more boy than girl." Both were skilled riders, and good shots. And both prized their independence and shunned marriage proposals in favor of making their own way in a world hostile to single working women. But the differences between the two women are striking too: Clara was nearly twenty years older than Emma, and while Emma despised her father, Clara loved hers, a retired soldier, to the point of hero worship. That one fact may explain why, while they both hated the limitations imposed on their gender, they took very different approaches to overcoming them.[28]

When the war broke out, Clara Barton was a salaried clerk in the U.S. Patent Office, one of the few women employed by the government in that capacity, a position she obtained through a combination of steely determination and family connections. From the moment that the first regiments from her native Massachusetts arrived in the city, she took it upon herself to make sure that they had the best care that she could provide.[29]

But if the thought of actually enlisting in the army under an alias had ever crossed her mind, she would have quickly rejected it. It would not have been easy to pull off, given her matronly figure, and despite all of her independence and stubbornness, Barton also had a strong sense of propriety and family honor. She was, as her father expected her to be, a lady, and, "no lady would ever impersonate a man in order to become a soldier, so that option for serving her country was out."[30] It was one thing for Barton to gather supplies for the soldiers, or visit the camps near Washington in the company of a suitable chaperone; it would have been quite another for her to travel, unescorted, to the field. Later, when things became more desperate, she would do so, but in the early part of the war, Barton limited herself to visiting the camps around Washington with medicines and supplies, which she paid for out of her own meager salary, and always in the company of a suitable chaperone.[31] Barton wrote to a friend that she longed to be more involved, to nurse the men herself, and that "nothing but the fear of finding myself out of place or embarrassing others restrains me."[32] In this, Barton's sentiments were not unlike Emma's, when Emma said that one of the reasons that she had enlisted as Frank Thompson was so that she could nurse men with less embarrassment to them as men than she could as a woman.

By the end of June, Washington had taken on a bustling, martial air. Emma recorded that "every hillside and valley for miles around was thickly dotted with snowy white tents. Soldiers drilling, fatigue parties building forts, artillery practicing, and the supply trains moving to and from the various headquarters, presented a deeply interesting picture." Emma could have been speaking for many when she wrote that, as she surveyed the scene, "I could but feel assured of the speedy termination of the conflict, and look forward with eager anticipation to the day when that mighty host would advance upon the enemy, and like an overwhelming torrent sweep rebellion from the land."[33]

That was certainly the predominant view in Washington on the first Fourth of July of the war, which dawned hot and hazy along the Potomac. The day was marked by a suspension of all unessential military duties, replaced with picnics, berry-picking expeditions, and formal dress parades. But even as regimental bands played patriotic songs, and fireworks lit up the night sky, a Confederate flag could be seen waving above Alexandria on Munson's Hill. Thirty miles to the west, at the railroad junction at Manassas, Confederate general P.G.T. Beauregard, who had been in command of the South Carolina forces that subdued Fort Sumter, was now ensconced with a force of nearly twenty thousand men on the far side of a creek called Bull Run. Nearly nine thousand more rebel soldiers, under the command of General Joe Johnston, loitered just upriver within striking distance of the Federal forces at Harpers Ferry.

As July wore on, public pressure was mounting in the North to put the nearly thirty-five thousand Union soldiers now amassed in and around Washington into action. As a veteran of the War of 1812, and the stand-out hero of the Mexican War, General in Chief Scott was one of the few men in Washington who was intimately familiar with the realities of war. He knew that it was too soon, that all the enthusiasm in the world could not adequately prepare his collection of green volunteers for battle. Scott practically begged President Lincoln for more time to train his men, and to allow the Federal blockade of Southern port cities to take its toll on the Confederate economy. But every day, the battle cry grew louder. Northern papers were demanding action. Horace Greeley's influential New York *Tribune* began running "the Nation's War Cry" of "Forward to Richmond" under its daily masthead. Some papers ridiculed Scott as a dotard, or worse, suggested that the native Virginian was secretly sympathetic to the Confederacy, and would never willingly move against it. The Republicans in Congress were growing increasingly restless, as well. For his part, Lincoln feared that the rebels might not wait for him to make the first move. Any day, he worried, Johnston could swing down from Harpers Ferry, join forces with Beauregard, and advance on Washington. Even if Lincoln's army could hold the city, an attack on Washington would take away his ability to maneuver, not to mention be a huge public relations disaster. And he feared, too, that if the Confederacy were allowed to survive unmolested throughout the summer, England and France would legitimize it by granting it diplomatic recognition.[34]

Lincoln concluded his army must act first, and soon. They must go out to meet Beauregard at Manassas, before Johnston could come down from Harpers Ferry to reinforce him. Not insignificantly, they would also take control of the important junction of the Orange and Alexandria and Manassas Gap railroads, a move that would both isolate Johnston to the north, and provide a way to maintain Union supply lines on a march south toward Richmond. The importance of Manassas was so obvious that even as early as May 31, the Detroit *Free Press* had announced, "Federal troops will occupy Manassas Junction tomorrow night, driving away the rebels who have congregated there."[35]

It took Lincoln several more weeks to convince Scott to act. Finally, Scott relented, and ordered General Irvin McDowell to lead an attack on Manassas. (Scott was once a dashing field general, but now, at seventy-four years old, and nearly crippled by gout, he was strictly an armchair warrior.) McDowell, another regular army veteran, also expressed strong reservations about sending the green troops into action so soon. Lincoln famously dismissed him, saying, "It is true that you are green. But they are green too. We are all green alike."

On July 15, the Second Michigan received orders to prepare to march. For the boys eager for a fight, it was welcome news. One member of the Second recorded in his journal that day, "Great excitement is kept up expecting the coming day to . . . march as orders have been given to be ready at 3 o'clock to start on a light march taking nothing but arms and blankets, rations for 3 days. Hearts are beating fast with the novelty of a march and prospects for a skirmish." [36] Emma, too, remembered the electric effect of the news on her comrades. "Oh, what great excitement and enthusiasm that order produced. . . . Nothing could be heard but the wild cheering of the men, as regiment after regiment received their orders. As the news spread throughout the camp, the troops, eager to prove themselves in battle, let out whoops of excitement. At last, they were to face the enemy." [37] Most, convinced of the righteousness of their cause and confident in their as yet untested skill as warriors, believed the end of the war was one decisive victory away, and that they were the ones who would win it.

The next afternoon, with blankets rolled, haversacks filled, and spirits soaring, the Second Michigan formed into lines, just as they had practiced so many times, and smartly marched out of camp toward the Chain Bridge that connected Georgetown with Virginia. As they went, they were joined by other regiments of their newly formed brigade: the Third Michigan, First Massachusetts, and the Twelfth New York among them, as well as by citizens in hacks and carriages with picnic baskets in their hands who were determined to witness what they, too, thought might be the only battle of the entire war.

"In gay spirits the army moved forward," Emma wrote, "the air resounding with the music of the regimental bands, and patriotic songs of the soldiers. No gloomy forebodings seemed to damp the spirits of the men." But Emma felt "strangely out of harmony with the wild, joyous spirit which pervaded the troops." As she looked into the happy, eager faces of her young comrades, Emma could only think that "many, very many" of those faces would not return to tell of their adventure.[38]

CHAPTER FOUR

July 1861

EVEN FOR the most eager, it did not take long for the novelty of the march to wear off, and when it did, the impressive martial appearances went along with it. With the hot July sun beating down, men sweltered in their woolen uniforms. Dirt roads dry from lack of rain turned into clouds of dust that settled over everyone and everything. New boots chafed. The parched and hungry soldiers, not used to conserving water, drained canteens and broke ranks to go in search of more. Some wandered off to pick berries. Others simply sat down to rest, and were not easily prodded back into action. Many of those who did keep up the pace came down with heatstroke, and had to be driven back to Washington in the already-scarce ambulances that were supposed to have been used for ferrying wounded from the battlefront.[1]

With all the stops, the columns moved slowly, reaching the village of Fairfax—less than halfway between Washington and Manassas—on the evening of the seventeenth, where they were ordered to camp for the night. Emma noted, "Notwithstanding the heat and fatigue of the day's march, the troops were in high spirits, and immediately began preparing supper. Some built fires while others went in search of, and appropriated, every available article which might in any way add to the comfort of hungry and fatigued men."[2] In other words, despite orders to the contrary, they ransacked neighboring farms, raiding chicken coops, shooting grazing livestock, tearing apart fences for fires, and generally destroying the rolling green countryside as only the sudden appearance of thirty-five thousand foot soldiers can do.[3]

They were now fifteen miles from Bull Run creek, which lay between them and their destination at Manassas Junction. The creek itself was not wide or deep, but its banks were steep and rocky, and higher on the far side, giving defenders a significant advantage. The best crossing point was a stone bridge on the Warrenton Turnpike, the main road that ran from Washington to Manassas, but, based on intelligence reports, McDowell knew that the rebels were guarding it in force, and that he would have to find another place where he could cross unimpeded. The creek was dotted with natural fords where his infantry could cross easily when not under fire; the question was how far north and south from the stone bridge the Confederate defenses stretched. The only way to find out was to try to draw their fire.

Emma's regiment was one of four that formed a brigade under the command of the Second's Colonel Richardson, who in turn reported to Brigadier General Daniel Tyler. Early the next morning, while the rest of the army was just beginning to stir, Tyler ordered Richardson to head out in advance toward Centreville, the next village to the south. Richardson's task was twofold: to determine if Centreville was occupied by the enemy, and to probe the strength of their presence along the creek south of the stone bridge, with an eye to finding an undefended ford. As Emma recalled, "Considerable excitement prevailed throughout the day, as we were every hour in expectation of meeting the enemy. Carefully feeling [our] way, [we] moved steadily on, investigating every field, building and ravine for miles in front and to the right and left."[4] Although they passed various signs of recent enemy presence—abandoned entrenchments, recently extinguished campfires, even a few forgotten tents—they discovered that Centreville itself was unoccupied.

Richardson sent word back to the main column, and then, after stopping for water, they pressed on through the woods toward one of the potential crossing points, called Blackburn's Ford. As they neared the creek, the terrain became increasingly wooded and steep, making it hard to see what, or who, lay in front of them on the far side. Just after noon, when the sun was directly overhead, the roar of artillery from a hidden Confederate battery announced that this was not the place McDowell was looking for. For the next three hours, Emma's regiment was pinned under enemy fire, while two other regiments to its right were able to maneuver into a position protected enough to return fire. After several hours, Colonel Richardson concluded that the enemy presence on the far side was not as formidable as it first seemed, and wanted to charge the creek and secure the crossing for the rest of the army. Fortunately for Emma and her comrades, General Tyler would not allow it, and instead ordered them to fall back out of enemy range. When it was over, the brigade had suffered sixty casualties, although only one from the Second Michigan.

By evening, the main columns reached Centreville, and, as Emma recalled, "our surgeons began to prepare for the coming battle, by appropriating several buildings and fitting them up for the wounded."[5] Word of the day's skirmish, and the casualties, spread quickly, and a more sober mood descended on the camp. Emma noted that night a notable "lack of that picnic hilarity which had characterized the [troops] the day before."[6] And while Emma's brigade was afforded a certain amount of new respect among the rest of the untested recruits, the day's encounter had an even more profound effect on General McDowell, who concluded that the enemy had a much larger force at Manassas than he had thought.

In fact, on the night of the eighteenth, the Union forces still outnumbered the enemy by almost two to one, and had McDowell gone ahead and thrown his main force across Bull Run that day, he might well have been able to roll on to Richmond. But instead he hesitated, spending two full days rethinking his plans, a delay that would cost him dearly; it allowed fifteen thousand Confederate reinforcements to arrive by train from Harpers Ferry to reinforce Beauregard. By the time McDowell finally tried to cross Bull Run, the two forces were nearly equal in size.

Well before dawn on Sunday, July 21, McDowell ordered three divisions forward. He sent one division directly down Warrenton Turnpike, to make the Confederates think that he was crossing the stone bridge in force, and two more divisions to a ford at Sudley Springs, well north of the turnpike. Emma's division was sent to guard the crossing it had tried to take several days before, to make sure the Confederates did not try to cross it themselves and attack the Union from the rear, but the Second did not go with them. Instead, Emma and her comrades were kept in reserve at Centreville. From her camp, Emma watched as the solemn procession of the scared and the stoic passed by. "Sunday morning before dawn, those three divisions moved forward, presenting a magnificent spectacle, as column after column wound its way over the green hills and through the hazy valleys, with the soft moonlight falling on the long lines of shining steel. Not a drum or bugle was heard during the march, and the deep silence was broken only by the rumbling of artillery, the muffled tread of infantry, or the low hum of thousands of subdued voices."[7]

The Second Michigan spent the rest of the day in a state of anticipation, expecting any minute to be called to the front. They were too far from the action to be able to see anything, but they could hear it well enough. "Nothing," Emma wrote, "could be heard save the thunder of artillery, the clash of steel, and the continuous roar of musketry. Oh, what a scene for the bright sun of a holy Sabbath morning to shine upon! Instead of the sweet influences which we associate with the Sabbath—the chiming of church bells calling us to the house of prayer, the Sabbath school, and all of the solemn duties of the sanctuary—there was confusion, destruction, and death."[8]

Emma did not know it, but for a good while that day, it looked as though General Scott would be proved wrong, and his green volunteers would win the day. The two divisions sent north had successfully crossed at Sudley Springs, and were making headway well into the day. But in the mid-afternoon, just as the Union was about to punch through rebel defenses on the high ground of Henry House Hill, the Confederates rallied under the leadership of General Thomas Jackson—a moment that earned him his nickname, "Stonewall." From then on, the tide shifted in favor of the Confederates. The Union army's fate was effectively sealed when, late in the day, two Union batteries were captured, at least in part due to confusion over uniforms. The commander of a Federal battery saw troops in the woods, and, judging by their blue jackets, assumed them to be reinforcements. In fact, they were the Thirty-third Virginia, which had flanked the Federal left. By the time the battery commander realized his mistake, it was too late, and his unit's key position was overrun. In Emma's recollection, and that of many others present, that was the last straw. "The news of this disaster spread along our lines like wildfire; officers and men were alike confounded; regiment after regiment broke and ran, and almost immediately the panic commenced."[9] General McDowell had no choice but to sound the retreat, and to try to restore some order to the withdrawal.

Finally, at five in the evening, the Second Michigan were called into action, not to go to the front, but to guard the retreat from what everyone assumed would be a Confederate counterattack. Well into the night, the Second stood their ground while the rest of the army made haste toward Washington. It was a duty that they performed well. The New York *Tribune* noted that the Second Michigan was one of the few regiments that managed to "come in fair order."[10] But it was a depressing and demoralizing task, nonetheless. One member of Company I recalled the dispiriting scene as they brought up the rear of the retreating army. "Government wagons tipped over, some broken boxes of provisions strewn about, beef and pork destroyed or left to fall into the hands of the enemy together with ammunition etc. All through the cowardice of the soldiers that commenced the retreat . . . I hope I may never see such again." [11] To make matters worse, a heavy rain began the next morning, and they were soaking wet and famished when they arrived near Arlington the next evening.

Emma was not among them. When the wounded began to arrive in Centreville during the battle the day before, she volunteered to help the surgeons at the hospital they had established several days earlier, in a small stone church on the Warrenton Turnpike. Although Emma was used to caring for the sick, this was her first encounter with the horrific effects of battle. "But how shall I describe the scene within the church at that hour? Oh, there was suffering there which no pen can ever describe." As the surgeons operated at a furious pace, and the "stacks of dead bodies piled up, and arms and legs were thrown together in heaps," Emma spent the day and night cleaning bandages, offering water, listening to dying men's final words, giving any comfort she could. In some cases, she recalled, she was "obliged . . . to use my teeth in order to tear the thick woolen garments stiffened with blood." [12]

One case Emma recalled with particular clarity nearly twenty years later. "It was that of a poor fellow whose legs were broken above the knees, and from the knees to the thighs they were literally smashed to fragments. He was dying, but, oh, what a death was that. He was insane, perfectly wild, and required two persons to hold him. Inflammation had set in, and was rapidly doing its work; death soon released him, and it was a relief to all present as well as to the poor sufferer." Another man, bearing his suffering in silence, touched Emma with his stoicism. "Poor pale face, I see it now, with its white lips and beseeching eyes, and then the touching inquiry, 'Do you think I will die before morning?' I told him I thought he would." Emma placed a high priority on being honest with dying men. She saw no usefulness in giving false hope; to the contrary, she believed it was her duty to help those who were beyond physical aid to prepare mentally and spiritually for the next, and she often took the hands of those who were slipping away and led them in prayer.[13]

Emma, like so many other wartime nurses, found an inner courage and fortitude that day that allowed her to overcome her fear and revulsion; she felt herself to be "simply eyes, ears, hands and feet." She and the doctors and other nurses were so engaged in their work that they were not aware that the retreat had been sounded. "Our hearts and hands being fully equipped with such scenes as these, we thought of nothing else. We knew nothing of the true state of affairs outside, nor could we believe it possible when we learned that the whole army had retreated toward Washington, leaving the wounded in the hands of the enemy, and us, too, in rather an unpleasant situation."[14]

Well after dark, Emma went out to where her regiment had been encamped that morning. "No troops were there. I thought then that they had merely changed position, and that by going over the field, I should certainly find them." After trying for nearly an hour to locate her regiment, she concluded that the rumors were true; they had been deserted. For the first time that day, fear began to rise within her, but she could not bring herself to abandon the wounded and dying men in the church. Even when the regimental chaplain departed, telling those remaining that they would "soon be in the hands of the enemy," Emma refused to leave. "Oh, how brave those men were. What moral courage they possessed. Nothing by the grace of God and a right appreciation of the great cause in which they had nobly fought could reconcile them to such suffering and humiliation."[15]

As the night wore on, several of the men urged their nurse to go, reminding "him" that he would surely be imprisoned and not allowed to care for them once the enemy arrived. Reluctantly Emma put water within reach of those who could drink on their own, and turned to leave. Her last act was to honor the request of a mortally wounded young officer from Massachusetts to open a gold locket in his pocket, and put it where he could see the enclosed picture of his wife and infant child. As she did so, Emma could hear the sound of horses clattering on the road outside. Peering outside, Emma found that the road was filled with Confederate cavalry. A gentle rain was falling, and the night sky was moonless. Quietly she slipped out the back window, and into a field. After climbing several fences and cutting through several fields, she emerged on the main road again only when she felt sure she must be well past the Confederates' most advanced lines. Following the detritus of the retreating army, she found her way back to Washington alone.[16]

It was still raining when Emma found her regiment the next morning, encamped on the Arlington farm of Confederate general Robert E. Lee, ground that would one day become Arlington National Cemetery. Her comrades were pleased to see young "Frank," whom they feared had been taken prisoner. The mood pervading the dreary camp, and indeed all along the banks of the Potomac, was one of exhaustion and despair. Across the river, the city of Washington was in a state of panic. Men with severed limbs, or partially missing faces, straggled through the streets in search of medical attention. Others, their bodies intact but their morale destroyed, sought refuge in the bars, pubs, and bawdy houses. Officers rode drunkenly through the streets firing their weapons into the air in a vain effort to restore discipline. Meanwhile, the rebel flag was flying across the river, and most civilians and troops believed a Confederate attack was imminent.[17]

But the Confederate troops were also in a state of disarray after their surprising victory, and the feared invasion never came. The respite was a relief for the Federals, but as the days and weeks went on, morale plummeted. Emma recalled that "Washington at that time presented a picture strikingly illustrative of military life in its most depressing form . . . and military discipline nearly, or quite, forgotten for a time in the Army of the Potomac."[18]

The number of casualties from what Northerners would eventually call the First Battle of Bull Run (in the South it would be known

as First Manassas—the Union tended to name battles after prominent geographical features, while the Confederates more often used
the names of nearby towns) were relatively small, at least in comparison to later engagements. Of the nearly eighteen thousand federal
troops actively engaged in combat, fewer than seven hundred were
killed, and approximately a thousand more were wounded. But the
loss had taken a devastating toll on the confidence among Northerners that the war would be short and sweet. Gone forever was the
hope that the war would be won in a single afternoon.

President Lincoln recognized that General Scott had been right.
The volunteer regiments that had come whistling into Washington
were not yet a real army, and should not engage the enemy again
until they were.[19] He also realized that while Scott had been right
about that, he was not up to the task at hand. General Scott agreed,
and recommended that Lincoln send for George McClellan, a brilliant young engineer commanding the Department of the Ohio. Mc-
Clellan was young, only thirty-four, but he was widely regarded, by
himself as well as by others, as one of the shiniest of the regular
army's golden boys. Second in his class at West Point, McClellan had
served under, and greatly impressed, General Scott in the Mexican
War. More important, from Lincoln's perspective, was that McClellan was fresh from a victory, albeit a minor one, in western Virginia.
Although the skirmish at Rich Mountain had been a relatively in-
consequential engagement in the grand scheme of things, at the
moment it was the only good news Lincoln had to tout. In fact,
McClellan had less to do with the victory at Rich Mountain than
did General William Rosecrans, but McClellan, more adept at self-
promotion, took the credit, and the Northern press was only too
happy to have someone, anyone, to lionize.[20]

When McClellan reached Washington a week later, he was given a
hero's welcome. He was not only young, but also handsome and full
of bravado—some called him a young Napoleon for his rather
grandiose airs and his habit of putting his right hand in his coat, just

as the famous emperor had done. But bravado was just what was needed, and from the moment he arrived, he was idolized by his troops, Emma among them. He was dashing, decisive, and self-assured. As a soldier, he seemed to be everything his men aspired to be, everything he now convinced them they could become. An excellent horseman, McClellan could be seen riding from camp to camp on a large black stallion, barking commands, bringing order out of chaos. "When General McClellan took command of the Army of the Potomac"—a name he himself gave it; prior to McClellan's arrival the collection of forces around the Capitol had no official name—"he found it in the most lamentable condition," Emma wrote. "I think even his enemies," of whom there were many by the time the war was over, "are willing to admit that there is no parallel case in history where there has been more tact, energy and skill displayed in transforming a disorganized mob into an efficient and effective army."[21]

McClellan was undoubtedly the man for the job—his specialty was military organization—but he had one thing going for him that his predecessor had not. The volunteers themselves now realized, after the debacle at Manassas, that they actually did need some training before they headed out again. Soon every camp was brought to order, and drilling and marching occupied most of the soldiers' time. Discipline was strictly enforced; when members of the Seventy-ninth New York Volunteers—a rowdy Scottish regiment known as the Highlanders—mutinied in early August against their new colonel, McClellan dealt with them quickly and firmly, depriving them of their colors and sending the ringleaders to the Dry Tortugas to do hard labor for the duration of the war. Word spread quickly among the rank and file that McClellan was not a man to be trifled with, but his heavy-handed tactics did not provoke anger, as they might have done before Bull Run.[22] Instead, the troops saw them as a sign of competence and decisiveness. And so it was for McClellan throughout the war. No matter how many mistakes he made, or how he was

treated by the politicians and the press, he would be almost universally revered by his men. As Emma recalled, under his leadership,
"the army . . . began to assume a warlike aspect—perfect order and
military discipline were observed everywhere among the soldiers. It
was a splendid sight to see those well drilled troops on dress parade—
or being reviewed by their gallant young commander, upon whose
shoulders the 'stars' sat with so much grace and dignity."[23]

By August, Emma was once again detailed for nursing duty. This
time, she was assigned to one of the general hospitals in Georgetown,
which, like all hospitals in Washington, was filled beyond capacity
with the sick and wounded. As she noted, "[T]hat extraordinary
march from Bull Run, through rain, mud, and chagrin, did more toward filling the hospitals than did the battle itself."[24] Her duties were
much the same as before, but now there were combat wounds to treat
as well as the still-rampant cases of disease. It was gruesome work,
made harder by the doctors' lack of modern knowledge. Sterilization
was unheard-of. Infection was considered a sign of healing; oozing,
pus-filled sores were met with sighs of relief, until the poor soldier
died of "unknown causes." Compounds of dangerous substances,
such as mercury, were also used to treat open wounds; many soldiers
died with symptoms that have since been determined to have resulted
from mercury poisoning. Anesthetics were primitive: Ether had been
in use since the Mexican War, but there was often not enough to
go around, and even when used, dosages were not uniform. Whiskey
was considered a viable substitute, but above all, surgeons needed
speed. A good surgeon was one who could remove a leg in under
thirty seconds.[25]

"Oh, what an amount of suffering I am called to witness every
hour and every moment. There is no cessation, and yet it is strange
that the sight of all this suffering does not affect me more. . . . It does
seem as if there is a sort of stoicism granted for such occasions. There
are great, strong men dying all around me, and while I write there
are three being carried past the window to the dead room." Emma

was proud of her hospital. "This is an excellent hospital –everything is kept in good order, and the medical officers are skillful, kind and attentive." But she also noted that "[t]here is a vast difference in surgeons; some are harsh and cruel—whether it is from habit or insensibility I am not prepared to say—but I know the men would face a rebel battery with less forebodings than they do some of our worthy surgeons."[26]

Despite the suffering around her, it was a point of pride for Emma that she be as cheerful as possible. "I was not in the habit of going among the patients with a long, doleful face, nor intimating by word or look that their case was a hopeless one, unless a man was actually dying, and I felt it to be my duty to tell him so. Cheerfulness was my motto." And it was not all grim work. "There were a great many pleasant things in connection with camp hospital duties." She enjoyed writing letters and providing small comforts for convalescing soldiers. She also tried to satisfy the whims of her patients whenever possible. One day, an old Dutchman recovering from typhoid declared that he desperately wanted a piece of fresh fish for dinner, so Emma headed off to a nearby creek, where she caught an eel for the soldier's dinner.[27]

In the weeks and months after Bull Run, Washington remained under the shadow of a possible attack from the rebels who were still amassed just south and west of Arlington. There were skirmishes with pickets. Inside the city, McClellan had restored calm and order. Passes were hard to come by, and the provost guards were ordered to inspect the papers of every soldier in the city proper.[28] In Virginia, white tents made for what one historian called a "continuous military city" from the Chain Bridge, north of Georgetown, south to Alexandria and beyond. The same was true in Maryland as well.[29] The Second Michigan was one of the "veteran" regiments—having seen action at Blackburn's Ford and been present at Bull Run—that were given primary responsibility for serving as the first line of defense on the Virginia side of the Potomac, while the newer regiments pouring into Union Station daily were kept in the rear until they could be brought up to speed.[30]

That fall McClellan introduced a new form of pageantry, called Grand Reviews, enormous parades staged mainly for the psychological impact they had on the viewing public.[31] Entire divisions marched up Pennsylvania Avenue to martial music as large crowds cheered them on. Day by day, with each such scene, and the ever-increasing fortifications around the perimeter of the city, the despair over Bull Run began to recede, replaced by a new, more mature sense of optimism.

In late October, Emma moved back across the river to the regimental hospital, at the Second Michigan's camp, which was now south of Alexandria. Shortly after her return, she became better acquainted with a young man from Company I named Jerome Robbins, a twenty-year-old college student from Matherton, Michigan. A handsome man, with dark wavy hair, strong cheekbones, and dark, inky eyes, Robbins had enlisted shortly after Fort Sumter, and he and Emma had been mustered into Federal service at Fort Wayne on the same day. They knew each other casually, to say hello in passing, until one evening when Robbins visited the hospital in search of a friend who was a patient there. They struck up a conversation, and soon realized that they had much in common—much more than they had with the vast majority of their comrades. They were both well educated, highly literate, and loved reading and debating. Despite his rugged good looks, Robbins was at heart a gentle and compassionate man, with the heart of a scholar rather than a warrior.

Above all, they were both intensely religious. Almost all Civil War soldiers were, or pretended to be, religious to some degree or another. In the decades before the war, America experienced a second Great Awakening, which revitalized the role of religion in general, and Christianity in particular, in the daily lives of many citizens. Revivalism took many forms, but its universal characteristic was the predominance of religion in the daily lives of Northerners and

Southerners alike. In rural areas, the church was the touchstone of the community, and Sunday services were often the only time in the week that neighbors saw each other. In Northern urban areas, revivalism was predominantly focused on social reform activities, including the temperance movement, indigent relief efforts, and the abolitionist movement. Much of the debate over slavery, both for and against, was rooted in the language of Christianity. Northern anti-slavery Christians were convinced that slavery was both a personal and a national sin, while Southern Christians believed, or claimed to, that, to the contrary, slavery was not only ordained by God, but that humane slave-ownership was in fact a Christian duty. But regardless of whether slavery was seen as prohibited or sanctioned by God, Christianity was a central, dominant facet of public, and private, life. Rare was the man who did not at least profess to be among the faithful.

But that did not mean that most Civil War soldiers held themselves to a particularly high standard of "Christian" behavior. Most soldiers honored at least the more minor proscriptions of their church in the breach. Emma and Robbins, however, were not among them. Neither of them drank alcohol, smoked, played cards, or swore, and both took every opportunity available to attend religious services. Robbins frequently wrote in his journal about his near-constant efforts to perfect his faith and to improve his relationship with God. They agreed on other things, too, particularly the subject of slavery, which they both abhorred. That alone made them different from most of their comrades, who were largely indifferent to it.

That first night in his journal Robbins wrote that he had had "a pleasant conversation with Frank Thompson on the subject of religion." Robbins had high praise for his new friend's "value in conversation," as well as his nursing skills, noting admiringly that "Frank" seemed to easily "win the hearts of those about him." But something—something—about Thompson nagged at Robbins. "A mystery," Robbins scribbled at the bottom of the page, "seems to be connected with him." The mystery must not have bothered him too much, because from that day on, Robbins visited the hospital regularly, sometimes as often as three times a day, ostensibly to visit his sick friend, but also to seek out the company of his new friend. On November 1, Robbins again visited "my friend Thompson this evening and was highly entertained," and came away more impressed than ever, describing him as "a good noble-hearted fellow as far as limited acquaintance will allow." [32]

For Emma, too, a friend like Robbins was an unexpected and welcome gift. For months, she had been keeping her distance from her comrades. Frank Thompson was universally well liked for his cheerfulness, his eagerness to take on jobs that others did not want, and even for his ability to laugh at himself when teased about his small features. But so far, she had not had a real friend, someone she could talk to about things that mattered most to her. She had not had a real friend since she left home. In Robbins, though, she felt that she had discovered a soul mate.

She was also touched by his devotion to his sick friend; no doubt he was among those she was describing when she later wrote that "the kindness of soldiers toward each other is proverbial, and is manifested in various ways." When men were brought to the hospital with "fever preying upon them" their comrades "come several times a day to inquire how they are, and if there is anything they can do for them. And it is touching to see those men, with faces bronzed and stern, tenderly bending over the dying, while the tears course down their sunburnt cheeks." [33]

After Bull Run, Robbins had frequently been assigned to picket and guard duties, and there is no indication that he was not an effective soldier, or that he did not acquit himself well at Blackburn's Ford or on the retreat from Manassas. Nonetheless, whether his superiors noted his new interest in visiting the hospital, or whether it was simply a coincidence, they apparently concluded that Robbins, like his new friend Frank Thompson, was a man more suited to saving lives than taking them. On November 6, Robbins was assigned to permanent duty as a steward in the same hospital as Emma.[34]

The reassignment was apparently not at Robbins's request; he noted in his journal that he accepted the assignment reluctantly (it is not clear that he had a choice, but he may have), and "came near regretting it" immediately afterward. The one consolation was that he could now spend more time with his friend Frank. The morning after he reported to the hospital, Robbins recorded that he "arose greatly refreshed after a good sound sleep on a couch with my friend Frank Thompson," and as he watched Emma go about her duties so cheerfully and with such compassion, he had a change of heart. "I had some misgivings about my new employment, but as the day increased my gloomy thoughts were dispelled and I am hoping that I may be as useful" as Frank. From then on Robbins and Frank were nearly inseparable. That evening, they were both off duty, and went to a prayer meeting together. The next day, they took a walk across the Long Bridge, and into Washington.[35]

When they arrived back at the hospital after one such walk, Robbins found that he had three letters waiting for him, including one from a former student of his, Anna Corey. Anna, the younger sister of one of Robbins's closest friends, had begun writing to him several months earlier, and he eagerly awaited her letters. Robbins may have shared his excitement at finding another one waiting for him at camp with Frank, although perhaps he did not, knowing that Frank did not receive many letters.

Whether it was the letter from Anna, or the outing with Frank, Robbins was in a cheery mood when he sat down to write in his journal that night. "I begin to like my new situation better daily," he wrote. "My duties consist of keeping the tents . . . in order, assisting in waiting upon the sick, especially at mealtime. No duties for the night unless some of the regular nurses should be unfit for duty." But no sooner had he written those lines than he was interrupted in his writing, and summoned to the hospital. "Little did I expect," he continued later, "my duties with the last expression would so soon take place." Frank, he noted, also "sits up the first part of the night," a duty that Emma, unlike Robbins, regularly volunteered to perform to avoid the forced and risky intimacy of sleeping side by side with her tent mates.[36]

As the midnight hour came and went, Emma and Robbins worked side by side, watching over their patients, and speaking together in hushed tones. "Oh how sweet to be where one may while away a few hours in thought. . . . How infinitely wise was the great Author in designing man," Robbins mused. The next evening, Sunday, November 10, after their hospital shift was over and they had each had a rest, Emma and Frank attended another prayer meeting, which Robbins described as "a delicious morsel for our thirsty souls."

But the more time Robbins spent with his new friend, the more convinced he became that there was something strange about him. The next day, Robbins noted that although "the society of a friend so [dear] as Frank I hail with great joy, though foolish as it may be, a mystery appears to me connected with him which it is impossible for me to fathom. Yet these may be false surmises—would that I be free of them for not for worlds would I wrong a friend who so sincerely appreciates confiding friendship."[37] He did not let these thoughts interfere with his new friendship. Later that evening, Emma and Robbins, and two other friends, watched a fireworks display in honor of McClellan's promotion. General Scott had, with some pushing from the ambitious McClellan, finally retired, and Lincoln made McClellan general in chief of the entire U.S. Army, in addition to his duties as commander of the Army of the Potomac.

McClellan had been able to convince Lincoln that Scott was an impediment for quick action, but even after he took over Scott's job, McClellan gave no sign of putting his army on the offensive. As before, Lincoln was eager for a military victory. The army had more than tripled in size since the Battle of Bull Run, and the men now had several long months of additional training under their belt. In addition, maintaining an idle army of that size was getting expensive. The quartermaster and his staff were having to feed, clothe, arm, and outfit more than a hundred thousand men, and despite widespread skimming, if not outright graft, they managed to do a pretty good job. But the citizens of Washington, once so pleased to have the protecting presence of so many troops, were beginning to wish that at least some of them would move out. Sanitary conditions in the city, poor to begin with, were getting worse with the daily arrival of more troops. A slaughterhouse was situated right under the base of the unfinished Washington Monument, and offal was piled up within sight and smell of the White House. The stench was so bad that Lincoln had taken to spending large stretches of time at a retreat several miles north of the center of the city. Water supplies were becoming contaminated, leading to another outbreak of typhoid and dysentery.

But worse than the logistics, the static army was again becoming a political liability. Public pressure was building for McClellan to move against the Confederate forces still at Manassas, a force of only fifty thousand. As they had with Scott the previous summer, some of the more radical Republicans even hinted that McClellan, a Democrat, was keeping his army idle out of sympathy for the rebel cause. Lincoln did not believe that, but he did continue to fear that if the Confederates were allowed to remain unmolested throughout the winter, the new country would gain legitimacy in the eyes of England and France. McClellan resisted all efforts to make him move, however, in large part because he was laboring under the false impression that the Confederate force was more than twice its actual size.[38]

As November wore on, Robbins was liking his new duties more and more, and he and Emma were closer than ever. One afternoon, he noted that he had just returned from a "very pleasant stroll . . . with Frank. How invaluable is the friendship of one true heart!" It was a happy time for Robbins, perhaps the happiest of his time in the army. Throughout the war, he was given to powerful bouts of homesickness, but "Frank" eased the pain. In another entry, Robbins wrote, "The morning is so beautiful that I could not allow words to express my thoughts. My time is greatly eased by conversations with Frank, which to me bind his friendship more firmly." And in still another, he wrote, "Each day I become better suited with my situation, as all around me are pleasant. Scarcely a profane oath is uttered and card playing is not known. . . . [N]o greater blessing at present could be mine than the society of a friend like Frank, fully appreciating the noblest sentiments that the heart should possess" and "ever ready" to defend "the right." [39]

Perhaps during these talks with "Frank," Robbins felt close enough to his new friend to share his growing feelings for Anna Corey, with whom he was now corresponding regularly. In the same journal entry, Robbins noted that he wrote a long letter to Anna, whom he described as "the only young lady correspondent I have had since I enlisted and well worthy of the highest esteem of any who appreciates virtue and true nobility." [40] But listening to her handsome, gentle Jerome, to whom Emma was closer than she had ever been to any man, other than perhaps Thomas, patter on and on about Anna's virtue and nobility was not what Emma wanted. The more time they spent together, the more her feelings for him were becoming confusing, and she found it harder and harder to keep the truth about her identity and gender from him.

The day after Robbins's entry about Anna, Emma told Robbins that she felt unwell, and asked him to take her shift at the hospital, which he did willingly. While Robbins was tending to his patients, Emma must have been lying awake in her tent, struggling with a difficult decision. For the first time in her life, she had found a man she could trust, a man she did not view as the enemy, a man completely unlike her father. Apparently now that she had found him, the thought of losing him to another was becoming unbearable. The next evening, Emma told Robbins that she felt much better, and suggested another walk. Perhaps she had already made up her mind, or perhaps she decided on the spur of the moment, but sometime during that stroll, she told him who she really was. It must have been hard; the words surely did not come easily. Emma was not used to being honest—she had been telling lies big and small for years, and it had become a habit. In all her life, before or after that moment, she was perhaps never as willingly vulnerable as she made herself that day.

There is no record of what exactly transpired between them. It is easy to imagine them walking together in the evening, as they often did, their heads close, their voices hushed. And to picture the look in Robbins's eyes—of bewilderment, surprise, and finally, comprehension. In *Fanny Campbell,* Emma's personal guidebook, the heroine did not reveal herself immediately to her lover once she had rescued him. Only after they had worked side by side for several weeks, and she had earned his respect as well as his gratitude, did she tell him the truth. William Lovell's reaction to Fanny Campbell's revelation was, of course, unmitigated joy and love, and, after several more adventures together, they married and lived happily ever after. When Emma first read it, this was the part of the book that she scorned; pitying poor Fanny for risking life and limb for "only a lover." But now, Emma may have been hoping that Robbins's reaction would be something like William Lovell's.

But if Emma did hand Robbins her heart that evening, he handed it right back to her. That night, he wrote for several pages, unusual for a man who was normally careful to conserve his precious paper. On the first, he wrote in thick, bold script, "Please allow these leaves to be closed until the author's permission is given for opening." Below that, he wrote several lines about the weather, as he usually began his entries, and filled the remainder of the page with a discussion about recent military news. But on the next few pages, which he then sealed, he changed the subject. "Had a long and interesting conversation with Frank, in which he described his childhood in New Brunswick." Emma told him everything: How she had run away from her cruel father, how she had come to be Frank Thompson. After repeating these salient facts, Robbins got to the point: "My friend Frank is a female."[41]

The next page is nearly illegible. In tight, dense script, so different from his usual loose and flowing handwriting, Robbins filled the sheet of paper, then turned the journal on its side, and wrote even more over what he had just written. Some lines are underlined for emphasis—the word "heart" in several places, as well as "her," "feelings" and "real." What is clear from these scribbles is that the conversation ended badly, that when it was over, Emma was hurt and angry. "God knows my heart that towards her I entertain the kindest feelings, but it really seems that a great change has taken place in her disposition or that the real has been unmasked." Then, after a few illegible words, "Perhaps a knowledge on her part that there is one in a Michigan home that I do regard with especial affection creates her disagreeable manner."[42]

For the next two days there is no mention of Emma at all. But on the nineteenth, Robbins revisited the strange conversation he had had with Emma, as though he was only now ready to try and make sense of it. "The evening I passed . . . in solitude my mind engaged in thoughts of the past and the future . . . and also upon a conversation which occurred with Frank." (Robbins had clearly decided not to reveal Emma's secret, and from then on, only referred to her in his journal as Frank.) It was dangerous information for Robbins to know; in some, albeit rare, cases, soldiers were court-martialed for helping a woman soldier hide her sex. He knew, too, that his friend was in a dangerous position herself. Women who were discovered were subject to a wide array of treatment—some were simply sent home, but others, particularly single women with no family ties to the regiment, were labeled prostitutes and even criminally charged with solicitation.

Robbins's entry that night suggests that there had been some kind of rapprochement between the two of them since their last stormy meeting. His initial shock and sense of betrayal were replaced with an almost brotherly, protective tone. He wrote of the "star of Christian hope" that "ever binds the links of friendship more firmly with friends true to the confidence of each other and to their God. A brief sketch of the history of this friend is already given yet I might write pages in giving conversations had with this dear friend of our past lives." But, he wrote, "suffice it that our confidence in each other is bound by Christian love and [I] may hope some future time when better convenience allow, a few leisure moments will be given in speaking of this friendship as one of the greatest events of my life." But confusion still lingered. The next day, he asked plaintively, "Do we look to the future to supply happiness in the manner we ought?"[43]

Emma's own feelings about what had transpired between them during those several days were never recorded. It is safe to assume that she was brokenhearted, at least at first. Whatever her initial disappointment and anger had been, it seemed that, at least on the surface, she had gotten hold of herself, and all seemed well. On the twenty-first, they attended a prayer meeting together, and, when "Frank" went to Washington with several other friends on November 25, Robbins wrote that "I missed his presence much but this evening brought his pleasant face again." By the end of November, the weather turned cold, and with it came a renewed iciness between Robbins and Emma. Robbins did not mention Emma again for several days, and apparently after their initial truce, the relationship once again began to show signs of strain. On December 6, Robbins noted, in a tone suggesting he was now used to it, that "Frank seems somewhat displeased about something. I am very sorry but guess it won't last." But it did. When Robbins mentioned Emma again a week later, he recorded that "Frank [is] very reserved, don't know what the difficulty is but I am afraid I have offended him in some way. Am very sorry if so." He went on, noting that he was now "fearful our natures are not as congenial as first supposed by me. Yet I feel he is the same friend. Towards him I entertain the same friendship. But I have my faults and nearly as I can figure he has discovered a new one which is to him unpleasant, as I am but a part of erring humanity it may not be strange." Emma's mood may have had something to do with the fact that, more than ever, Robbins was spending what little free time he had writing to, and about, Anna Corey.[44]

The weeks before Christmas were busy ones, as the orders to establish winter quarters arrived and the soldiers went about the business of winterizing their tents to ward off the coming cold. Most built wood floors and some erected stockades of split logs around the lower half of the tents to serve as walls. Others built platforms for their bedrolls for additional insulation from the frozen ground. Many of them complained about the cold, but not Emma, who was inured to the climate by her years on the banks of Magaguadavic Lake.

The Army of the Potomac's first Christmas was a festive occasion. Evergreen arbors were constructed and decorated; musicians played hymns and carols. Memories of Bull Run were now quite distant. The future was unknown, but for the moment they were safe. On Christmas Day, the soldiers were served an unusually good dinner of chicken, turkey, and cider. But Robbins learned, to his surprise, that Emma was not there to share it. On December 25, Robbins wrote that "Frank has this morning gone to Alexandria as nurse in the Mansion House hospital." Robbins guessed that her departure, which apparently was at her request, was due to sensitivity about her small stature. "Some difficulty has arisen owing to the selection of cook for the nurses' mess. His nature being so timid that he dislikes to be joked about his feminine appearance, which caused him to take this step." But, given that there is no record of anyone in the regiment yet suspecting the truth about young Frank, it may be that there was more to it than that, that perhaps the proximity to Robbins had finally become too painful for Emma to bear. If Robbins was aware of this, he pretended not to be, adding somewhat smugly that "I fear I have been somewhat deceived by his disposition yet as before intimated the fault may be mine but certain it is there is not so warm friendship existing between us as there formerly has been."[45]

Emma serving as an orderly at the Battle of Fair Oaks, May 1862. (As drawn and engraved on wood by R. O'Brien, New York. Originally published in Emma's memoirs, *Nurse and Spy in the Union Army*.)

CHAPTER FIVE

March 1862

EMMA spent the first two months of the new year working in the Mansion House hospital at Alexandria. In early March, Colonel Orlando Poe, who was given command of the Second Michigan when Israel Richardson was promoted to brigadier general, appointed Emma as regimental mail carrier. She was eager for a change of pace from her nursing duties. Poe, a personal friend of McClellan's—they were both regular army engineers before the war—said that he chose Emma to serve as mail carrier because, "as a soldier, Frank Thompson was effeminate looking" and he wanted to "avoid taking an efficient soldier from the ranks."[1] Poe would be something of a mentor to young Frank Thompson for the remainder of Emma's time in the army.

Emma loved her new duties. They allowed her an inordinate amount of freedom for a private. She was given her own horse, and was able to come and go—from camp to camp, to Washington—with few questions asked, as long as the mail was picked up and delivered in a timely manner. It also gave her a much-needed respite from the incessant suffering and death in the hospital, a chance to spend time out of doors in the fresh spring air. Above all, it meant that overnight, she became one of the most popular and recognizable figures in the entire regiment. Mail was extremely important to the troops, and the appearance of the mail carrier was always a cause for great excitement. Soon almost everyone in the regiment knew Frank Thompson by sight.

Soon after Emma took over her new duties, General McClellan was finally persuaded, with some prodding from President Lincoln, that his new army—the largest, best-trained, and best-equipped the country had ever seen—was as ready as even he could hope it to be. It was time to see what it could do. On March 14, he issued an announcement to be read to all of his troops at roll call. "The army of the Potomac is now a real army, magnificent in material, admirable in discipline and instruction, excellently equipped and armed. Your commanders are all that I could wish. The moment for action has arrived, and I know that I can trust in you to save our country. The period of inaction has passed. I will bring you now face to face with the rebels, and only pray that God may defend the right."[2]

Rumors swirled in the camps in and around Washington as to when and where that face-to-face meeting would occur. Some guessed that they would head back to Manassas, to try again to accomplish what they had failed to do the summer before. Others believed that they would march on Richmond by way of Fredericksburg.[3]

Emma's regiment found itself marching to the wharf at Alexandria. There, "to the utter astonishment of all," Colonel Poe announced they would board a steamer that would take them down the Virginia coast to Fort Monroe, at the tip of the Virginia Peninsula, an eighty-mile-long, slightly crooked finger of land that pointed southeast from Richmond. The Peninsula was bounded on the north by the York River and on the south by the James. At its tip, where Chesapeake Bay met the Atlantic Ocean, sat the Federal stronghold of Fort Monroe. Between Fort Monroe and Richmond were Yorktown, and, farther up, the town of Williamsburg.[4]

McClellan's plan, then still unbeknownst to Emma and her comrades, was to amass his army at Fort Monroe, and push up the Peninsula toward Richmond, using the York River to maintain supply lines. The James, on the south side of the Peninsula, would have been preferable, as it flowed directly from Richmond, but it was then heavily guarded by the fledgling Confederate navy. The beauty of McClellan's plan was that it would allow his army to make an end run around the ever-strengthening Confederate forces lying between Richmond and Washington.

It was a bold plan, the kind of thing at which McClellan excelled. But logistically, it was a nightmare. It would require one of the most massive maritime movements in American military history. In all, it would take more than three weeks for more than 350 vessels— steamers, barges, sloops, and canal boats—to ferry the 150,000 soldiers, 300 pieces of artillery, 3,600 wagons, 700 ambulances, 2,500 cattle, and more than 25,000 horses and mules to Fort Monroe.[5]

Emma's regiment arrived at Alexandria on the morning of March 17, a cold, blustery day. Soldiers and citizens alike crammed onto the docks to watch the chaotic scene unfold. A massive traffic jam of all types of watercraft packed the wharf, where Emma and her regiment had to cool their heels for several hours, until around three in the afternoon, when they were finally ordered aboard the steamer *Vanderbilt*. The boarding process itself took several hours, and by the time it was finished, the steamer was packed. "Regiment after regiment," Emma wrote, "were huddled together on board until every foot of room was occupied, and there remained but little prospect of comfort for either officers or men." Still, despite the crowded conditions, the air was full of confidence and excitement. "The troops" after nearly nine months of camp life, "were eager for a campaign."[6]

Jerome Robbins was one of the lucky ones; he was able to secure a makeshift seat on the deck that afforded him a good glimpse of the commander of the Army of the Potomac. "This afternoon we were greeted with a view of McClellan. A very intelligent-looking countenance marked with determination and decision. He was greeted with shouts from the men, and 'Hail to the Chief' from the band."[7]

By 10 p.m., the *Vanderbilt* was finally ready. A signal was given, and soon the packed steamer, guarded by gunboats, joined the flotilla moving downstream, "with the Stars and Stripes floating from every mast-head."[8] But after the initial pomp and circumstance, the trip turned tedious. It took two days to arrive off the coast of Fort Monroe, and in the rough and stormy March weather, many of the troops spent the voyage violently seasick. Once they arrived, they had to wait at anchor for another two days until there was room at the crowded harbor for them to disembark. By then, the troops were cranky and eager to get ashore. At one point, a fight broke out between members of the Second Michigan and the Thirty-seventh New York, which was only resolved when Colonel Poe personally threw two of the New Yorkers down a set of galley stairs, and closed the hatch.[9]

To pass the time, Robbins filled several pages in his journal describing the massive stone fort. It was an imposing structure. Built during and immediately after the War of 1812, the seven-sided building perched on the rocky point surrounded by a wide moat. The pride of coastal Virginia, the fort was now garrisoned with six thousand troops under the command of General John Dix, and provided a critical Federal toehold on the otherwise hostile Peninsula.

The Second Michigan finally disembarked the *Vanderbilt* in a driving rainstorm on the evening of March 20. Instead of seeking shelter at the fort, which could not accommodate all of the newly arriving troops, they had to march several miles beyond before setting up camp in what Emma remembered as "a fair specimen of Virginia mud." It had been raining steadily for twenty-four hours, and the mud was now knee-deep in places. It would not be their last encounter with the waxy, sticky mud of the Peninsula, where the typical summer weather pattern alternated between oppressive heat and torrential downpours. For their entire stay, the few roads that crisscrossed the sparsely populated, heavily forested Peninsula would either be dry dust bowls or nearly impassable bogs.[10]

On the way to their campground, Emma and her regiment passed through the burned-out remains of what was formerly the town of Hampton. Hampton had once been a pretty, thriving colonial village, but at the outbreak of the war, its residents, fearing their proximity to the Federal fort, abandoned it. Shortly thereafter, Confederate general John B. Magruder burned it to the ground when he learned of Union plans to turn it into a settlement for runaway slaves.[11]

Despite the mud and rain, Emma remembered that it was "a great relief" to be off the crowded transports. Upon reaching their campground, "fires were soon built, coffee made, and fresh bread served," which did much to ease frayed nerves and restore some semblance of morale. Although Robbins does not mention Emma in his journal during this time, suggesting that the coolness between them continued, they were in close proximity and must have seen each other regularly. The cold March rain continued for days on end, and both Emma and Robbins recorded that they were among the many stricken with a severe fever, or what was generally called miasma. For days, both lay in their tents, alternately shivering or roasting.[12]

They also both described an event that happened not long after their arrival on the Peninsula, one that made a strong impression on them both. One evening, Dr. E. J. Bonine, who had replaced Alonzo Palmer as regimental surgeon in the fall when Palmer returned to Ann Arbor for the start of the new medical school year, took a walk after supper. Before long, he came to a creek about a mile and a half from camp. On the opposite bank, he noticed a small band of men, whom he assumed at first to be rebel pickets. He quickly went back to camp to report their presence, and then led a small force of Federal guards to the spot where he had seen them. But when the men arrived, the guards realized that the figures across the creek were runaway slaves trying to make their way to the fort. As Dr. Bonine and the guards watched, it appeared that the men could not swim, and the creek was too wide for them to cross safely. Quickly Dr. Bonine and his party made a small raft, which they tied to a rope and sent across the water. The fugitives caught it, and, one by one, they were pulled to safety.

When all of the fugitives were across, the eldest of them explained to Dr. Bonine that they were slaves, and had been forced to work on the rebel fortifications at the James River, but, hearing that the Federals had landed in force, they escaped, and for the past ten days had been slowly making their way east under the cover of darkness. Afraid that if they came out of the woods they would be recaptured, they had eaten only what they could forage in the forest for nearly a week. Worse, the men had been fired upon as they were making their escape; one was killed, and another was so weak that he could barely walk. Dr. Bonine and the Federal guards made an improvised stretcher out of tree branches, and carried him and escorted the others back to camp.

It was nearly midnight, and beginning to rain, when they arrived. As they entered the Federal enclave, the fugitives, realizing that they were safely at their journey's end, fell to their knees, and began to pray, one of them shouting, "Glory! Glory! Glory!" Emma wrote that "notwithstanding the stormy night, the whole camp was aroused, everyone rushed to find out the cause of the excitement." Robbins, too, emerged from his tent to see what the fuss was about, quickly dressed and came to assist Dr. Bonine in tending to the weak and wounded man. Meanwhile, as an ever larger group of soldiers gathered, a large fire was made, and the contrabands—the common Northern term for escaped slaves—were given food and hot coffee. Then the old man repeated the story he had told Dr. Bonine. The soldiers, many of whom had never seen contrabands, or for that matter, many free blacks, listened intently. Robbins, moved by their suffering, noted that night, "After all which has transpired under my observation, no one need ever tell me that a slave is happy in bondage, if so why have these endured everything but death, even part of their number suffering that, for blissful freedom?" Emma, too, witnessed the scene, which she recorded in her own memoirs. Suddenly, in the company of people who had actually suffered under the "sin" of slavery for the first time, the issue of slavery became real to her in a way it had never been before, and she seethed at its injustice. Why, she asked, "should blue eyes and golden hair be the distinction between bond and free?" [13]

From then on, Emma made a point to spend time with the contrabands, and the many other escaped slaves who made their way to the protection of the fort, near which they occupied a long row of board buildings. The men were hired to load and unload military ships, while the women found work washing clothes and cooking. Emma was struck by the fact that although most of them lacked a formal education, many of them knew the Scriptures well. "Almost all whom I conversed with today were praying men and women." Listening to their stories, Emma was struck, too, by their hunger for education, which she wished she could provide. "Oh, how I should like to teach these people," she wrote. [14] Many years later, when she did have an opportunity to do so, she would take it.

The tip of the Peninsula around Fort Monroe was Federal territory, thanks to the presence of the fort's large garrison, but between the fort and Richmond lay sixty miles of hostile, unfamiliar territory, much of it heavily forested. The land itself was low-lying and swampy, crisscrossed by innumerable creeks, gullies, and ravines. The most logical way to get the massive army and its heavy artillery and supplies to Richmond was not overland but by water. The James, the southern boundary of the Peninsula, was the most appealing water route, but that approach was blocked by the Confederate ironclad gunboat *Merrimac*. That left the York River, the northern boundary of the Peninsula, which did not go directly to Richmond, but forked into a narrower tributary, the Pamunkey, at West Point, the terminus of the railroad that ran from the river to Richmond. This, McClellan decided, would have to do. [15]

The first step in taking control of the York was to dislodge the Confederate presence at Yorktown, the colonial town that commanded the eastern portion of the river. This would be no easy task. Ever since the Federals began arriving on the Peninsula, the Confederates had been building up the old Revolutionary War fortifications defending the town. And McClellan had no idea what kind of enemy force he was facing. He knew that Yorktown was commanded by Magruder, who had fallen back on the town when he left Hampton, but he had no idea how many men Magruder had.

At the beginning of the war, there was no formal Federal intelligence agency; although there were several attempts to create one, they did not take hold until much later. During the first year and a half, intelligence activities were generally ad hoc, and completely uncoordinated among the various commands. McClellan's main source of military intelligence was Allan Pinkerton, a well-known railroad detective whom McClellan knew from his days as a railroad executive before the war. When the war broke out, Pinkerton went to work for McClellan in Ohio, and came with him to Washington when McClellan was given command of the Army of the Potomac. Pinkerton's talents were best suited to counterintelligence work—interviewing deserters and escaped slaves, ferreting out double agents and spies. He was no expert at the proactive work of ascertaining enemy troop strength and positions. McClellan was not very good at it either, and had a natural tendency to overestimate, both in his own mind and in his reports to his superiors, the size of the forces he faced. Whether Pinkerton actively contributed to McClellan's false assumptions, or merely validated what his boss wanted to hear, the fact remained that between the two of them, they severely and repeatedly misjudged the number of Confederates on the Peninsula at every turn. McClellan also had at his disposal the aeronautical services of Dr. Thaddeus Lowe, who pioneered the use of hot-air balloons for reconnaissance purposes. Emma recalled seeing "Professor Lowe . . . making balloon reconnaissances, and transmitting the results of his observations to General McClellan by telegraph from his castle in the air, which seemed suspended from the clouds, reminding one of the fabled gods of old looking down from their ethereal abodes upon the conflicts of the inhabitants of this mundane sphere." But the balloons' utility was limited by the weather conditions, which continued to be horrendous, and Lowe was no more able to ascertain the actual number of Confederate troops at Yorktown than were Pinkerton and McClellan.[16]

Thus, based on not much more than rumor, McClellan came to the erroneous conclusion in early April that Magruder had over a hundred thousand at his disposal; the actual number was less than thirty thousand. By then McClellan had amassed around Fort Monroe nearly four times as many men as Magruder actually had. Nonetheless, he decided that he could not risk an infantry assault when the two sides were, in his mind, so evenly matched. Instead, he spent most of the month of April demanding even more troops be sent to him, and getting those he already had close enough to Yorktown to mount a siege, a slow and laborious process that involved not only moving his men, but all 114 heavy guns and mortars to within range of Yorktown.

The twenty-three miles from Hampton to Yorktown were heavily contested, not by the Confederates but by the weather. "The Yorktown road is one long to be remembered," Emma recalled. "[I]t required all the determination and energy of veterans to march half that distance in two days. With two days' rations in their haversacks, the men marched until they arrived in front of Yorktown, where they bivouacked on the ground, over which the water was running like a flood."[17] Emma was among the lucky ones; as mail carrier, she was mounted.

As the infantry waited for the siege guns to be brought to the front, the Second settled into camp in front of Yorktown. During this lull, McClellan and Pinkerton were still trying to get a better idea of what lay in front of the army, although the main focus of their intelligence efforts was in putting spies in Richmond, rather than on the other side of the picket line directly in front of them. Then, at the end of March, news arrived from Richmond that one of Pinkerton's most valuable agents, Timothy Webster, had been captured, and was to be hanged. According to Emma, she was shortly thereafter approached by a friend, whom she identified only as "Chaplain B.," who informed her of an opportunity of "great danger and of vast responsibility," if she had the "moral courage." The opportunity, she soon discovered, was to become an agent in the "Secret Service of the United States." Presumably in reaction to the loss of Webster, who was executed on April 29, and the capture of most of his comrades in Richmond, McClellan intended to enhance his on-the-ground reconnaissance efforts. After a great deal of thought, Emma said later, she "made up my mind to accept [the assignment] with all its fearful responsibilities. The subject of life and death was not weighed in the balance; I left that in the hands of my Creator, feeling assured that I was just as safe in passing the picket lines of the enemy, if it was God's will that I should go there, as I would be in the Federal camp." [18]

After that, Emma later said, that her "name was sent in to head-quarters, and I was soon summoned to appear there myself." She was ushered into the presence of General McClellan and two others, whom she only identifies as "M" and "H." It is odd that Pinkerton was not among them, and that Emma does not mention Colonel Poe. As her immediate commanding officer, he would have had to be involved in the decision to use his mail carrier for intelligence work. In fact, if Emma's claims are true, it was likely that Poe—a close personal friend of McClellan's who had formerly done his own "secret service work" for the general outside Pinkerton's auspices—was the one who recommended "Frank Thompson" for the job.

Emma was "questioned and cross-questioned with regard to my views of the rebellion and my motive for wishing to engage in so perilous an undertaking." McClellan was, by all accounts, deeply paranoid about double agents, and often interviewed potential agents himself. After her interview with McClellan, Emma said, she was subjected to a test of her skill with firearms, which she easily passed. Finally, there was a medical examination, which, fortunately for Emma, consisted only of a manual examination of her skull, which was believed to reveal intelligence and character.[19]

When she passed all three ordeals, she was instructed to disguise herself as a slave. To do so, she obtained suitable clothes from the contrabands near Fort Monroe, and then darkened her skin with silver nitrate, which was easily obtained from hospital medical supplies. The last piece of her disguise was a black wig, which she obtained through the quartermaster at Fort Monroe, explaining that it was needed for some "reconnaissance business." When her disguise was completed, she returned to camp, where "I found myself without friends—a striking illustration of the frailty of human friendship." But she was nonetheless pleased; if her own friends could not recognize her, then, she concluded, her disguise must be good enough to fool perfect strangers. "At half-past nine o'clock I passed through the outer picket line of the Union army, at twelve o'clock I was within the rebel lines, and had not so much as been halted by one sentinel." She stayed hidden until morning, when she came upon a party of slaves who were returning from bringing breakfast to the rebel picket lines. Apparently, the small group was not the least bit surprised to be suddenly joined by another slave, and together, they returned to camp.[20]

Inside the rebel camp, Emma, like the other slaves, was ordered to work on fortifications, which she did for the remainder of the day. "I was soon furnished with a pickaxe, shovel, and a monstrous wheelbarrow." Unsure at first what to do with them, Emma watched the others for a moment or two, and then tried to follow their lead. But the work was backbreaking. Emma struggled as best she could to push her wheelbarrow full of gravel up the steep incline to the top of the defense works, but the task, which was hard even for the strongest men, was nearly impossible for her. Several times, she had to be helped by other slaves, and was impressed by their silent but compassionate aid. By evening, her hands were raw and bloody, and she was afraid that she would not be able to work at all the next day, which would surely lead to the discovery of her deception.[21]

She solved that problem that evening by negotiating to pay one of her "companions in bondage," whose job was to carry water for the troops, to switch places with her the day; otherwise, she was certain that her "assumed African complexion" would have been detected by the overseer. Now she was able to wander more freely through camp. She tried to note the number of mounted guns and troops, but vastly overstated both. Based on her own observations, as well as snatches of overheard conversations, she estimated the latter to be 150,000—nearly a third more than even McClellan believed, and five times as many as were actually there.[22]

Once Emma had accomplished all that she believed she could, she was eager to get back to the safety of her own camp. It dawned on her, however, that it was easier to get into the rebel camp dressed as a slave than it would likely be to get out of it. For the next two days, Emma worked, listened, and watched for a moment to escape, each day becoming more and more fearful of being discovered. Her skin was beginning to blister and peel from the silver nitrate solution, revealing so much of her natural skin tone that one slave jokingly commented to another, "Well, I'll be darned if that feller ain't turning white!" Emma mumbled a reply and slipped away before they could examine her any further, but the comment made her realize that it was just a matter of time before she was discovered.[23]

Fortunately for Emma, she was among a group of slaves sent out to carry supper to the men on the Confederate picket line. Once there, Emma loitered as long as she could, hoping for an opportunity to escape, but before long, an orderly sergeant took notice of her, and ordered her to follow him to a gap along the line where one of the Confederate pickets had been wounded. To her surprise, the sergeant handed Emma a rifle, "which I was told to use freely in case I should see anything or anybody approaching from the enemy" until a replacement arrived. As he was leaving, the orderly sergeant gave her a hard kick, and said, "Now, you black rascal, if you sleep on your post, I'll shoot you like a dog," to which Emma responded, "Oh, no, Massa, I'se too feerd to sleep."[24]

As night fell, Emma could scarcely believe the absurdity of her position—armed, in bondage, and facing her own picket lines. The Confederate pickets were placed about twenty-five yards apart, hidden from both the Federals across from them, and from one another, by thick brush and trees. All night, Emma listened and waited for a moment when the men on either side of her were distracted, or sleeping. Finally, it came. Deep into the night, it started to drizzle, and she heard both of them pull back to the shelter of the trees. Emma took the opportunity to slip from behind her protected position and slide forward into the dark stillness of the forest that separated the two lines. But Emma did not "dare to approach very near the Federal picket lines, for I was more in danger of being shot by them than by the enemy." At first light, however, she was able to convince her own pickets to let her through the line. Once back in camp, she surreptitiously resumed her own uniform, but she must have drawn some odd stares from her friends. According to Emma, her "complexion was a nice maroon color" for several days. Despite the painful blistering, which presumably was assumed to be the result of a nasty sunburn, Emma was exhilarated by the success of her mission. "I am," she explained, "naturally fond of adventure, a little ambitious, and a good deal romantic, and this together with my devotion to the Federal cause and determination to assist to the utmost of my ability in crushing the rebellion, made me forget the unpleasant items, and not only endure, but really enjoy, the privations connected with my perilous positions."[25]

The strategic benefits of her success were less clear. The most valuable piece of information Emma claims to have passed on when she returned to camp on May 2 was the rumor circulating in the Confederate camp that Yorktown was about to be evacuated. If she did come forward with this rather startling piece of news, it fell on deaf ears; McClellan and Pinkerton both received and ignored similar reports from other sources around the same time. On May 1, a reporter for the Philadelphia *Inquirer* interviewed an unidentified slave who apparently escaped Yorktown at about the same time that Emma did, who told him the same story, but when he passed it on to McClellan's chief of staff (and father-in-law) Robert Marcy, Marcy replied that the story was certainly false, because they had "positive intelligence" that the Confederates were planning to hold Yorktown at all costs.[26]

That "positive intelligence" was wrong. On the night of May 3, Magruder's force began to slip silently away from Yorktown under the cover of darkness and a heavy diversionary artillery barrage. Then the guns fell silent, and by the time the sun came up, they were gone. The first reaction of the Federals was ecstatic. Emma recalled that "the news spread throughout the Federal army like lightning; from the right to left and from center to circumference, the entire encampment was one wild scene of joy."[27] Likewise, Jerome Robbins noted in his journal on May 4 that "[u]nequalled excitement prevails this morning as the flying rumors about the evacuation of Yorktown has been confirmed as a reality. Their boasted strong works are now in possession of our troops." By mid-morning, the Stars and Stripes was raised over the fort at Yorktown, and bands played "The Star-Spangled Banner."[28]

But if the soldiers on the Peninsula viewed the evacuation of Yorktown as an unqualified victory, Lincoln and the Republican Congress saw it differently. Yorktown, after all, was not the goal; Richmond was, and to their eyes, it looked more as though Magruder had simply been allowed to escape destruction to live to fight another day.[29] Meanwhile, the long delay had allowed Confederate reinforcements to arrive from the Shenandoah Valley to help defend Richmond. As

Lincoln had feared, there were now sixty thousand men between McClellan and the Confederate capital. McClellan still had a two-to-one advantage, but the ten-to-one moment was lost forever.[30]

McClellan himself shared the view of his men rather than his bosses. He was so emboldened by the sudden turn of events that he sent a large detachment of his infantry forward to give chase to the fleeing enemy. His advance column caught up with Magruder's rear guard at Williamsburg, twelve miles from Yorktown, on May 5. Hunkering down behind another line of reinforced Revolutionary War fortifications, Magruder turned and made a stand in a short but intense engagement that became known as the Battle of Williamsburg.

The Second Michigan, under the command of Colonel Poe, was the tail end of the force sent forward from Yorktown in pursuit of Magruder. By the time they arrived on the scene, around two in the afternoon, the rain was coming down in torrents, and the fighting was reaching its most fevered pitch. For Emma and her comrades, the scene was unlike anything they had witnessed before. This was their first taste of full-on combat; at Blackburn's Ford, they had been under hostile fire, but were essentially pinned down and on the defensive. At Bull Run they had been held in reserve, and although Emma came face to face with the horrible effects of combat in the stone church at Centreville, she herself had not been in on the fight.

As Emma described the scene, "The thick growth of heavy timber was felled in all directions, forming a splendid ambush for the rebel sharpshooters. The Federals moved forward in the direction of the enemy's works, steadily, firmly, through ditch and swamp, mud and mire, loading and firing as they went, and from every tree, bush and covert which could conceal a man, the rebels poured a deadly fire into the ranks of our advancing troops."[31]

For a time, confusion reigned. Emma "was subject to all kinds of orders. One moment I was ordered to the front with a musket in my hands; the next to mount a horse and carry an order to some general, and very often to take hold of a stretcher with some strong man and carry the wounded from the field."[32] These last duties suited Emma best; in a pattern that she would repeat throughout the war, she consistently put herself in physical danger that day to carry messages or retrieve the fallen wounded in the midst of heavy fire, but she avoided having to inflict harm herself.

Among the first casualties Emma helped was the colonel of another regiment; Emma did not record his name. The colonel was a heavy man, and Emma and another medic, a "stripling of a soldier," carried the wounded man "for about a quarter of a mile through a terrific storm of bullets" to the nearest surgeon, whom Emma identified as "Dr. E." "We laid him down carefully at the surgeon's feet, and raised him tenderly from the stretcher, spread a blanket and laid him upon it, then lingered just a moment to see whether the wound was mortal." But upon examining the man, the doctor could find no wound, mortal or otherwise. The doctor ordered the colonel back to his regiment, whereupon, much to Emma's amazement—and anger—the man they had just "saved" jumped to his feet and threatened the harried surgeon, who nonetheless replied firmly that if the colonel were not back with his regiment in fifteen minutes, he would report him to the commanding general. Emma "turned and left the spot in disgust, mentally regretting that the lead or steel of the enemy had not entered the breast of one who seemed so ambitious of the honor without the effect." From then on, Emma was careful to "ascertain whether a man was wounded before I did anything for him."[33]

But there was no doubt that the next man she helped was seriously injured. It was her captain, and friend, William Morse, whose "leg was broken and shattered from the ankle to the knee." Unlike the anonymous colonel, Captain Morse bore up bravely, expressing concern for his fallen men all the while being carried away from the front. Morse's bravery restored Emma's faith. "Oh, how glad was I to hear those words from his lips," she recalled. "I believed him honest and brave, and those few words on the battlefield at such a moment spoke volumes for the faithful captain's heroism and love for his men." [34]

Hour after hour, in incessant rain, Emma ferried the wounded to the rear for medical attention, then promptly returned to the front as fast as she could to repeat the process, each trip made harder by the ever-deepening mud. The contest was nearly matched, and seemed to be about to tip in favor of the Confederates, when Federal reinforcements arrived late in the day and, in one enormous push, drove the rebels out of their defenses and back on their way toward Richmond. It was a victory, but there was no celebrating when it was over; unlike the one at Yorktown the day before, this triumph came with a startlingly high price. The Battle of Williamsburg was considered by most who were not there to have been a minor skirmish, but for many of those who were, it would be remembered as one of the most intense engagements they were ever in. When it was over, more than two thousand Union troops, and close to as many rebel soldiers, lay dead or wounded in the tangled underbrush, amid the trees, and on the open fields that had separated the two armies.[35] For the Second Michigan, it was one of the bloodiest days of the war, with seventeen killed, thirty-eight wounded, and four missing. For Emma, the loss was particularly hard; in addition to Captain Morse, her good friend Damon Stewart was among the seriously wounded, shot clear through the thigh.

That night, there was no time for rest. As darkness fell, the rain picked up again, "drenching alike the living and the dead." [36] A temporary truce was arranged to allow both sides to collect their casualties from the field. "It was indescribably sad," Emma wrote, "to see our weary, exhausted men, with torches, wading through mud to their knees piloting ambulances over the field, lest they should trample upon the bodies of their fallen comrades." All night long, soaking wet and exhausted, Emma and her comrades "toiled in this manner, and when morning came still there were hundreds upon the field.

Those of the enemy were found in heaps, both dead and wounded piled together in ravines, among the felled timber, and in rifle pits half covered with mud. . . . The dead lay in long rows on the field, their ghastly faces hid from view by handkerchiefs or the capes of their overcoats, while faithful soldiers were digging trenches in which to bury the mangled bodies of the slain." [37]

Jerome Robbins was among those combing the field that night, bending down over each slumped body he came to, searching for signs of life. Robbins wrote in his journal that he did not sleep more than fifteen minutes. "Such a scene as presented itself here God grant I may never again witness. Friend and foe literally piled in heaps. It seemed that wherever either showed itself in range of the other's guns he fell." The work continued all night and well after sunrise. The next afternoon, Robbins came across the body of a friend. "This afternoon I have assisted in burying the dead, some I were quite well acquainted with. Poor Wallace has gone, how heartrending will be the sad news to his mother." [38] Much of the terrain was so heavily wooded that finding casualties was difficult. For the two days following the battle, the sun shone hot and bright, drying the field so well that, on the third day, the underbrush caught fire, burning an untold number of injured men to death before they could be found. [39]

Once the wounded were removed from the field, they were brought to one of the many impromptu hospitals hurriedly established in the small town of Williamsburg, where Emma and Robbins both spent the better part of the next two weeks. McClellan allowed Confederate surgeons to enter the town under a flag of truce, where side by side with Federal medics, in the college buildings, churches, and private homes, they worked for days to tend to the wounded on both sides—sometimes Federal doctors treating Confederate soldiers and vice versa.

In one of the college buildings, Emma came across a young boy from Massachusetts, no more than sixteen, who had been shot in the temple. Emma doubted that he could live, but for once, her habit of complete honesty about prognoses failed her. She "took his feverish hand, and told him that I was glad that his wound was not mortal." He thanked her, and responded, "I would rather have been killed than to have lost the battle." Emma noted that the boy was wearing shoulder straps; he had already been promoted to sergeant for his bravery under fire.[40]

Left: Colonel Orlando Metcalfe Poe, Emma's commanding officer and
mentor. Poe's testimonial about "Frank's" exemplary wartime conduct
helped tip the scales in favor of the effort to have deserter status expunged
from Emma's service record. (Library of Congress, Prints and Photographs Division.)
Right: General George B. McClellan. Although McClellan's leadership has
been judged harshly by history, Emma's loyalty to her beloved "Little Mac"
never wavered. The resemblance between Robbins, Poe, and McClellan is
striking. (Source unknown.)

CHAPTER SIX

May 1862

HAVING WON control of the York River, McClellan spent the next few weeks moving his base of operations to West Point, at the junction of the York and the narrowed Pamunkey that fed into it, and then even farther up the Pamunkey to White House Landing, a large plantation that was the childhood home of Martha Custis Washington, and the place of her courtship with the country's first president. It now belonged to William "Rooney" Lee, the son of Confederate general Robert E. Lee, whose wife was the great-granddaughter of Mrs. Washington. Rooney Lee was, like his father, currently serving in the Confederate army; he was a colonel in the Ninth Virginia Cavalry. Mrs. Lee was living in the house when the Federals first landed at Fort Monroe, but left shortly after the fall of Yorktown. When McClellan arrived, he found a note pinned to the door of the house, beseeching the Federals not to destroy the place of George Washington's "first married life." McClellan, who had served under General Lee in the Mexican War, honored her request, and gave strict orders that the house was to be unharmed.[1]

The sweeping green grounds of the Lees' home, however, were soon trampled down to dirt, and jam-packed with tents, wagons, horses, and ever-accumulating Federal supplies brought upriver by a steady stream of barges and vessels of all varieties. Emma, who was still acting as regimental mail carrier, was often at White House Landing to retrieve and deliver mail, and was struck by how quickly an entire village had taken root. "The grounds were laid out in broad streets and squares, and there were long rows of snow-white tents, with their neatly printed cotton signboards 'to guide the traveler on his way' to the different headquarters, provost marshal, hospital, sutlers, blacksmith, etc."[2]

It was now mid-May, and although it had taken nearly two months, McClellan had achieved his objective of getting control of the terminus of the railroad at White House Landing. That was vital, because although McClellan continued to outnumber the rebels by a margin of almost two to one, he was still convinced that it was the Confederates who had that same margin in their favor, and that they were constantly adding to that margin through reinforcements arriving from the south. This meant, in his mind, that an infantry assault on Richmond was bound to fail. Instead, he planned to use the railroad to bring his heavy artillery pieces to within shelling distance of the city and lay siege to it, as he had at Yorktown. To do this, he needed two things.

The first was more men. Almost daily, McClellan barraged Lincoln with telegrams alternately demanding and begging for more men. On May 10 he wrote, "From the information reaching me from every source, I regard it as certain that the enemy will meet us with all his force on or near the Chickahominy. . . . If I am not reinforced it is probable that I will be obliged to fight nearly double my numbers strongly entrenched." And, four days later, a similar missive: "I will fight the enemy, whatever their force may be, with whatever force I may have, and I believe we shall beat them; but . . . [s]trong reinforcements will at least save the lives of many of them. . . . For obvious reasons I beg you to give immediate consideration to this communication." Although Lincoln doubted McClellan's estimates of enemy troop strength, and was reluctant to weaken the force defending Washington, he finally concluded that agreeing to McClellan's request was the only way to get him moving. On May 18, Lincoln ordered General McDowell, who was then less than thirty miles north of Richmond at Fredericksburg, with forty thousand men, to march south to join McClellan's left flank.[3]

The other thing McClellan needed was to get the railroad running, and to take control of the tracks to Richmond, so that he could get his siege guns in place. While he waited for McDowell to arrive, McClellan brought up dozens of railroad cars and locomotives by water from Fort Monroe, and set about repairing the railroad lines that ran southwest to Richmond. His engineers soon had the tracks open as far as the Chickahominy River, a normally languid ribbon of water that bisected the northern third of the Peninsula from north of Richmond southeast to the James, and that now lay between McClellan and his objective. The Chickahominy was normally not much more than a creek, and although it was bordered by wide, swampy banks on either side, it was generally fordable by infantry. But the artillery required bridges, which the rebels had burned on their retreat to Richmond.

As work on the bridges progressed, McClellan sent one of his corps, commanded by Erasmus Keyes, across the river to hold the far banks and allow the engineers to do their work in peace. Keyes expected to find the river crossing contested, but it was not, and they were able to push seven miles along the railroad, past Savage's Station to the depot at Fair Oaks, putting the most advanced Federal divisions less than ten miles from Richmond. Meanwhile, the four corps on the north side of the river were pushing forward as well, close enough that their most advanced divisions on the left could see the church spires of Richmond.[4]

It was during this lull that Emma claimed she undertook another foray into enemy territory. Whether McClellan, or Poe, or someone else ordered or blessed it, she did not say, but there is evidence that McClellan was making use of every available source of intelligence to determine what, exactly, waited for him on the other side of the river. Emma concluded that the slave disguise was too risky, not to mention too hard on her skin. This time, she would pretend to be something that came more naturally, and less painfully, to her: an Irish peddler woman. On one of her mail trips, she passed through Williamsburg, and procured proper clothes, as well as several baskets, wares, and various other items that would supplement her disguise. Her plan was to pass through the Confederate picket line by claiming to be fleeing the advance of the Federal army, find out what she could, and then sneak back across to her own lines as quickly as possible.

Emma set out, crossing the river on horseback, with her disguise packed in a basket that she held carefully over her head to keep dry. But her horse stumbled, and the basket and all of its contents were soaked. When she reached the other side, she sent her mount back to the far bank, and set out on foot. Finding a secluded spot in the woods, she put on the wet clothes, and buried her uniform beside a tree.[5]

By now it was nearly dark. Deciding to wait until daybreak before going any farther, she wrapped herself in a thin, wet blanket, and tried to sleep. In the night, though, she was overcome with fever and chills from what was most likely a recurrence of malaria she had contracted during the first few weeks on the Peninsula, a condition that would plague her intermittently for the rest of her life. "My mind began to wander, and I became quite delirious. There seemed to be the horrors of a thousand deaths concentrated around me; I was tortured by fiends of every conceivable shape and magnitude." In the morning, still weak with fever, she discovered she had lost her bearings. For several days, she wandered near the swamp in a feverish daze, searching for something to point the way.[6]

Finally, she came upon a farmhouse that looked abandoned, but once inside, she found a Confederate captain, suffering from an advanced case of typhoid fever. He told her, in a weak, soft voice, that he had become separated from his company while in retreat from the skirmish at Cold Harbor, and unable to make it back to the army, took refuge in the farmhouse. Emma's experience in the hospitals told her instantly that he was on his deathbed. She gave him water, found some flour to make some small pancakes for him to eat, and soothed his brow. "It is strange how sickness and disease disarm our antipathy and remove our prejudices. There lay before me an enemy to the government for which I was daily and willingly exposing my life and suffering unspeakable privation . . . and yet, as I looked upon him in his helpless condition, I did not feel the least resentment, or entertain an unkind thought to him personally, but looked upon him only as an unfortunate, suffering man, whose sad condition called forth the best feelings of my nature." For the next several hours, Emma comforted the man, whose name, he told her, was Alan Hall, and listened as he talked about his life, and the home he would not return to. She agreed to deliver his gold watch to a Major McKee, on General Ewell's staff. Eventually he began to fall in and out of consciousness. At one point, he opened his eyes and asked, "Am I really dying?" "Yes," she replied. "Is your peace made with God?" He answered that his trust was in Christ, that God would not forsake him. Emma wrote later in her memoirs that she was struck by the similarity of his words to those of a dying Union soldier she had comforted only days before at Williamsburg, and noted that while in life they had been enemies, in death the two soldiers trusted in "the same Savior."[7] From then on, Emma seems to have had a more acute sense of the humanity of the enemy, and perhaps lost some of her earlier certainty that God was on the Union side alone.

The man died shortly after midnight, "his hand clasping mine in the painful grip of death, my arm supporting him, and his head leaning on my bosom like a wearied child. I laid him down, closed his eyes and straightened his rigid limbs; then folding his hands across his breast, I drew his blanket close around him and left him in the silent embrace of death." It was an eerie, almost mystical moment for Emma, as she described it. "Profound silence reigned supreme, and there was naught to chase away the darkness of that gloomy midnight hour save the consciousness that God was there."[8]

Exhausted, Emma wrapped herself in a patchwork quilt, and fell into a sound sleep next to her late patient. At sunrise, she scoured the house for supplies and found several useful items for her costume as a peddler woman. Once outside, she decided to bury her pistol, for fear that she would be searched when she presented herself, as she intended to do, at the rebel pickets as bearing a message for Major McKee. It did not take her long to reach them.[9]

Her ruse worked, and she was permitted to pass behind enemy lines. Again, she says, she was able to learn details about troop placements and battle plans. She also sought out Major McKee, who was not in camp, and did not reappear until around five in the evening. To Emma he appeared "rough and stern," and for a moment, her courage sank. But when she handed him Captain Hall's watch, Emma was surprised to see him overcome with emotion; he dropped his face in his hands, and "sobbed like a child." McKee thanked her profusely, saying, "You are a faithful woman, and you shall be rewarded." Offering her "a ten-dollar Federal bill" he asked her if she could lead them to his friend's body. "If you succeed in finding the house, I will give you as much more." Emma declined the money, saying, in her best Irish accent, "Oh, Gineral, forgive me! But me conshins wud niver give me pace in this world or the nixt, if I wud take money for carrying the dyin missage for that swate boy that's dead and gone!" She did, however, ask that she be allowed to ride, explaining that the farmhouse was a bit of distance away, and she had not been feeling well. The major readily agreed, and ordered a horse be brought up for her. When her escorts were ready, Emma mounted, and, looking at the grief-stricken face of the major, she recalled, "I really felt mean, and for the first time since I had acted in the capacity of spy, I despised myself for the very act which I was about to perform. I must betray the confidence which that man reposed in me."[10]

When her party—twenty-four members of McKee's cavalry—arrived at the farmhouse and dismounted, Emma stayed on her horse, waiting for the chance to escape. Suddenly she was not at all

Emma behind enemy lines disguised as an Irish peddler, with a Confederate officer, May 1862. (As drawn and engraved on wood by R. O'Brien, New York. Originally published in Emma's memoirs, *Nurse and Spy in the Union Army*.)

sure how to do it; while some of the men went inside to retrieve the body, the rest stayed outside, guarding the road. Surely, if she simply turned and rode off, they would try to stop her, if only to retrieve their horse. To her great relief, however, one of the men, seeing that Emma was still mounted, asked her to ride down the road a bit to keep a look out for Federal cavalry. Gratefully she did as she was asked, and then some, not stopping until she had crossed back through her own lines.[11]

By the time she returned to her regiment, McDowell still had not arrived—Lincoln countermanded the order sending him to the Peninsula when Stonewall Jackson appeared to be threatening Washington from the Shenandoah Valley—but the engineers had completed the railroad bridge and were in the process of completing two others for use by the wagons and troops.

At this point, in the last week of May, McClellan must have appeared to the Confederates to be an imposing enemy. He now had

four corps north of the Chickahominy, and one to the south, forming a semicircle around the north and east of Richmond. And he was
about to have control of a railroad that ran straight to the heart of
the city. None of this was lost on Confederate general Joe Johnston,
who was now in command of the forces defending the city. If Mc-
Clellan was able to mount his siege, it was only a matter of time before Richmond would fall. Johnston concluded that the only thing
to do was to go on the offensive; specifically, he would try to take advantage of the fact that McClellan's army, at least for the moment,
lay divided by the Chickahominy by launching a surprise attack designed to destroy the corps on the south side before reinforcements
could come to their aid.

On May 29, the first of the two remaining bridges was completed,
and McClellan sent General Samuel P. Heintzelman's corps, of which
Emma's regiment was a part, across the river to join Keyes in preparation for a final push toward Richmond. To many of the rank and file
on the Peninsula, it seemed, as it did to Johnston, as though the fall of
Richmond were just days away. But the next night, May 30, "a most
fearful storm swept over the peninsula, accompanied by terrible exhi-
bitions of lightning and thunder. The water came down all night and
all day in perfect floods, completely inundating the valley through
which the Chickahominy flows, turning the narrow stream into a
broad river, converting swamps into lakes, and carrying away one
bridge and rendering another unsafe."[12] The storm was truly terrible—many diaries and journals recorded it as the worst the authors
ever experienced in their lives. Four members of one Alabama regiment were killed simultaneously by a single bolt of lightning.[13]

For McClellan, it was a terrible setback. But the ferocity of the
storm was viewed as auspicious by at least one person on the Peninsula that night: Joe Johnston knew that the rising floodwaters would
leave the two corps he was planning to attack out of reach of reinforcements. In what would be remembered as the Battle of Fair
Oaks, the Confederates struck two days later, around one in the af-

ternoon, when the storm was over but the river still dangerously high. The most advanced Federal regiments, taken by surprise, fell back, and after several long hours of intense fighting, seemed on the verge of being driven into the swollen river. At what was very nearly the last minute, however, Edwin Sumner, commander of the Federal corps nearest the river on the other side, pushed his men across one rickety bridge that still held by a thread, to come to the rescue. Although the Confederates had started the day with a large numerical advantage, many of their troops never managed to get in on the action, and when Sumner crossed and evened out the numbers, the rebels fell back at last.[14]

As she had during the Battle of Williamsburg, Emma made herself useful under heavy fire, but without returning it. At one point, she carried messages for brigade commander Philip Kearney; later she again ferried casualties to the rear. When the fighting finally began to die down, she took up position at an old sawmill that had been converted to a field hospital. The hospital was severely understaffed; at one point, Emma was the sole nurse, and had to enlist two men who were less seriously wounded than the others to help her.[15]

As dusk fell, she was relieved to see a chaplain, whom she knew, approaching—presumably, to help. But instead of pitching in, he hitched his horse, ate a hearty meal in front of the famished soldiers' eyes, and promptly fell fast asleep, without ever offering his assistance to any of the wounded. This made Emma furious, and when she discovered in the morning that he had ridden off again "without so much as inquiring whether the men were dead or alive," she was livid. "Oh, what a stumbling block that man was to my soul," she recalled, "for weeks and months Satan took occasion to make this a severe temptation and trial to me. I was tempted to judge every Christian by that unholy example, and to doubt the truth of every Christian experience that I had heard related from time to time." Although she eventually recovered her faith, she never "recovered from my feelings of disgust for that particular chaplain."[16]

The day's fighting had been inconclusive; no significant ground gained or lost. All night long, the men at the front lay on their arms, the two sides separated by only yards in some places. The fighting did indeed resume the next morning, but with Sumner's entire division now across the river, the Federals were able to beat the Confederates back, and by noon the field fell silent.[17]

Jerome Robbins was not with his regiment at Fair Oaks; several weeks before, he had been assigned as a steward at one of the several "general" brigade hospitals set up in the rear to care for the sick, to free the regimental medical staff to treat combat casualties. Robbins's hospital—really a collection of tents in a clearing at Talleysville, near White House Landing—was on the north side of the Chickahominy, well out of danger, but he could hear the incessant thunder of artillery and musketry, and, knowing his own regiment was likely engaged, was desperate for information. Finally, as the battle was petering out, a patient who had been released a few days earlier to return to his regiment came back, having been deemed still unfit for duty by Dr. Bonine, and carrying with him some news. "We have indulged in a great deal of speculative curiosity respecting the heavy firing of yesterday and today. . . . Some of the most fabulous reports have been brought in today," including that McClellan "was driven back across the Chickahominy."[18]

That report was wrong; McClellan was not driven back across the river. Although he was sick the day of the main contest, he was well enough to ride onto the battlefield just as the rebels were falling back on June 1. Emma arrived on the field from the sawmill about the same time, and "saw him ride along the entire battlefront, and if I had not seen him, I could not have long remained in ignorance of his presence—for the cheers from all parts of the Federal lines told as plainly as words could express that their beloved commander was with them, amid that desperate struggle for victory."[19]

But despite the relief at the outcome, the price was high. In all, Federal casualties from Fair Oaks were more than 5,000; 790 killed,

3,594 wounded, and 647 missing; the Confederates nearly 1,000 more.[20] As Emma surveyed the detritus on the field, she was struck afresh by the horror of war. "It was a terrible slaughter . . . enough to make Angels weep, to look down upon that field of carnage."[21]

When it was over, Emma took several of her most seriously wounded patients from the sawmill to a larger "hospital" set up under a large tree at Fair Oaks station. The sight there was staggering. As Emma recalled,

> [There] was an immense tree under whose shady, extended branches the wounded were carried and laid down to await the stimulate, the opiate, or the amputating knife, as the case might require. The ground around the tree for several acres in extent was literally drenched with human blood, and the men were laid so close together that there was no such thing as passing between them; but each one was removed in their turn as the surgeons could attend to them. I witnessed there some of the most heartrending sights it is possible for the human mind to conceive.[22]

All day long, and well into the next, Emma helped load the most severely wounded onto railroad cars bound for White House Landing, where they were transferred to hospital ships for the trip north. Many died before even reaching the supply base. As one observer recalled, "They arrived, dead and alive together, in the same close boxcar, many with awful wounds, festering and alive with maggots."[23]

McClellan was, like Emma, greatly affected by the sight of so much suffering. Publicly, he swaggered and boasted about the "great victory." On June 3, a warm and sultry day, McClellan issued an address to his troops that was read to all regiments. "Soldiers of the Army of the Potomac! I have fulfilled at least a part of my promise to you. You are now face to face with the rebels, who are held at bay in front of their Capital. The final and decisive battle is at hand. . . . Let us meet and crush [them]!"[24] And his men believed him; almost all of them expected to be in Richmond in time to celebrate the Fourth of July.

But McClellan's private reaction was far less bombastic. Immediately after the battle, he wrote his wife that "I am tired of the sickening sight of the battlefield, with its mangled corpses & poor suffering wounded! . . . Victory has no charms for me when purchased at such cost."[25] This, as some historians have speculated, may explain why, poised on the brink of success, McClellan did nothing—nothing, that is, except continue to badger Lincoln for more men, and blame the weather for his inaction. It rained steadily for the first ten days of June. In one message, on June 7, he explained that

> [The] Chickahominy river has risen so as to flood the entire bottoms to the depth of three to four feet; I am pushing forward the bridges in spite of this, and the men are working night and day, up to their waists in water, to complete them. The whole face of the country is a perfect bog, entirely unpassable for artillery, or even cavalry, except directly in the narrow roads, which renders and general movement, either of this or the rebel army, entirely out of the question until we have favorable weather. . . . I shall be in perfect readiness to move forward and take Richmond the moment [reinforcements reach] here and the ground will admit the passage of artillery.

Two days later, he sent a similar message, begging for more men while simultaneously promising action at the first opportunity. "I wish to be distinctly understood that whenever the weather permits I will attack with whatever force I may have."[26]

But other than move two more corps to the south side of the Chickahominy—leaving only one, that of General Fitz-John Porter, on the north side to guard the supply lines from White House Landing to the river and beyond from any possible flank attack—McClellan would not budge. Finally, Lincoln agreed to send two additional divisions, those of Generals McCall and McDowell, which would allow McClellan to fill in any possible gaps in this northern right flank and, presumably, get on with his advance on Richmond. They would, Lincoln promised, arrive by the end of the third week in June.

McClellan's reaction to the carnage at Fair Oaks, the first large-scale battle during his entire command of the Army of the Potomac, may explain much of what happened next. He was a brilliant organizer, and loved war as a chess game, moving pieces here and there. His plan—fantasy, really—was to win the war through one essentially bloodless siege, as he had taken Yorktown. But the truth was that McClellan had no taste for the realities of actual warfare, and could not get used to the unfathomable responsibility of ordering men to their death. It may not have been the most desirable characteristic in a combat general, and may have, in fact, caused the death of many more men on both sides, by prolonging a war that might otherwise have ended much sooner. But his evident desire to save his men, which so angered Lincoln and the other politicians in Washington, made him even more beloved by the rank and file, most of whom had no more desire to be sent into danger than he had to send them there. As one soldier noted approvingly in a letter to his mother after Fair Oaks, "You can plainly see [he] dont go in to the field and get half his men killed off. . . . How ever plainly to be seen General Mc-Clellan is a General that economizes life." [27]

As McClellan waited, for his bridges to be rebuilt, for his reinforcements to arrive, an odd lull ensued. Union and Confederate pickets posted in the swampy river lowlands on the south side of the Chicka-hominy, in some cases separated by less than a hundred yards, reached informal agreements not to shoot at each other, as long as nobody tried to advance past their posts. Some even got friendly enough to trade newspapers, share coffee, or just pass the time in conversation. [28] When it wasn't raining, it was unbearably hot and muggy, often in the 90s for days at a time. The bouts of heavy rain filled the ditches and swampy lowlands with pools of stagnant water, creating perfect conditions for the mosquitoes that came out in full force at dusk. Every day, more and more soldiers were succumbing to the miasma, or swamp fever, but few realized that the mosquitoes were responsible. Fortunately for the thousands of soldiers who contracted malaria during the war, it was a relatively mild strain and, unlike modern malaria, was usually responsive to treatment with quinine.

During these long weeks in June when the army was idle, the routine of camp life reasserted itself, and Emma noted that such periods provided ample opportunity for the "study of human nature. As I looked around upon that mass of busy men, I thought I could discover almost every trait in the human character. . . . There was the selfish man, only intent on serving himself . . . by himself building a fire of his own especial benefit." But, Emma noted, "that class of character, thank heaven, was a very small minority. There, too, was the cheerful happy man, who had been several hours engaged in cutting up and serving to others" yet "looked as good natured as if he had dined on roast beef and plum pudding." And she was, in essence, describing both herself, and her friend Jerome Robbins, when she noted another character "who always made it the first duty, under all circumstances, to look after those who were not able to look after themselves." [29]

Emma also continued with her duties as postmaster and mail carrier, which often required her to spend long hours in the saddle, covering the nearly sixty miles from the front lines to Fort Monroe and back again, alone. It was dangerous work; although the territory was occupied by the Federals, there were plenty of Southern sympathizers among the civilian population, as well as less ideological, but no less hostile, thieves. Emma wrote that "I was often compelled to spend the nights alone by the roadside. It was reported that the bushwhackers had murdered a mail carrier on that road [to Fort Monroe] and robbed the mail, and there seemed to be evidence of the fact, for in the most lonely spot of the road the ground was still strewn with fragments of letters and papers, over which I often passed when it was so dark that I only knew it by the rustle of the letters under my horse's feet." [30]

Through the month of June, Jerome Robbins was still at the auxiliary hospital at Talleysville. But for the most part, his twelve patients were recovering nicely, and he was frequently bored. When time permitted, he went for long walks, often with a tin cup in hand to pick strawberries. When he was successful in finding a patch, he tried his hand at making strawberry shortcake for his patients, at which, in his own opinion, he "succeeded admirably." But despite these diversions, Robbins was listless and melancholy. "Begin to feel quite lonely," he wrote, "so long a time has elapsed since I received a letter from home." One evening, he complained that he was too bored and listless even to write to his beloved Anna. "I should write Anna a letter . . . but I usually feel dull with sitting up so constantly. I will defer it until tomorrow, hoping I may produce something of more interest to one so highly esteemed than my drowsy nature will allow tonight." [31]

He did not hope in vain. Robbins would soon find himself in the middle of one of the most dramatic episodes of the entire Peninsula campaign. Joe Johnston had been severely wounded at Fair Oaks; with Johnston out of commission, overall command of the Confederate force on the Peninsula fell to Robert E. Lee. Lee understood McClellan, and guessed that his former subordinate would not risk a massive infantry assault on Richmond. Instead, Lee reasoned, correctly, McClellan would try to inch within shelling range of the capital and lay siege to it. Lee also knew that while McClellan might be cautious, he was also highly efficient, and if he were given the time to implement his plan, Lee knew, just as Johnston had, that it would just be a matter of time until Richmond fell. He must, therefore, disrupt McClellan at all costs—if he could not defeat him outright, he could perhaps harass him enough to throw him off balance. He could not now try to attack on the south side of the Chickahominy, as Johnston had done, with four corps firmly entrenched there. But he was wondering how vulnerable McClellan's supply lines on the north side might be. It was just the sort of attack that McClellan most feared.

To find out, Lee sent his brilliant, flamboyant cavalry commander, James Ewell Brown "Jeb" Stuart, on a secret reconnaissance mission to probe into Federal territory on the north side of the river, with an aim of ascertaining the vulnerability of the Federal supply lines to a flank attack, as well as the prospects for an approach from the north by Stonewall Jackson, whom Lee was planning to bring down from the Shenandoah Valley. Stuart, grasping the danger inherent in riding straight into territory occupied by the largest army ever assembled in the history of the country, leaped at the chance. Before he left, Lee, knowing Stuart's propensity for dramatic action, cautioned him not to do anything rash. But Lee's warning fell on deaf ears.[32]

On the morning of June 12, well before dawn, Stuart and about twelve hundred cavalry, including the two Colonels Lee—General Lee's son, Rooney, and his nephew, Fitzhugh, mounted their horses in silence and headed out as quietly as so many horses can. Riding north, they crossed the Chickahominy well above the Federals' most western position, and then turned east. The first day, they covered nearly twenty-five miles with no opposition, or even any sight of the Federals. But on the next, they ran into a squadron of the Union's Fifth Cavalry. After a brief clash, the rebels, who had the bigger force, pushed their way past, leaving the squadron fairly well cut up in its wake. Soon thereafter, they came upon the camp of the same unit they had just decimated, and set it ablaze. But Stuart knew that it was just a matter of time until the entire Union cavalry, commanded, oddly enough, by his own father-in-law, would close in and give chase. He also knew that they would be expecting him to head back the way he came.[33]

Instead, Stuart decided that the safest, not to mention most dramatic, course of action was go farther into Federal territory, rather than to retreat from it. He announced to his officers that he intended to continue east, and then, when they had gone far enough away from where the Union cavalry would likely be amassed and waiting for them, they would turn south, cross the Chickahominy, and loop back up toward Richmond along the banks of the James. On their way east, they managed to attack the Federal train depot at Tunstall's Station, just five miles south of White House Landing, and to burn two schooners in the Pamunkey loaded with stores and supplies. Emma was at White House Landing when a train arrived in a rush from Tunstall's Station, where it had narrowly escaped attack from Stuart's men. "Everything was thrown into wild confusion by the arrival of the train and the news of the attack. The troops at White House were immediately called out under arms to protect the depot. All this excitement had been produced by a detachment of Stuart's cavalry." [34]

Stuart briefly toyed with the idea of attacking White House itself, which would have given Emma even more "excitement," but he thought better of it and continued east. Just after midnight, they reached the hospital clearing at Talleysville. Jerome Robbins was awake, sitting beside a critically ill patient, when he heard the sound of horses' hooves disturb the quiet night air. When he peered out of the tent, he was surprised beyond description to see, in the light of a full moon, the advance unit of Stuart's cavalry appear out of nowhere.

In his journal the next day, he recorded, "A squad of Va. Cavalry rode up and called our surgeon out when quite a conference ensued. The sensation caused by this unexpected call from rebels can hardly be described. Where they came from and where they were going was indeed a mystery." Fortunately for Robbins and his comrades, "through their entire call they were with 3 or 4 exceptions, very gentlemanly." The rebels assured Dr. Weisel, the head surgeon, that his hospital "would not be molested if they turned over everything in their possession which was not necessary for the care of their pa-

Jerome John Robbins, Emma's confidant during the war. (From J. Robbins Papers, Bentley Historical Library at the University of Michigan.)

tients, to which Dr. Weisel replied that he had no supplies that fit that description." Robbins was thankful for Weisel's calm demeanor in the face of the unexpected visitors. "Our surgeon," Robbins noted, "deserves much praise for the excellent manner in which he got through the $3\frac{1}{2}$ hours the rebels were here and about us, and I really believe had it been almost any other surgeon in the service, much more difficulty would have arisen." In addition to being a Marylander, and therefore a "neighbor" of Stuart and his Virginians, Dr. Weisel knew at least one of the Confederate officers from before the war. In the end, the rebels were satisfied to carry away the few guns on the hospital grounds. Although Stuart returned to Richmond with more than 160 prisoners, he left the medical staff at Talleysville, and their patients, alone.[35]

By the time Stuart arrived back at Lee's headquarters on June 14, the news of his audacious escapade was everywhere. In the Southern papers, it was heralded as one of the greatest feats in the history of warfare; in the North, it was labeled an utter humiliation. At the very least, it gave Robbins something to write to Anna about. Perhaps nobody was more amused by the whole affair than Stuart who no

rong defenses, and when the sun went down, the day belonged to
e Union. The Confederates had tried several times to turn McClel-
n's right flank, and failed each time; the result was 1,475 rebel ca-
alties to 391 on the other side.

Mechanicsville should have been the beginning of the end for Lee.
ad McClellan ordered his main force to Richmond, Lee, badly
t up and disorganized at the end of the day on the twenty-sixth,
uld not have begun to stop him. Lee had exposed his hand, and
me up short. And feeling "invincible" after Porter's victory,
cClellan later claimed that he was about to do just that, until he
rned late that night from various scouts that Stonewall Jackson
d in fact arrived, but too late to have been in the fight that day.
at meant that Porter had faced down only a portion of what
e had available, and worse, now that Jackson had finally come,
e was likely to try again the next day. He also learned that the
esident was withholding McDowell's division near Washington
er all. All of these bits of news seem to have paralyzed McClel-
; he again neither gave orders for an advance on Richmond nor
a consolidation of his forces. What he did do was begin to
ic, concluding, in the wee hours of the night, that the single
st imperative goal was to change his base of operations from
ite House on the York to Harrison's Landing on the James.
e that was done, he told himself, once his supply and commu-
tions lines were safe, then he would turn his attention back to
mond.⁴²

etween midnight and dawn, McClellan sent a flurry of mes-
s—one to Porter to fall back to a heavily fortified rise called
es' Mill, the better to fend off the renewed Confederate assault
e the base change was accomplished; another to the chief quar-
aster of the Army, who in turn instructed Rufus Ingalls, in
ge of White House Landing, to get ready to move, fast. "Run
ars to the last moment, and load them with provisions and am-
ition. Load every wagon you have with subsistence, and send

doubt got a kick out of thinking about how much grief McClellan
would take when the word got out that Stuart's twelve-hundred-
member cavalry had been able to completely circumnavigate the
mighty Army of the Potomac while the latter was knocking on Richmond's door.

The immediate effect of Stuart's ride was to put the Army of the
Potomac on edge. Emma's regiment still lay where it had a month
before, less than ten miles from Richmond on the south side of the
Chickahominy. Many, many soldiers wondered aloud why they were
not moving. When the month opened, they had been absolutely certain that they would be in Richmond by the end of it; now they were
beginning to wonder if they ever would see the Confederate capital
up close. To keep them in place, their counterparts fired a steady
round of warnings, adding to their frazzled nerves. In Emma's recollection, "I think [that was] the most trying time that the Army of the
Potomac ever had on the peninsula. . . . A heavy and almost incessant
firing was kept up day and night, along the entire left wing, and the
men were kept in those rifle pits (to say in water to the knees is a very
moderate estimate), day after day, until they looked like fit subjects
for the hospital or lunatic asylum, and those troops in camp who
were not supposed to be on duty . . . were often called out ten times
a night." ³⁶

Another effect of Stuart's ride was to give Lee the information he
wanted: McClellan's right was weak. With the imminent arrival of
Stonewall Jackson from the north, Lee believed that it was worth a
try to push down the York River side of the Peninsula, cut off Mc-
Clellan's main force in front of Richmond from its supply base, and
ideally, turn McClellan's right flank so that the Army of the Potomac
would be sandwiched between the two halves of Lee's forces. Lee's
army was still outnumbered, but with Jackson's additional twenty
thousand veterans, the margin would be narrowed enough to make
it worth a try. At least, Lee concluded, it was better than sitting in
Richmond waiting for McClellan to mount his siege.³⁷

In fact, McClellan was finally on the verge of doing just that. Even before Stuart's probe, he had been considering moving his supply depot from the York to the James. The James had the advantage of directly linking to Richmond, but when the army first arrived on the Peninsula, it had been blocked by the Confederate naval base at Norfolk on the James's far bank. Norfolk was abandoned after the fall of Yorktown, and now the James was clear if not all the way to Richmond, at least a good part of the way. Even if McClellan still mounted his main attack by land, a supply line running from the James would be much shorter, and easier to defend, than the long railroad line that ran from White House Landing. But for now, this was still just an idea, one that he would not likely put into action unless his right flank was pressed. As a precaution, he did order eight hundred thousand rations and other supplies to be brought by water from White House to Harrison's Landing on the James, but his immediate plan was to advance on Richmond via the railroad. South of the Chickahominy, a mile or so in front of the Federal lines, was a high point of ground that would put McClellan in shelling range of Richmond. On June 25, he ordered two divisions of Heintzelman's corps to move forward and take a dense oak grove that lay between the Union and Confederate front lines, the first step in McClellan's multi-step plan for capturing the coveted rise. It was a small step; McClellan was asking for only a twelve-hundred-yard gain; but it was, in McClellan's mind, the beginning of his grand siege. If he could accomplish this, he wrote, "the game is up for the Secesh." [38]

Emma's regiment was held in reserve in the ensuing clash at Oak Grove, but could hear the sounds of battle well enough. It was a surprisingly intense fight: The Federals had the numerical advantage, but the Confederates were shielded by thick trees and redoubts they had spent a month reinforcing. At the end of the day, McClellan's troops were able to give him half what he asked for—six hundred yards, gained at a cost of one casualty per yard. [39]

McClellan rode out to the field late in the afternoon, and declared

himself thrilled with the result, although he might
pleased had he realized that he was, at that moment,
mond as he was ever going to get. He could not kno
Grove marked the beginning of what history refers
Days, a weeklong series of daily contests that would
the Peninsula campaign. But he did soon learn that
an advance of his own, against General Porter's
strong corps on the north side of the river, and tha
son was on his way to reinforce Lee. Still, had McC
grasped the situation, even this might not have t
was on the verge of taking a terrible risk, throwing
his eighty thousand men at McClellan's flank,
thirty thousand to protect Richmond from the
thousand troops McClellan had now less than six
ital. If anyone else had been in command of th
tomac, those would have been unacceptable odds
understood that McClellan would not attack
right flank was hit; he would act defensively, as h

Lee was right. When McClellan learned that
way, he knew that it would be Porter's corps
brunt of the Confederate assault. But, as Lee p
pull Porter across the river and march into Ric
rush reinforcements back across the river to
night of June 25, he told Porter to hold his
had been heavily fortified over the past two mo
alone. [41]

Lee planned for the attack on Porter near t
chanicsville, a scant six miles northeast of Rich
light on June 26. But Jackson, apparently no
portance of his division in Lee's complicated
ing, and the coordination between Lee's othe
as well. As a result, the assault did not get un
afternoon. Porter's well-organized line did

them to Savage's Station, by way of Bottom's Bridge. If you are obliged to abandon White House, burn everything that you cannot get off. . . . It will be of vast importance to establish our depots on the James River without delay, if we abandon White House."[43]

This set in motion the bizarre tableau that unfolded over the next four days, in which Lee, whose capital was on the brink of capture, chased McClellan's 120,000-man army, with its wagons and supply trains, its guns, even its 2,500 head of cattle, as it fled to the safety of the James River. All day on the twenty-seventh, in the largest and fiercest fight on the Peninsula, Porter fended off the Confederates' renewed assault at Gaines' Mill, buying time while the evacuation of the north side of the river began. But by nightfall, his defenses collapsed and he was driven, at great cost, from his elevated defenses, and ended the day in a fighting retreat across the Chickahominy, burning the bridges behind him.

While the Battle of Gaines' Mill was under way, Emma was ordered—or may have volunteered—to ride to the various auxiliary hospitals on the north side of the river and warn "the surgeons, nurses, and such of the patients that could walk, to take care of themselves as best they could, for no ambulance could reach them; that the army was retreating to the James River, and that if they remained longer they would fall into the hands of the enemy."[44] Among those she visited was Robbins's hospital at Talleysville; she rode into the clearing with a clatter just after noon. There is no record of what transpired between Emma and Robbins that day, amid the confusion, the chaos, the sound of heavy fighting drawing ever closer. All that is known is that she urged him to leave with her, and that he, like the other medical staff, refused to abandon his patients. Emma likely pleaded with him, but with the sound of approaching cannon, she finally decided to leave herself, knowing that if she was taken prisoner, she would be revealed as a woman. Finally, with great reluctance, she rode off at a gallop, leaving the man she loved best, and sometimes hated, to an uncertain fate.[45]

Emma caught behind enemy lines after leaving Talleysville during the Seven Days' Battle, June 1862. (As drawn and engraved on wood by R. O'Brien, New York. Originally published in Emma's memoirs, *Nurse and Spy in the Union Army*.)

CHAPTER SEVEN

June 1862

AFTER LEAVING Talleysville, Emma rode southwest toward the Chickahominy. The bridges were burned, but the river had receded in the recent sunshine, and it was easily fordable in several places. As she headed toward one, near the old Bottom's Bridge, Emma discovered that she was now behind enemy lines. After helping to drive Porter off the rise at Gaines' Mill, the most forward Confederate divisions had pushed farther down and closer to the north bank of the river than she had thought. Emma turned her horse off the main road, and cut through a wide swath of woods, but when she emerged into a clearing on the other side, she found that she had stumbled into the midst of a rearguard action. She was now "between two fires, and tremendous hot ones at that, for the whole lines were a perfect blaze both of musketry and artillery." Nothing, she said later, "but the power of the Almighty could have shielded me from such a storm of shot and shell, and brought me through unscathed."[1] Miraculously, she managed to reach the Federal lines unharmed.

That night, as Emma was making her way back to her regiment, and Porter was bringing what was left of his combat-weary corps across the Chickahominy, McClellan called his remaining corps commanders together. With his right flank collapsed, and the enemy on the verge of encircling his army, there was no choice but to pull back and retreat to the safety of Harrison's Landing and the navy gun-boats in the James. As word spread along the lines, so, too, did con-fusion, as thousands of men who expected to be in Richmond any day now found themselves moving, quickly, in the other direction.

After he dismissed his generals to begin carrying out his order, McClellan, realizing that Lincoln might judge his decision harshly, fired off an intemperate telegram to the president and to Secretary of War Edwin Stanton, telling them, in effect, that the disaster that was befalling his army was entirely their fault.

Had I twenty thousand or even ten thousand fresh troops to use to-morrow, I could take Richmond; but I have not a man in reserve, and shall be glad to cover my retreat, and save the material and per-sonnel of the army. If we have lost the day, we have yet preserved our honor, and no one need blush for the Army of the Potomac. I have lost this battle because my force was too small.

I again repeat that I am not responsible for this, and I say it with the earnestness of a general who feels in his heart the loss of every brave man who has needlessly been sacrificed today. In addition to what I have already said, I wish only to say to the President that I think he is wrong in regarding me as ungenerous, which I said that my force was too weak. I merely intimated a truth which today has been too plainly proved. If, at this instant, I could dispose of ten thousand fresh men, I could gain the victory tomorrow. I know that a few thousand men would have changed this defeat to a victory. As it is, the government must not and cannot hold me responsible for the result.

I feel too earnestly tonight. I have seen too many dead and wounded comrades to feel otherwise than the government has not sustained this army. If you do not do so now, the game is lost. If I save this army now, I tell you plainly that I owe no thanks to you, or to any other persons in Washington. You have done your best to sac-rifice this army.

The telegraph operator in Washington who received this emotional message deemed the last line so inflammatory that he struck it from the version that went to Lincoln, although the original was preserved.[2] It was ludicrous for McClellan to be demanding more men when more than half his army had not been engaged that day. But Emma, for one, trusted McClellan's judgment implicitly, and took his view of things when she later wrote about his decision to evacuate White House Landing, which she described as "necessitated" by the "employment of General McDowell's force in the defense of Washington, and its failure to co-operate by land with McClellan."[3]

It took the better part of the day for Lee to figure out that McClellan was abandoning his entire position on the north side of the river. Lee assumed that the Federal forces retreating from Gaines' Mill would fall back to defend the supply base at White House Landing, or even back to Williamsburg; he did not expect them to cross the river in a full-scale retreat. But soon enough, Lee's scouts informed him that the Federals were in fact moving everything out of White House—some by way of the York River, but most by land across the Peninsula. Lee thought it was worth a chase; if he could catch and destroy even a significant portion of McClellan's army while it was attempting its lateral move, it would significantly lessen the likelihood that McClellan would try again to attack Richmond once he had regrouped.

Sending Jeb Stuart to retrace the same route he had taken earlier in the month toward White House Landing, Lee ordered the rest of his force across the river in pursuit of McClellan's retreating army. For the next three days, a pattern emerged. The Federals moved slowly and steadily toward the James, with Lee in pursuit; when he came close enough—first at Savage's Station on the twenty-ninth, then Glendale on the thirtieth—the Federal rear guard would turn and hold the rebels off until nightfall. Then, they, too would skedaddle after the rest of the army under the cover of darkness.

From their current positions, most of the corps were within

twenty miles of Harrison's Landing, but the roads were so poor, and indirect, and the terrain so heavily forested and marshy that it would take three full days to cover that ground. The greatest obstacle was the vast wetlands known as White Oak Swamp, which lay between them and the James. When the Federals were pushing west up the Peninsula toward Richmond, the swamp had guarded their left flank; the Confederates, McClellan knew, would not try to turn his left, as they had his right because they would not be able to maneuver through it. Now, though, McClellan's only avenue of escape cut right through the heart of the murky swamp. All through the day and night of the twenty-eighth, and again on the twenty-ninth, the long, slow Federal column made its laborious way through the gloomy, forested muck, without taking the time to eat or sleep. Even if they had had time to rest, the swamp was so wet—with water up to their ankles or higher—there was no place to lay a bedroll. Some men literally died of exhaustion. Emma, who caught up with the main column during the night of the twenty-ninth, recalled seeing one man, leaning against a tree, still holding his rifle, dead. To make it worse, nobody seemed to understand where they were going, or why.[4]

Finally, by daylight on June 30, the main body of McClellan's army began emerging exhausted, wet, and bedraggled, on the far side of White Oak Swamp; by evening they were entrenched atop a rise overlooking the James called Malvern Hill, where McClellan planned to turn and face the enemy in force. All day and into the night, while the rear guard, including the Second Michigan, desperately held off the advancing rebels at Glendale, troops streamed up Malvern Hill. Those who had arrived first and had had time to rest were busily engaged in erecting defense works, and positioning batteries for optimal advantage.

Emma, who had not found her own regiment in the confusion of the retreat, reached Malvern Hill at two in the morning of July 1, and was pleased by what she found. As she described it, "Malvern Hill is an elevated plateau, about a mile and a half by three fourths of a mile in area, nearly cleared of timber. . . . In front there are numerous ravines. The ground slopes gradually toward the northeast to the wooded plain beyond." The artillery, more than 250 guns, "was already in position, and the weary troops were in the line of battle, but flat on the ground and fast asleep—all except the guards who were pacing backward and forward in front of the line, ready to arouse the sleepers at any moment." For the first time in nearly thirty-six hours, Emma felt safe enough to "consign myself to the arms of Morpheus." Wrapping herself in her blanket, she fell sound asleep "until the thundering of cannon awoke me in the morning."[5]

The next day marked one of the few times—maybe the only one— that McClellan clearly got the better of Lee on the Peninsula. Lee, failing to appreciate how well fortified the Federal position was, ordered a headlong infantry attack. Perhaps he was influenced by his success at Gaines' Mill, where the Federals had also been on well-fortified ground. But this time, his army had been marching and fighting, marching and fighting, for six days in a row, and they, too, were exhausted and hungry. In addition, at Gaines' Mill, Lee had been facing only a fraction of McClellan's force; this time he confronted nearly four times as many men.

Lee had hoped to soften up the Federal position with his own artillery, but his guns were soon rendered useless. Instead of giving up, however, for some reason, Lee ordered his infantry to do what his batteries could not. All day on July 1, the Confederates charged up Malvern Hill in wave after unsuccessful wave, each mowed down in turn. The battle "raged all day with terrible fury," Emma recalled.

The battle of Malvern Hill presented, by far, the most sublime spectacle I ever witnessed. All the battles I had seen before, and those which I have seen since, were nothing to be compared to it. The elevated position which the army occupied, the concentration of such an immense force in so small compass, such a quantity of artillery on those hills all in operation at the same time, the reflection of the flashes of fire from hundreds of guns upon the dense cloud of smoke which hung suspended in the heavens . . . and the deafening roar of cannon combined to make a scene which was *awfully grand*.[6]

Although the tide of the battle was very much in the Federals' favor, Emma herself only narrowly escaped harm. In the late afternoon, there was a sudden lull in the Confederate onslaught, and it appeared that the action might be winding down. Emma, always looking for ways to be useful without actually inflicting harm herself, took the opportunity to try to secure food for the famished men around her; there had been no time to eat yet that day. Spying a farmhouse between the two front lines, but not in the direct center of the action, Emma made her way down the hill to see what she could find there. Inside, to her delight, the house appeared as though it had only just been evacuated—dishes were set on the dining table, and the cupboard was full. Quickly she began to load ham, flour, and other items onto a bed quilt, and was just wrapping up her treasure to carry it back to her lines when "a shell came crashing through the side of the house . . . then another and another in quick succession." Soon the roof of the house was ablaze, and Emma "thought it prudent to make an attempt to escape." Dragging her precious bundle behind her, she carefully stepped out the door, which was fortunately on the side of the house facing her own lines, but she soon determined that the shells had been misfired, and that the house itself was no longer a target. She made her way halfway up the hill, then was met by several of her comrades who helped her carry the heavy cargo the rest of the way, where it was greeted with a great deal of enthusiasm.[7]

The errant shells signaled a renewal of hostilities, and for several more hours the Confederates again tried to push their way up the hill. But by nightfall, when the firing died away, the dead were lying "in heaps upon the field" with no ground lost or taken. If McClellan had been an opportunist, he might have followed the decisive defensive victory with a counterattack on the badly cut-up rebels, and perhaps even have reversed his retreat and pushed his way on to Richmond. Several of McClellan's subordinates argued for doing just that. But McClellan was anything but an opportunist. Since reaching the James on the twenty-ninth (he had gallantly led the retreat), he had spent most of his time safely ensconced on a navy gunboat in the James. He did briefly appear on the battlefield in person late in the afternoon, but after a brief inspection, he again removed himself well to the rear, and shortly after nightfall, was on his way to Harrison's Landing, eight miles south of Malvern Hill, where he planned to set up his new headquarters. Without orders to the contrary, McClellan's generals had no choice but to stick to the original plan. Near midnight, the Federals slipped down the backside of Malvern Hill and followed the James downriver to the safety of the Union gunboats at Harrison's Landing.

When the rank and file found themselves again marching away from Richmond after such a clear-cut victory, what was left of their morale evaporated. Despite the odd movements of the past few days, until that moment, most still expected to be in Richmond in time to celebrate the Fourth of July. But it was July 2, and they were headed in the wrong direction. "The troops presented a most distressing appearance as they drew up in line and stacked their guns at Harrison's Bar. The rain had been pouring down most of the night, and was still drenching the poor battleworn, footsore soldiers, and turning the roads into beds of mortar, and the low marshy ground from the landing into such a condition that it was impossible to get along dry shod, except for those who rejoiced in the possession of high boots."[8]

McClellan continued to call the events of the past week a "change of base," rather than a retreat, and to insist that the Army of the Potomac would yet move on Richmond. On the Fourth of July, McClellan issued an optimistic, albeit self-serving, statement to his troops, in which he praised them for overcoming "superior forces," and for having "in every conflict beaten back your foes with enormous slaughter." He also assured them that "this army shall enter the Capital of the so-called Confederacy." But the truth was that since arriving on the Peninsula, McClellan had rarely gone on the offensive, and had reacted to almost every victory by retreating. There was little in his past conduct to give the men, or their officers, much hope that anything would be different in the future.

In those first few days at Harrison's Landing, Emma had no way of knowing what had happened to Jerome Robbins since she left him at Talleysville. After she passed through with her warning, he and the other staff and patients had waited nervously for what they expected would be another visit from the rebels. They were right. The next evening, members of Jeb Stuart's cavalry suddenly entered the clearing; this time, led by Colonel Fitzhugh Lee, General Lee's nephew. Colonel Lee had every reason to be angry: He had only just learned that, despite McClellan's orders to the contrary, his aunt's family home at White House Landing had been torched to the ground by the retreating Federals. But to Robbins's surprise, Lee and his men were nonetheless "very gentlemanly" with the hospital staff and patients, "making no disturbance even being anxious to please. One young fellow entirely emptied his pockets to give the patients each a relic. I exchanged buttons with a Mr. Spotts."[9]

Again to Robbins's surprise, instead of taking them prisoner, Colonel Lee gallantly offered to "parole" them. Parole was a European custom, dating back to the Middle Ages, of allowing captured opponents to go free, so long as they took an oath swearing not to bear arms against their enemy until they had been formally ransomed or released from their vow by the exchange of another prisoner of the same rank. The practice seems quaint now, but in a day when oaths were not taken lightly, it was still relatively common, at least for captured hospital staffs and their patients. It had not always been that way; at the beginning of the war, medical personnel were treated as combatants, and routinely imprisoned when captured. But Stonewall Jackson, a deeply religious man, believed this practice to be immoral, and insisted that hospital personnel captured by his men be allowed to go free, with the promise that they lobby their own officers to adopt the same practice. By the summer of 1862, Jackson's approach had taken hold with both armies.

Robbins and his comrades readily accepted the offer of parole. Still, "it was with some difficulty" that he and his comrades realized that "our services" were "no longer needed. . . . Now we are prisoners, yet free." A detachment of the Virginia cavalry stayed at Talleysville, "guarding" the parolees until arrangements could be made to send them north. The next day, Robbins caught a glimpse of the famous Jeb Stuart himself. "This morning Genl. Stewart [sic] was here. . . . He presented a very pleasant appearance except disclaiming all friends between the opposite parties. Our Surgeon had quite a number of friends in the cavalry who greeted him very cordially." When Stuart saw one of his men visiting amiably with Dr. Weisel, he asked his subordinate to whom he was talking. Robbins recorded that when the man explained to the general that Dr. Weisel was a friend, Stuart replied, "He is not now." Nonetheless, Robbins was able to have "a very pleasant conversation with a 2nd Lieut. Smith of the 4th Cavalry. He expressed a warmness for his cause which was very creditable. Yet all of either party expressed an earnest desire for the war to close." [10]

For the next several days Robbins and his comrades were in the dark about the fate of their army. On July 1, the day of the heavy fighting at Malvern Hill, they could hear the artillery fire, but had no way of knowing what was happening. The Confederates told them that McClellan was fleeing down the James, a report that Robbins had trouble believing. "We are really at a loss to determine the meaning of the strange movements within the past few days. We can hardly believe our Potomac is totally defeated but we have to conjecture everything." The day after the battle, they heard even more wildly disparate rumors, "one that McClellan had surrendered at six this morning with his entire army," another that "he is surrounded," and still another that "he had fallen back to the James River." Robbins proved to be an astute judge of the situation. "The first I can not believe, the second we doubt, but the last may be so."[11]

As the days wore on, Robbins became lethargic and depressed, and worried that because they had taken the parole oath, the Federal government "might regard us as deserters."[12] In fact, General Dix, the Federal commander of Fort Monroe, which was still firmly in Union hands, had learned of their fate, and was working with the Confederates to arrange their transportation to Camp Parole in Annapolis, a facility set up to house parolees until they could be exchanged. At the beginning of the war, parolees were sometimes allowed to simply return home, but when a fair number failed to return to their regiments when exchanges were arranged, the Federal government instituted the practice of keeping the men in an army camp for the duration of their parole. The result was that each side was essentially assuming the costs of detaining their own men, but for the men so detained, it was infinitely preferable to being in an actual prisoner-of-war camp.

On July 9, Confederate Colonel Thomas Goode, now in command of White House Landing, gave General Dix permission to send a steamer under the flag of truce to retrieve the 106 parolees from Talleysville, who, according to Dix's report on the transfer to General McClellan, "are nearly all well and speak in strong terms of the kindness with which they were treated by the insurgent officers."[13] The steamer arrived on July 11; three days later, Robbins and his fellow parolees disembarked at Camp Parole, on Chesapeake Bay. The camp consisted of a single frame building, for the guards and officers in charge, surrounded by a collection of tents for the "inmates." Food was plentiful, and there was access to medicines. It was not unlike a regular army camp, except that the men were not allowed to drill, or work in any way that might be considered beneficial to the Union cause. Robbins noted that "our present camping ground is quite pleasant; a point extends into an arm of the Chesapeake, so we have water on three sides of us." But by his second day, Robbins was becoming bored; "the place" he wrote, "is too monotonous which is its greatest fault," a complaint that would become a recurring theme of his journal entries for the next several months. A week after he arrived, he noted, "About the same transpires daily in camp. We have nothing to do but eat our rations and lounge about." Out of boredom, Robbins and some of his fellow parolees asked if they could take over guard duty—essentially, to guard themselves— just so they could have something to do. But they were told that "in performing any duties for our government we break our parole. It seems very strange; we can't do enough to keep us healthy." Mostly, they simply hoped to be exchanged. Even that hope dwindled when they learned in late July, from an article in the Richmond *Examiner* that was widely circulated through camp, of "a suspension of the exchange in prisoners." [14]

About the same time that Robbins was arriving at Camp Parole, Emma was sent by steamer from Harrison's Landing to Washington, on a working furlough to deliver mail to members of the regiment who were in hospitals there. Having spent the past three months on the Peninsula, confronting a myriad of dangers and hardships, she was shocked at the cosseted pomposity of the brass in Washington. "The military display made in Washington is certainly astonishing, especially to those who are accustomed to seeing major generals go round in slouched hats and fatigue coats, without even a star to designate their rank. But cocked and plumed hats, scarlet-lined riding cloaks, swords and sashes, high boots and Spanish spurs, immense epaulets, glittering stars, and gaily caparisoned horses are to be seen by the hundreds around Willard's Hotel and other places of resort." [15]

While in Washington, Emma also did some sightseeing, visiting the Capitol and the Smithsonian. At one point, she found herself in a camp of former slaves, where she encountered a Northern woman who was teaching a group to read. Emma struck up a conversation with one elderly man, and asked him how he thought he would get along, now that he was free. The man laughed heartily, and replied that as he had been taking care of both himself and his master for the past fifteen years, he believed he would do just fine taking care of himself alone.[16]

When Emma returned to Harrison's Landing, at the beginning of August, she again volunteered her free time in the hospitals.

> I used to watch with much interest the countenances of those men as they lay fast asleep, and I often thought I could read their characters better when asleep than when awake. Some faces would grow stern and grim—they were evidently dreaming of war, and living over again those terrible battles in which they had so recently participated; some groaned over their wounds, and cursed the rebels vigorously; others grew sad. . . . Often the roughest grew young and pleasant when sleep soothed away the hard lines from the brow, letting the real nature assert itself.[17]

Shortly after she returned, Emma learned where Robbins was, possibly from Colonel Poe, or from reading about him in the newspaper. On July 30, Robbins noted in his journal that his name had been mentioned in a Michigan paper. "We were greeted by several home papers" in one of which "is a list of the Michigan soldiers taken at the hospital near Talleysville." It is possible that the same paper made the rounds among the Michigan troops at Harrison's Landing. Robbins noted that he received a letter from "Frank Thompson," which he "enjoyed exceedingly." And he noted with appreciation that she had enclosed a $5 note. "The money came most acceptably as I was entirely destitute." Robbins wrote to thank her; from then on, the frostiness between them was gone, and they shared a regular and affectionate correspondence.[18]

As July came to a close, and McClellan had not renewed his initiative against Richmond from his new "base," Lincoln began pressing

McClellan to fish or cut bait. By now, the Confederates had mostly fallen back on Richmond, but they had also taken over and heavily fortified Malvern Hill, which the Federals would have to take in order to approach Richmond from their present location. McClellan now had ninety thousand men at Harrison's Landing; with twenty thousand more, he said, he could take Richmond, despite the fact that it was, in McClellan's estimation, defended by a force of two hundred thousand. (In fact, the real number was closer to eighty thousand.) Perhaps to McClellan's surprise, Lincoln agreed; a day later, McClellan changed his mind, saying he in fact needed at least thirty-five thousand more men. This was the last straw.

On August 3, Lincoln ordered McClellan to abandon the Peninsula campaign and bring his army to Washington to reinforce General John Pope, who was being harassed by Confederate forces near Manassas. Lincoln feared, rightly, that Lee had also concluded that McClellan was a paper tiger, and was planning to go on the offensive while the Army of the Potomac whiled away the summer on the Peninsula. Leaving only twenty thousand men to defend Richmond, Lee turned his eyes northward. Lee knew that he could not reasonably attack Washington itself, but perhaps, if he could cross the Potomac higher upriver and slip into Maryland or Pennsylvania, and win a decisive victory there, on Union ground, he could force Lincoln to accept the existence of his new country.

Lincoln, too, was looking for a decisive victory, for a different reason. Since July, he had been planning to issue a presidential proclamation freeing the slaves, at least those in the rebellious states. It was an extremely controversial move, even in the North; it would transform the war from one principally about preserving the Union to one that was primarily about freeing the slaves, something it had not been until that point for most Union soldiers. McClellan himself spoke for many of his men when he said that he cared "not at all for the Negroes one way or another." Lincoln's desire to issue his proclamation was partly ideological, but also partly, perhaps largely, pragmatic—he wanted to ensure that England and France did not succumb to the pressures on their own economies from the shortage of cotton caused by the North's blockade of Southern ports, and come to the military and political aide of the Confederacy. Slavery was Lincoln's international trump card—both countries were vehemently opposed to slavery, and Lincoln knew that if he could recast the war from a political dispute to a moral one, they would be unlikely to take the South's part in the conflict. But Lincoln was convinced that his proclamation would look to his European audience like a sign of desperation, rather than a moral stance, if he issued it in the wake of the humiliation of the Peninsula campaign. In order for it to have its full effect, Lincoln needed a win.[19]

When McClellan received Lincoln's order, he was furious, both at having to return to Washington, and more particularly, at being ordered to reinforce Pope, a man he knew well and hated. Lincoln had not made clear who, Pope or McClellan, would have command of the combined forces, but McClellan feared, correctly, that it would be Pope, a fact that made him nearly insane with anger. In a letter to his wife, he essentially willed Pope to fail, noting that in that case, "they will be very glad to turn over the redemption of their affairs to me." Given how he felt about his orders, it is not surprising that McClellan took his own sweet time in getting his army back to Washington.[20]

Not until August 15, nearly two full weeks after Lincoln's order was received, did the Army of the Potomac begin the laborious process of reversing the monumental deployment of the previous March. The order, Emma noted, had "a demoralizing effect upon the troops, for they had confidently expected to advance on Richmond and avenge the blood of their fallen comrades, whose graves dotted so many hillsides on the peninsula, and whose remains would now be desecrated by rebel hands. The men were deeply moved; some wept like children, others swore like demons, and all partook in the general dissatisfaction of the movement."[21]

The Second Michigan arrived in Alexandria on August 21, in a driving rain, befitting their mood. It had been five months since they had started out in grand style; now the Peninsula campaign was over and it had been an utter failure, with nothing to show for their trouble other than the loss of fifteen thousand men. For Emma, it was a particularly lonely time. Her closest friends in Company F, including Damon Stewart, William Morse, and Will McCreery, had all been wounded and sent home; Jerome Robbins was a parolee. And now her beloved McClellan was about to be gone as well.

Two days after they arrived in Alexandria, the Second Michigan, under the leadership of Colonel Poe, was sent to join Pope. They boarded trains for Warrenton Junction on the twenty-third, and from there marched toward Manassas. This was depressingly familiar territory; the same place they had suffered their first, humiliating defeat just over a year before. Unsure of their orders, they did not arrive at Manassas until the night of the twenty-eighth. Two days earlier, Stonewall Jackson's division overran the lightly guarded Union supply depot at Manassas Junction, plundering all they could and torching the rest, including the railroad tracks running south from the depot. That sparked, three days later, what became known as the Second Battle of Bull Run (or Second Manassas), an intense, two-day contest on almost exactly the same ground as the first engagement there. This time, however, the Federals were the ones on the defensive. When it was over, Pope, who had started the week on the south side of Bull Run creek, with full control of Manassas Junction, had been completely flanked, and very nearly encircled. He was lucky, in the end, to manage to escape back across the creek in a fighting retreat to Centreville, then to Chantilly, where another intense skirmish occurred in a terrible rainstorm, and finally to Fairfax. Unlike its experience during First Bull Run, the Second Michigan was actively engaged every day, and saw particularly heavy action during the retreats to Centreville and Chantilly. The result of the three days of battle was a complete victory for Lee—and a humiliating defeat for Pope, just as McClellan had predicted, and possibly hoped.

Emma's own actions during the last ten days of August are somewhat mysterious. The muster roll for the month of August reflect that she was "absent—mail carrier by order of Col. Poe." In her memoirs, she claimed that she went behind enemy lines three different times during the five days between when her regiment reached Warrenton Junction on the twenty-third and the beginning of the engagement on the twenty-ninth. This time, she was in the guise of a female slave, and claimed to have collected important information while she helped the other slaves make and serve meals. According to Emma, "I was ordered by General H. to pass through the rebel lines and return as soon as possible. I took a train at Warrenton Junction, went to Washington, procured a disguise, that of a female contraband, and returned that same night. I passed through the enemy's lines in company with nine contrabands," who, Emma claimed, preferred to voluntarily return to bondage rather than live free without their families or friends. "I had no difficulty getting along, for I, with several others, was ordered to headquarters to cook rations enough, the rebels said, to last until they reached Washington." The assignment was fortuitous, Emma claimed; it allowed her to steal critical battle plans from the unattended jacket of a Confederate officer.[22]

"General H." may have stood for Samuel P. Heintzelman, who was commander of Pope's Third Corps, of which Poe's brigade was now a part. Unlike McClellan, who relied primarily on Allan Pinkerton to coordinate his intelligence operations, Pope authorized his generals to direct their own espionage activities, and encouraged them to send their own spies and scouts behind enemy lines. Because their activities were rarely fruitful, they were rarely recorded, and their exact numbers are not known. One exception was a member of the First Indiana Cavalry, named Thomas Harter, who managed to insert himself into the oncoming Confederate army in the days before Second Bull Run, and then to slip away and warn Pope of certain vital information.[23] But whether General Heintzelman ordered Emma to assume a disguise and infiltrate enemy lines is less certain, and there are reasons to doubt her claim. For one thing, she says that she emerged from "rebeldom" with critical battle plans, which she claims to have stolen from the unattended jacket of a Confederate officer. There is no record of any such plans being discovered under such circumstances, and her story is oddly similar to a widely repeated, but not wholly accurate, incident in which a detachment of Union cavalry supposedly surprised Jeb Stuart and his staff while resting at a farmhouse several days before the main engagement. Stuart fled, but left behind his coat, which contained a letter from Robert E. Lee. (In fact, the Federals did nearly capture Stuart, and did manage to capture his famous plumed hat, but the letter in question was taken from the satchel of one of Stuart's deputies. Still, it is highly possible that Emma heard, and remembered, the rumor about Stuart's coat pocket.)[24]

If Emma did go behind enemy lines, it must have been before the main engagement began on the twenty-ninth; it is well documented that on that day, while she was riding to the front with messages and mail, she was involved in a riding accident. Her mount for the day was not a horse, but an army mule. Rushing with messages that she hoped to deliver before the fighting began, she took a shortcut off the main road, riding wildly through ditches and over fences and fallen trees. When she came to a particularly wide ditch, she tried to jump it, but she was asking of a mule what only a horse could do. The mule reared and then slipped. Emma was flung against the far side of the rocky ditch. The mule fell in on top of her, stepping on her as it tried to scramble out. As she pulled herself out of the ditch, Emma could hear the cannon booming in the distance. Her left leg had been broken, and there was an excruciating pain in her chest. Still, she managed to drag herself back on the mule, and eventually arrived at the front lines with the "precious" mail. But even after she regained some strength, her injuries continued to be painful, and she had to convince the medical staff to give her medicine for the pain without giving her an examination, which she was afraid would lead to her discovery. Although she would soon be able to ride again, her leg never completely healed, and her foot remained so deformed that, for the rest of her life, she had trouble wearing shoes.[25]

The Second Michigan spent the next several days near Fairfax Station, where a large field hospital had been set up near the train depot. As during First Bull Run, a number of civilians had come from Washington to witness combat, or at least its aftermath, for themselves. While thousands of wounded lay in wait for trains to take them back to Washington, Emma recalled seeing several government clerks, a "class of individuals," she said, who were incomparable "for importance and absurdity." That day, she noticed that a number of "those pompous creatures" were

distressed beyond measure because they could not return to Washington on a train that was crowded with the wounded. After the carts moved off there they stood, gazing after it in the most disconsolate manner. Said one, "I came out here by invitation of the Secretary of War, and now I must return on foot, or remain here." One of the soldiers contemptuously surveyed him from head to foot, as he stood there with kid gloves, white bosom, standing collar . . . in all the glory and finery of a brainless fop, starched for display. "Well," said the soldier, "we don't know any such individual as the Secretary of War out here, but I guess we can find you something to do; perhaps you would take a fancy to one of these muskets," laying a hand on a pile beside him.[26]

The debacle that was, for the Union, the Second Battle of Bull Run, resulted in more than sixteen thousand casualties. In the days following, the wounded flooded the hospitals in Washington, which were already overflowing. At one point even the rotunda of the Capitol building was used, and lawmakers had to lift their feet to avoid

stepping on them. Once again, Washington braced for what was sure
to be an attack by Lee and Jackson, just as it had the summer before
after the first debacle at Bull Run. And once again, the rank and file
were utterly demoralized. Lincoln reluctantly, but with certainty,
concluded that McClellan was the only one who could put the army,
and the North's, confidence back together. He might not be able to
mount effective offensive campaigns, but he knew how to organize
and energize a defeated army. He had done it before, and, Lincoln
hoped, he could do it again. McClellan apparently agreed with that
assessment, writing to his wife that his predictions had come true,
and that "again I have been called upon to save the country."

At Camp Parole, Jerome Robbins, with little else to do, was following news of the army carefully. On August 29, the day after Robbins marked his twenty-first birthday with very little cheer, he
received reports of the engagement "on the old battleground of Bull
Run," but in the accounts Robbins read, it was reported to have
been a Union victory. The news made him eager to get back in action. "How ardently do I hope we may soon be exchanged that we
may contribute our role to our country. . . . I often get to thinking of
our situation being idle and fruitless . . . but the ministers of our government have as much as they can master and it should be far from us
to complain." Robbins also followed with great interest the news of
McClellan's removal and subsequent reinstatement as commander of
the Army of the Potomac; like Emma, he greeted the latter with
great pleasure. "It does our hearts good to hear that General Mc-
Clellan has command of the fortifications about Washington," he
noted, and prayed that "our glorious cause be made to prosper
under the masterly supervision of our beloved General."[27] Apparently, Robbins did not hold McClellan responsible for his "situation."

During September and October, Emma wrote to Robbins eleven
times, and he responded eight times. By contrast, he received only
four letters from Anna Corey, and responded an equal number of

times. Emma's letters were always well received. On September 9, Robbins wrote, "Yesterday I received a letter from my friend F. Thompson, at the same time a choice work by Mrs. Hale presented by him. I have before mentioned this friend whose sympathies seem to be with me most earnestly."[28]

Imprisonment was not too taxing. In between prayer meetings, and taking care of the sick, which he apparently did voluntarily and unofficially, Robbins was allowed to take walks around camp, and he would frequently swim in the river on warm days. Occasionally he was allowed to visit Annapolis, to take in the sights of America's first capital city. The degree of freedom meant that some parolees took what Robbins referred to as "French leave." "I do not approve but it seems where a man has a family it is better for him to be there than here where he benefits no one. . . . I am quite lonely myself and long to be at home, yet until I can go with freedom I think I shall decline."[29]

While McClellan was resupplying his exhausted and hungry troops for the first time since they left Harrison's Landing, Lee was following up on his victory at Bull Run. On September 4, he forded the Potomac forty miles north of Washington, and headed into western Maryland near Sharpsburg. When the news reached Washington, panic ensued; this must be the start of the offensive on Washington that everyone there so greatly feared. But McClellan, with uncharacteristic speed, sent a large portion of his troops north to meet them. The Second Michigan were not among them; they remained near Alexandria for the next several days, and were not present on September 17 for what would be the bloodiest one-day engagement of the entire war, near a small creek southwest of Frederick, Maryland, called Antietam. The result was seen as a strategic Union victory—in what was perhaps McClellan's finest hour during the entire war, the Confederates were driven out of Maryland—but at an enormous cost to both sides. Nearly five thousand men were killed that day; nearly twenty thousand were wounded. But Emma and her regiment did share in the rejoicing that followed. Emma wrote later that the "brilliant and triumphant" victory "more than counterbalanced the disastrous campaign of Pope, and which sent a thrill of joy throughout the North." So did Robbins, who followed "the glorious news" of the victory closely.[30]

Later Emma claimed that she was on the field at Antietam, but it may have been a literary device to allow her to include a story that was most likely based on hearsay rather than her own experience. Emma claimed that during the battle, a dying soldier, who refused to be treated by anyone but Emma, confessed to Emma that she, too, was a woman. (In writing about this episode, Emma is vague about her appearance; the story suggests that Emma was at the time dressed as a woman.) In explaining herself, the dying woman said, "I have enlisted for the purest motives," presumably what Emma herself might have said had she been in the same situation.[31]

Particularly since there is nothing to suggest that Emma herself was present at Antietam, her story is strangely, and suspiciously, similar in some respects to that of Clara Barton's experience there. Barton had abandoned her early reticence at the start of the war about going to the field. Her first foray had been at Fairfax Station immediately after the Second Bull Run—she simply took a train to the depot and began ministering to the nearly four thousand wounded waiting to be sent into the city. From then on, she would be a regular fixture on eastern battlefields.

After Antietam, as the medics were collecting the wounded from the field, one approached Barton and said that he had found a soldier who refused to be treated by the doctor or any male medic; only a woman would do. When the soldier was brought in, she confessed to Barton that she was in fact Mary Galloway, a sixteen-year-old girl from nearby Frederick who had fallen in love with a Union officer while his regiment was in Frederick at the beginning of the war. When the fighting broke out at Antietam Creek, and she learned that his regiment was involved, she disguised herself as a soldier to come to look for him. In Emma's "experience" the female soldier died; in the case of Mary Galloway, Barton coaxed her into allowing the surgeon to operate, saving her life, and she and her lover were ultimately reunited.[32]

As at Yorktown, McClellan has since been faulted for not chasing the rebels and destroying the Confederate army, allowing it to fight another day. Still, driving Lee out of Maryland gave Lincoln the victory he had been waiting for. On September 22, he issued the Emancipation Proclamation, which pronounced that on January 1, 1863, all slaves held in "the rebellious states" would henceforth be free. Robbins made a passing note of it in his journal on the twenty-third, but Emma did not refer to it in her memoirs, rather a muted reaction from two passionate opponents of slavery. In fact, abolitionists tended to view the proclamation as too limited, as it applied only to slaves held in the Confederacy, and not those held in loyal slave states, such as Missouri. Union soldiers who did take note of it in their journals, tended, for the most part, to be those who were opposed to making the war about ending slavery rather than preserving the Union.

Robbins's seeming indifference to the Emancipation Proclamation may have had something to do with the fact that on the same day that he noted it in passing, more than three thousand paroled prisoners arrived at Camp Parole from a Confederate prison called Belle Island, in the middle of the James River. Most of them had been captured during the Peninsula campaign, and Robbins realized how lucky he was not to have shared their fate. "It is enough to make the heart bleed to look at the poor fellows, feet sore, dirty and ragged and nearly covered with vermin. One poor fellow told me he had been for 3 months as I saw him, which was barefooted, hat, pants and shirt in tatters, no blanket or other article to make him comfortable. I did what I could to make them comfortable."[33]

For the next month, Lincoln once again found himself in the now familiar dance with McClellan, urging his general to give chase to

Lee while he was still reeling from defeat, while McClellan argued that his army needed a rest after such a draining fight. At first Lincoln acquiesced, thinking that McClellan wanted a few days to resupply. But a month came and went, and McClellan was still resting. Lincoln was beside himself with anger. Lee was still in the northern Shenandoah, but Lincoln feared that after a month of recuperation, Lee's forces, so decimated at Antietam, would be strong enough to go on the offensive, or at least to mount a spirited defense of Richmond.

Finally, on October 25, McClellan gave Lincoln what he wanted. The Army of the Potomac left the safety of Harpers Ferry and headed into Virginia in pursuit of Lee. The goal was to reach Warrenton, just south of Manassas, and from there swing east to Richmond. The weather was warm and the countryside in full fall splendor. Emma's regiment, then at Edward's Ferry, started out to meet up with McClellan. According to Emma, "the army . . . now in admirable condition and fine spirits . . . enjoyed this march exceedingly." [34]

On the third day of the march, as the army neared Lovettsville, Emma, whose duties as regimental mail carrier often included serving as a courier, was given a message for headquarters, some twelve miles to the rear. She turned her horse around, and headed to the back of the long column. During the afternoon, the weather changed for the worse, and by the time she delivered her message, it had begun to sleet. She was tired, hungry, and shivering as she headed back to find her regiment in the fading daylight. She had not eaten since breakfast, but, knowing that the area was riddled with rebel scouts, she did not dare stop. [35]

Around 10 p.m. it began to snow, an unusual occurrence for that time of year. Emma had long since passed the place where she expected to overtake the rest of the army. Unbeknownst to her, they had shifted their march route after coming in contact with Confederate skirmishers. Not knowing what else to do, she rode on through the night. Around midnight, she came upon a tiny village. Just as she was about to approach one of the homes to ask for shelter and food, she realized that the entire town was occupied by a small band of Confederate scouts.[36]

Quietly she rode on. Finally, at 2 a.m., she decided she had no choice but to rest for the night. Near what appeared to be a deserted farmhouse, she dismounted, and, using her saddle blanket for cover, she lay down to sleep. By this time, nearly two inches of snow covered the ground. Emma would have frozen that night, if her horse, weary from the long day's ride, had not lain down beside her, and kept her warm.[37]

At daylight, she resumed her search for her regiment. Suddenly a party of Union cavalry approached from the other direction. After she identified herself to their satisfaction, they told her they were searching for a group of Confederate guerrillas. She told them what she had seen in the village she had passed the night before. Although she was eager to return to her regiment, which the soldiers were able to point her toward, they prevailed upon her to lead them to the town before she did so. After going only about five miles, her small party was fired upon. Two of her new comrades were killed. Her horse was also hit. He reared up and threw her, then fell on top of her, saturating her with his blood as he died.[38]

Emma, injured from the fall, and terrified, lay perfectly still, hoping that the enemy would take her for dead as well. It apparently worked; she listened, eyes closed, as the rebels gave chase to the members of her party who managed to escape. Just as she was deciding it might be safe to move, though, she heard the sound of approaching hooves. One of the rebels had returned. He dismounted and walked over the wet ground to where Emma and her fallen comrades lay. Emma held her breath as she listened to him rummage. Suddenly two hands grabbed her feet and pulled her lower body out from under her horse's legs. After examining her boots, which he undoubtedly decided were too small to be of use to him, he reached into her pockets and pulled out the small amount of money she had been carrying with her. Then he hastily remounted his horse and galloped away.[39]

After a long silence, Emma wriggled her way out from under her horse. For a moment, she felt pure relief. But that feeling was soon replaced with sadness over the loss of her brief acquaintances, whose bodies lay just a few yards from her own, and for her beloved horse. Then sadness was overtaken by fear as she realized that she was still in hostile territory, without mount or money, or even any idea in which direction she should head. Before she could decide what to do next, she once again heard the sound of fast-approaching horses. By now, she was standing up. This time, it was too late to play dead.[40]

Much to her relief, however, it was the surviving members of the cavalry party she had met earlier that morning. They had turned back when they were fired upon, and were now returning with reinforcements to pursue the guerrillas who had attacked them. Before they left, they told Emma where to find the rest of her regiment. One of them, noticing that the mail carrier was covered in blood and limping, offered Emma his horse, and walked beside her all day until they found the Second Michigan. Once in camp, she realized that she was more seriously injured than she thought; the left leg she had injured six weeks earlier during Second Bull Run was probably fractured again. She was, as always, unwilling to seek medical help, for fear that her gender would be revealed, and was back in the saddle, on a new horse, and serving as mail carrier again within the week.[41]

CHAPTER EIGHT

November 1862

McCLELLAN'S PLAN was to head south until they reached the Alexandria and Orange railroad line, which he would use to maintain supply lines as far as Culpeper. There they would turn west, toward Richmond. The army reached Warrenton, about twenty miles north of Culpeper, by the first week in November. But for President Lincoln, it was not soon enough. By then, the Confederates, under James Longstreet, had managed to slip down the Shenandoah Valley to Culpeper, and get between the advancing Union army and the Confederate capital. With that, the already intense pressure from politicians and pundits in Washington, many of whom were now openly questioning McClellan's loyalty, exploded into a firestorm of protest that Lincoln could no longer ignore. This had been McClellan's last chance. All fall, as McClellan kept his troops idle at Harpers Ferry, Lincoln urged him, begged him even, to follow Lee into Virginia, believing that Lee's army was in even worse shape after Antietam than McClellan's. Lincoln vowed to himself that if McClellan delayed long enough to let Lee block the road to Richmond, McClellan would once again lose command of the Army of the Potomac, this time for good. As Lincoln remarked, "He did so, and I relieved him."[1]

Lincoln issued the order relieving McClellan of his command on

November 7. Although the Republicans in Washington, and many of his own senior officers, were glad to see McClellan go, the rank and file were not happy. Despite everything, his troops almost universally adored him. It was he who had turned them from a disparate bunch of ragtag volunteers into an impressive, disciplined, well-equipped army, and while his caution exasperated his superiors, it made his troops feel that that their well-being was his chief concern.

Emma watched, with a lump in her throat, as McClellan said good-bye to his troops at Warrenton on November 9. "In parting from you I cannot express the love and gratitude I bear to you," McClellan said. "As an army you have grown up under my care. . . . The battles you have fought under my command will proudly live in our Nation's history. The glory you have achieved, our mutual perils and fatigues, the graves of our comrades fallen in battle and by disease, the broken forms of those whom wounds and sickness have disabled—the strongest associations which can exist among men—unite us still by an indissoluble tie. Farewell!"[2]

By the time he finished his remarks, many of the men were crying openly. So beloved was McClellan that some of his more devoted troops even urged him not to relinquish command, offering to support him in a military coup d'état.[3] McClellan refused, and urged them to support their new commander as faithfully as they had followed him. Emma spoke for many of them when she recorded the event as "a sad day for the Army of the Potomac."[4] Jerome Robbins, still at Camp Parole, shared that view. When he received the news three days later, he noted in his journal, "We were startled to read from the papers that Gen. McClellan had been removed from the army & Gen. Burnside has taken command. . . . We feel depressed indeed."[5]

Lincoln replaced McClellan with Ambrose Burnside, a well-respected thirty-eight-year-old regular army veteran whose distinctive muttonchop whiskers gave rise to the term "sideburns." Burnside no more wanted command of the Army of the Potomac than most of

the soldiers, devoutly loyal to the displac
have it. In fact, Burnside turned down t
cepting when formally ordered to do so,
he was simply not up to the job. After M
humility may have seemed refreshing to his
it was not false modesty: By the end of the y
be proved right.[7]

What Lincoln wanted from General Bur
though winter was fast approaching, and the
hunker down in winter quarters until the sp
choice but to follow Lincoln's orders. The pres
With the Orange and Alexandria line now bloc
tion for maintaining supply lines was the Fred
Potomac line, farther to the east. But that app
getting 120,000 men, their supplies, and heavy
Rappahannock River, a logistical nightmare giver
ates had burned all of the bridges earlier in the wa

Burnside's plan was to amass the entire army at
the appointed time, a small contingent would init
make Lee think that Burnside was preparing to take
Culpeper. Then, at the last minute, he would quickly
the army east toward Falmouth, just across the Rap
the town of Fredericksburg. There the army would q
pontoon bridges, and cross the river before Lee coul

Lincoln was skeptical. He had hoped that Burnside
take Lee head-on, believing that the key to ending th
was not to take Richmond so much as it was to destroy
Northern Virginia. It went against Lincoln's best judgn
the Army of the Potomac to march away, rather than t
but with the two armies in a virtual stalemate at Warre
action was better than nothing. By mid-November, he
agreed to Burnside's plan. But he cautioned Burnside
quickly. He understood that success would depend on gett

ppahannock River and through Fredericksburg before Lee
shift his own army and put up resistance. Lincoln also knew
experience that once the Army of the Potomac started mov-
would not take Lee long to figure out what Burnside had in
[9]

th the plan in place, Burnside sent orders that materials for
ontoon bridges be sent to Falmouth immediately. Burnside also
ome reshuffling of his army. He created three separate Grand
sions, the Right, Center, and Left. Emma's regiment, the Sec-
Michigan, became part of a brigade consisting of three other
ments, with the Second's own Colonel Orlando Poe as brigade
mander. Poe's brigade was assigned to the Right Division, com-
ded by General Edwin Sumner.[10]

On November 15, Burnside set his plan in motion. While a small
achment was sent to start a diversionary fight near Culpeper, the
t of the Army of the Potomac, led by Sumner's division, quickly
aded east toward Falmouth. Emma, however, was not among
em. Instead, she had orders to ride to Washington, to collect and
liver mail. On her way, she crossed the battleground at Manassas,
here the two battles of Bull Run had taken place. It had been more
an two months since the second, but still the battlefield was littered
vith evidence of carnage. Emma recorded later that "there were men
nd horses thrown together in heaps, and some clay thrown on them
aboveground; others lay where they had fallen, their limbs bleach-
ing." One in particular sent chills down Emma's spine. "A cavalry-
man; he and his horse lay together, nothing but the bones and the
clothing remained; but one of his arms stood straight up, or rather,
the bones and the coatsleeve, his hand had dropped off at the wrist
and lay on the ground; nor a finger or joint was separated, but the
hand was perfect." Later she passed the stone church at Centreville, a
sight "of great interest to me," where she had tended to the wounded
in the summer of 1861. As she rode on, the horrible sights still fresh
in her mind, Emma could not help thinking about how much had

changed—and how much more had not—since that first encounter with the enemy.[11]

To Burnside's immense satisfaction, his troops moved extremely quickly, covering fifteen miles a day through cold, muddy terrain. Sumner's division, thirty thousand strong, arrived in Falmouth on November 17, the same day Emma arrived in Washington. Falmouth was a sleepy village two miles north and across the Rappahannock from Fredericksburg. The river was unusually low, and, after some scouting, Sumner identified a spot where he believed his cavalry could ford the river on horseback, drive out the small number of Confederate troops—about a thousand—who had been there all along, and give the rest of the army the chance to cross the river in peace when they arrived. But Burnside thought this was too risky. In the first of many ill-fated decisions in the coming days, he sent word to Sumner to wait for the pontoon bridges that were due to arrive any day.[12]

Disappointed, Sumner established headquarters at Lacy House, an elegant Georgian mansion on the north bank of the river, directly across from the town of Fredericksburg. Almost instantly, the thousand-acre estate, and the surrounding countryside, were covered in a sea of white tents. Soon Burnside himself arrived, only to be greeted with bad news: His order for pontoon bridges to be sent to Falmouth had gone astray, and the materials were only now leaving Harpers Ferry. But if Burnside wished to reconsider Sumner's suggestion, it was too late. The chance to ford the river without bridges had been literally washed away by a heavy storm that made the river rise dangerously. There was nothing to do but wait, and hope that the bridges arrived before Lee did.[13]

They did not. The pontoon materials did not reach Washington until November 19. By then, the same rain that made fording the river unthinkable had turned the roads into mud, slowing the progress of the wagon trains bringing the pontoons and building materials to a glacial pace. They had still not arrived in Falmouth when the first large contingent of Confederate troops reached Fredericksburg on November 22.[14]

After transacting her business in Washington, Emma boarded a government steamer bound for Aquia Creek Wharf, a busy depot on the Potomac River, thirteen miles south of Washington. Once there, she continued toward Falmouth on horseback, rejoining the army on December 3. "I found the army encamped in the mud for miles along the Rappahannock." Except for the bitterly cold temperatures, it reminded Emma of the Peninsula campaign that summer, only worse. "It was now December and the weather was extremely cold, yet the constant rains kept the roads in the most terrible state imaginable. . . . All the mud and bad roads on the Peninsula could not bear the least comparison with that of Falmouth and along the Rappahannock." Emma passed though the town of Falmouth, which had become a busy military depot in the few weeks since the first Union troops had arrived, and made her way down the river in search of her own brigade.[15]

Emma soon found Sumner's division on the grounds of Lacy House, and reported promptly to Colonel Poe. The arrival of the postmaster was greeted with great expectation and enthusiasm by the men—she came not only bearing letters from home, but also packages full of priceless objects such as paper, socks, food, and tobacco. She also came bearing a special gift for Poe, who noted in a letter to his wife that day that "Frank Thompson (mail carrier) has just returned from Washington. He brought me a pocket full of apples and doughnuts, and a very nice orange." Whether the delicacies had anything to do with it or not, two days later, Poe appointed Emma postmaster and mail carrier for the entire brigade.[16]

The pontoon bridges finally arrived in Falmouth just a few days before Emma did. By then, Lee's entire army, nearly eighty thousand strong, were amassed in and around Fredericksburg. As Emma noted, "on riding along the brink of the river we could see distinctly the rebel batteries frowning on the heights beyond the city of Fred-

ericksburg, and the rebel sentinels walking their rounds within talking distance of our own pickets."[17] (Among those on the other side
of the river was James Horace Lacy, owner of Lacy House, now a
major in Lee's army. From his vantage point, he could clearly see the
Federal troops swarming over his property. The sight of Union officers coming and going through his gracious doors, and soldiers turning his beautiful gardens into a sea of mud, was so disturbing to him
that he begged Lee to shell his own house. Lee refused.) Now, despite Burnside's best intentions, the two armies were once again at an
apparent stalemate.[18]

While the armies eyed one another at Fredericksburg, Jerome
Robbins continued to languish at Camp Parole, outside Annapolis.
For months, he and his comrades heard a steady drip of rumors that
they would soon be released. The repeated rise and fall of false hopes
was making Robbins edgy and impatient. On December 10, they
heard another such rumor, this one more believable than most. The
rumor was confirmed the next day, when Robbins was ordered to
pack his few belongings—one set of clothes, two pairs of socks, several books, a blanket, and his journal—and prepare to return to his
regiment. As the reality of his imminent release began to sink in, his
thoughts turned to those to whom he would soon return. "Have
been somewhat busy with preparations for going away which report
seems well-authenticated. . . . I feel glad in the thought that I may
again meet dear comrades. . . . My dear friend Frank is last on the list
but not least. How very often do I think of you my dear friend, and
more than ever since I learned of your illness. Oh, how I have longed
to be there to care for you but God willed it otherwise and let us be
content." But the formal order of exchange did not come that day,
or the next. So Robbins continued to wait.[19]

Meanwhile, Burnside was formulating a new plan. Had Robbins
known of it, he would have had much reason to worry about his
"Dear Frank." By now, Lee not only occupied Fredericksburg, but
had also established a formidable twenty-mile semicircular line of de-

fense in the hills and ridges behind the city. Burnside could try to cross the river above or below the semicircle, but that would require a massive shift of position that Lee would easily be able to see and respond to. He could also call it a draw, go into winter quarters, and wait until spring, undoubtedly the decision his troops were hoping for. But Lincoln, and the Northern public at large, were more impatient for action than ever. With the stiff winds of political expediency at his back, Burnside would not seriously entertain that option.

That left only one choice. On December 9, Burnside convened his generals at his headquarters at Phillips House, another once-elegant home just downriver from Lacy House. He told them that he had made up his mind to attack head-on. The engineers would lay the pontoons, under the cover of darkness if possible, supported by heavy artillery on the near side of the river. The army would then cross in force, and once the town was taken, they would attack Lee's defenses and simply overpower them.

Burnside's officers objected strongly, some to the point of near-insubordination. Getting across the river in the face of stiff resistance would be hard enough, but even so, what Burnside was proposing might have been possible if the terrain beyond Fredericksburg was flat. But it was not. Lee occupied the high ground, which gave him an insurmountable advantage. Sending troops across open fields to charge up heavily fortified hills was unconscionable. For the rebels, it would be like shooting ducks in a barrel. But Burnside, short of options, could not be dissuaded.

The next day, he again convened a council of war, this time at Lacy House. Despite his officers' continued objections, Burnside stubbornly clung to the idea that his plan would work, convinced it would take Lee by surprise. The officers generally agreed with that assessment, if only because Lee would not expect them to do anything so stupid. That evening, the engineers received orders to begin laying three pontoon bridges before dawn.[20]

As word of the plan spread, a deep sense of foreboding overtook the army. Among those at Lacy House that night was Clara Barton, the patent-office clerk turned field hospital nurse. Barton had arrived in the area on December 7, shortly after Emma had. In all likelihood, Barton believed herself to be the only woman at Lacy House, but Emma was frequently there as well, carrying messages between Colonel Poe and General Sumner's staff. Late that night, Barton, having made as many preparations as possible for treating the coming wounded, stood on the veranda of the house. As she looked out over the sprawling tent city, she noticed lights still burned in tents here and there. She imagined that inside, men were writing farewell letters to their loved ones, as many in fact were, and her heart went out to those whose last night it would be.[21]

Around 3 a.m., those who had managed to sleep awoke to the sound of men and machinery splashing into the dark, cold waters below Lacy House. The engineers of the Fiftieth New York, also part of Sumner's division, were assigned to build the upriver bridge, almost directly in front of Lacy House. For the first few hours they were protected by darkness. Soon Sumner's entire division was roused, and fell into line on the grounds of Lacy House and beyond. Emma, as brigade mail carrier, was mounted, and almost certainly by Colonel Poe's side. Clara Barton stood above them, on the veranda of the mansion. All waited together in silence, waiting to see if the engineers would win their race with dawn. One soldier wrote later that he "was filled with more anxiety and dread than I have ever known since."[22]

Shortly after a church tower in the distance struck five, the heavy morning fog hiding the engineers began to break up. As it did, those on the north side of the river caught a glimpse of hundreds of Confederate guns on the opposite banks; they, too, had been waiting for first light. The fog closed once again, but Emma could now see that the upriver pontoon was only half-completed, and soon the engineers would be completely exposed. Then, another break in the fog. This time, a flash of muskets pierced through the mist, followed by the hissing of shot, and screams of agony.[23]

Some of the engineers were struck instantly, falling lifeless into the cold waters of the Rappahannock. The rest ran for cover. The Federals returned fire, but could not reach all the way across the river. Soon, though, the batteries of Union cannon overlooking the river, more than 170 guns in all, opened simultaneously on the town and the riverbanks, sending the Confederate marksmen scrambling for cover. The roar was deafening, drowning out all other sound for miles.[24]

Once the bombardment was fully under way, the engineers tried to finish the bridges. Emma watched, transfixed, as "the pontoon bridges were laid amid showers of bullets from the sharpshooters of the enemy, who were ensconced in the houses on the opposite bank. However, the work went steadily on, notwithstanding that two out of every three who were engaged in laying the bridges were either killed or wounded. But as fast as one fell another took his place."[25]

The town of Fredericksburg was soon burning, but the rebel sharpshooters kept firing from the buildings facing the river with remarkable accuracy. Finally, in a fit of desperation, 135 members of the Seventh Michigan were ordered into boats, and rowed across the river in an unrelenting hail of shot. Many were killed or wounded, but those who reached the other side stormed the town, and engaged the rebels house by house. This gave the engineers the time they needed. Less than an hour later, the bridges were finally finished. For the remainder of the day, the Union troops poured across the bridges, and drove the Confederates out of town, back to the heights where Lee's main forces were entrenched.[26] By nightfall, the once-quaint colonial town of Fredericksburg had been destroyed; most of the buildings were shelled or burning, and those that were not were thoroughly looted.

On the twelfth, both sides regrouped, tended to the wounded, and waited to see what Burnside would do next. Colonel Poe received word that for the remainder of the engagement, his brigade would be commanded by General William Franklin, who assigned them to guard the lowest of the three pontoon crossings south of town. That afternoon, when Poe's orderly fell ill, Emma volunteered to take his place in the battle that would surely begin tomorrow.[27]

News that the Army of the Potomac was shelling Fredericksburg traveled fast, reaching Camp Parole on the twelfth. Jerome Robbins, still waiting for his exchange order, noted the event in his journal. "Papers tell us our army is crossing the river at Fredericksburg & that the city was in flames from our bombarding 176 guns opening at once. God speed the right and end the terrible national rivalry."[28] Robbins's prayers for swift victory would go unanswered.

The next morning, Emma arose before dawn. Like everyone in or around Fredericksburg that morning, she knew that the day of battle had arrived. She dressed quickly, and managed to dash off a few lines in her journal before the fight broke loose. "[A]m now aide-de-camp to [Poe]. I wish my friends could see me in my present uniform. This division will probably charge on the enemy's works this afternoon. God grant them success! While I write the roar of cannon and musketry is almost deafening. This may be my last entry in this journal. God's will be done. I commit myself to Him, soul and body. I must close. [Poe] has mounted his horse and says Come!"[29]

But even as Emma mounted her own horse and took her place beside Poe, Burnside was still trying to decide what to do next. He had identified two points in Lee's defensive lines beyond the city that might be vulnerable to a frontal attack. One was a ridge called Prospect Hill, just south of town. The other was another ridge directly behind the center of town, called Marye's Heights. Since their arrival, Confederate troops had been fortifying both ridges. By now, Maryey's Heights was "such a favorable piece of terrain for Lee that he beleived no rational Union commander would send his troops to such a certain death."[30] Moreover, to take the heights, the Union troops first had to get to them. Between the town and the heights lay an open field, dotted here and there with clusters of trees, and one or two small outbuildings, but essentially a flat expanse that would leave any attacking troops fully exposed to the Confederate guns on the ridges above. To make matters worse, the field was bisected by a fifteen-foot-wide drainage canal. To cross it, the men would either have to run through waist-deep, ice-cold water, or slow down and cross one of the three narrow footbridges single-file. And, as if that were not enough, at the far end of the field, a stone wall stood at the base of the hill, which they would have to climb while taking what would surely be constant fire.[31]

Burnside decided to storm both Marye's Heights and Prospect Heights at the same time, hoping this would weaken Lee's defenses. In the early morning, as a chilly fog covered the ground, Burnside ordered General Franklin to attack Prospect Hill, while Sumner would lead the advance against Marye's Heights. But there was some confusion about Burnside's order to Franklin. Burnside later claimed that he intended Franklin to make a massive assault, while Franklin understood Burnside to have requested only a diversionary skirmish. Franklin sent one division out, which made some headway, but, because of Burnside's vague order, he did not commit any more troops. Eventually, his lead division was driven back, and Franklin spent the rest of the morning waiting for further orders.

Around noon, believing that Franklin was already fully engaged and drawing at least half of Lee's strength to the south, Burnside gave Sumner the order to attack. Soon the first of what would be fourteen futile attempts to storm Marye's Heights was under way. With a great yell, three brigades, one after another, charged across the field in the face of withering fire. They ran with heads down, as though into a cold and icy rain. As soon as they came within range of the Confederate guns, they began to fall in waves. Those who, by sheer luck, managed to make it most of the way across the open fields without being hit by the shot and heavy artillery coming from above were mowed down by two lines of Georgia marksmen hiding behind the stone wall at the base of the heights.

All day long, brigade after brigade was ordered out, each one having just witnessed the fate of the one before. The dead and wounded soon littered the field, another obstacle to slow the fresh attackers. Not one got within fifty yards of the stone wall. Some of the wounded, or simply scared, took cover in a small ravine in the middle of the field that offered some protection from the guns above them. Some crouched behind the dead or dying. Others lay perfectly still on the field all day, afraid that any movement would draw fire. Within the first hour, the Union had lost nearly three thousand soldiers, and still they kept coming. By 2 p.m., the number of casualties had nearly doubled.[32]

Amid the carnage, Emma's own brigade spent the day in relative safety, guarding the lower pontoon crossing for a possible retreat. But as Poe's orderly, Emma was in constant motion, often close to the hottest action. All day, she rode up and down the Union lines, to headquarters and back, carrying messages and relaying orders. "I was not out of the saddle but once in twelve hours, and that was to assist an officer of the 79th [New York], who lay writhing in agony on the field, having been seized with cramps and spasms, and was suffering the most extreme pain. He was one of the brave and fearless ones, however, and in less than an hour, having taken some powerful medicine which I procured for him, he was again on his horse, at the general's side."[33]

Major Byron M. Cutcheon, of the Twentieth Michigan, was one of many who noticed Emma's bravery that day. Many years later, he recalled that "Frank Thompson" rode during the Battle of Fredericksburg "with a fearlessness that attracted the attention and secured the commendation of field and general officers."[34]

Not everyone was heroic that day, as Emma noticed. "I never saw, til then, a man deliberately shoot himself, with his own pistol, in order to save the rebels the satisfaction of doing so, as it would seem. As one brigade was ordered into the line of battle, I saw an officer take out his pistol and shoot himself through the side—not mortally, I am sorry to say, but just sufficient enough to unfit him for duty; so he was carried to the rear—he protesting that it was done by accident."[35]

By mid-afternoon, Burnside's officers realized that they had been right; Burnside's plan was simply not feasible. General Darius Couch, watching the assault on Marye's Heights from a church steeple in town, recalled that the whole plain was covered with men, "prostrate and dropping, the live men running here and there, and in front closing upon each other, and the wounded coming back . . . I had never seen fighting like that, nothing approaching it in terrible uproar and destruction." To Couch, the waves of men falling before the stone wall looked from afar like "snow coming down on warm ground."[36]

In the early afternoon, Couch could not take it any longer. He sent a message to Burnside, begging that the whole enterprise be called off, saying, "It is only murder now." Sumner shared Couch's opinion, and rode over to Phillips House, where Burnside could not even see the action, to personally ask him to call a halt to the day's offensive. But Burnside refused, and when Sumner informed him that he had no more brigades to send out, Burnside sent a message ordering General Franklin to renew his attack on Prospect Hill with every company still held in reserve.[37]

There is still much confusion about what happened next, but Franklin did not do as ordered. Some attribute it to outright disobedience; others, to another vaguely worded order. At least one private in the Second Michigan thought that Poe had something to do with it. "We were commanded by Col. Poe, a graduate of West Point, a man thoroughly versed in the art of war. He saw the utter hopelessness of the struggle, and when the order came to advance, he flatly refused to sacrifice his men in the unequal contest. Of course, he was put under house arrest, and will be court-martialed, but he saved his men."[38]

There is no evidence that Poe refused an order to engage, or that he was subject to discipline after the battle. In fact, it was Franklin who either misunderstood, or intentionally ignored, Burnside's orders to renew his attack that afternoon, although he undoubtedly had Poe's support, either tacitly or explicitly, in reaching that decision. Instead, for the rest of the day, Franklin maintained a defensive position. His decision, or ineptitude, whichever it was, cost him his command, but it undoubtedly saved many lives, including Emma's.

Once night fell, Poe and Emma rode three miles south from their camp to Franklin's headquarters to obtain instructions for the morning. On the way, they were haunted by the constant moans from the wounded. As one historian described it, "The night of December 13th was bitterly cold, which caused extreme suffering for the wounded who could not be evacuated. Many died of their wounds and exposure, and, wrote General Couch, 'as fast as men died they stiffened in the wintery air and on the front line were rolled forward for protection to the living. Frozen men were placed like dumb sentries'"[39] Emma later wrote that "of all the nights that I can recall, that was the darkest."[40]

Burnside spent the night contemplating another attack, this time with him personally leading the charge. But when the next morning dawned cold and clear, Burnside did not move. Instead, a brief truce was negotiated so that the wounded could be removed from the field. When she was not carrying messages, Emma helped the ambulance corps ferry wounded to Lacy House, where Clara Barton waited to receive them. Since dawn, the surgeons had been working frantically in every room, and soon an inch or more of blood covered James Lacy's beautiful hardwood floors.[41]

Meanwhile, just downriver, at Phillips House, Burnside's generals spent the day convincing him not to renew the attack. Finally, they prevailed. Before dawn on December 15, Burnside, who seemed to those who were with him to have finally realized the enormity of what had happened, and his responsibility for it, gave the order to retreat under cover of darkness. Quietly the army crossed back over the Rappahannock River, which had been forded at such cost. The troops returned to their old camps, thirteen thousand men lighter than when they had set off three days earlier. It was more casualties than the Union had sustained at Antietam, the bloodiest day of the war, but this time, they had nothing to show for it. The Confederates, for their part, sustained fewer than half that number.

For Emma, as for many who were at Fredericksburg, it was one of the lowest moments of the entire war, not least because, more than ever before, they had lost confidence in their leaders. Many openly pined for their beloved McClellan, certain that he would not have gotten them into such a mess. As one member of Emma's regiment wrote in a letter home to his parents, "I suppose you would like to hear something about the battle. I don't know hardly what to say about it but I think that it was a rather foolish operation. . . . I think McClellan's plans are the best after all and I still think he is the man. He don't believe in rushing men in and having them killed for nothing." [42]

Emma expressed similar thoughts, although slightly more eloquently, when she later wrote:

Of course it is not for me to say whose fault it was in sacrificing those thousands of noble lives which fell upon that disastrous field, or in charging again and again upon those terrible stone walls and fortifications, after being repulsed every time with more than half their number lying on the ground. . . . But when it was proved to a demonstration that it was morally impossible to take and retain those heights, in consequence of the natural advantage of position which the rebels occupied, and still would occupy if they should fall back— whose fault was it that the attempt was made time after time until the field was literally piled with dead and ran red with blood? [43]

Meanwhile, on the morning of the fifteenth, Jerome Robbins, unaware of what was happening just to the south, finally got the word he had been waiting for. Five months and two days after entering

Camp Parole, he was now a free and active soldier once more. "All is excitement this morning, we are each moment expecting the orders to march." Robbins bade farewell to the friends with whom he had spent five months, but "the hope of meeting other dear friends made our separation tolerable." At a little after noon, Robbins and several others who had been captured at Savage's Station boarded the transport *Belvedere,* took up "quarters" around the foremast, and settled in for the voyage up the Potomac.[44]

As Emma and her comrades were reeling from their devastating losses, Robbins and his companions enjoyed their first taste of freedom since the summer. "Nothing of especial interest occurred" that evening, "except the beautiful sunset and the soft-mild atmosphere were like a cool summer evening than of Dec. 15." Other than a stray shot across the bow from Union sentries, which took them by surprise but did no damage, they slept comfortably that night. By the afternoon of the sixteenth, the *Belvedere* pulled within sight of Aquia Creek Wharf, where Emma had disembarked just two weeks earlier.[45]

The wharf was a hive of activity, filled with "all manner of crafts." Soon a smaller vessel pulled up alongside the *Belvedere* to bring Robbins and his companions ashore. As soon as they reached Aquia, they learned what had happened at Fredericksburg. Robbins was concerned about his comrades in the Second Michigan, and most particularly about Emma. But it was too late in the day to head south. Instead, he found an unused tent near the wharf and made his bed for the night. At first light, after a weak cup of coffee made with brackish river water, he and his comrades shouldered their knapsacks, and started out by foot down the railroad line toward Falmouth.[46]

All morning long, they asked the regiments streaming away from Fredericksburg for news of their own, but no one could tell them anything. Finally, toward evening, as they neared Falmouth, they encountered some troops who pointed them toward the Sixteenth Michigan, who in turn forwarded them in the general direction of the Second. A mile and a half farther, in a strip of woods, they encountered boys from the Third Michigan, many of whom they knew, making a fire. "It was really pleasing to see the cordial greeting of friends after so long a separation," Robbins noted. From them, Robbins learned that his own regiment was about three quarters of a mile farther toward the river. He shouldered his knapsack once again, and resumed his march. "About sundown, I came in view of my own company and it was with . . . pleasure that I saw the first familiar countenances of my old comrades," Robbins wrote. With great relief, Robbins found all of the schoolmates with whom he had enlisted in good health, except one, George Southworth, who was in the hospital suffering from dysentery.[47]

After a brief rest and a hot cup of coffee, Robbins walked around the camp, looking in vain for Emma. "Did not find my friend Frank; learned he was mounted orderly for acting Brig. General Poe." He also learned of other changes that had taken place. His friend Dr. Cleland had been promoted to assistant surgeon, and Dr. Bonine had become brigade surgeon.[48]

It was not until late the next afternoon that Robbins finally saw Emma for the first time since that horrible day at Savage's Station. It was no doubt a joyful moment for both of them. They spent the rest of the evening catching up. "Found Frank after the day was well passed. In the evening, walked with him over to General Burnside's headquarters for the mail."[49] Time had mended their feud—time, and the maturity each had gained from the hardships of the past six months. In the chilly December twilight, on the banks of the Rappahannock, they were once again each other's dearest friend, and closest confidant. Emma had been Robbins's most loyal correspondent while he lay idle at Camp Parole. And Robbins was, after all, the only person in the entire world who knew who Frank Thompson really was, the only person Emma could really trust. Or so Robbins thought.

CHAPTER NINE

December 1862

AS ROBBINS soon discovered, in his long absence, his friend "Frank" had become "extremely fond" of a young, attractive—and recently married—lieutenant in the notorious Seventy-ninth New York Highlanders, the primarily Scottish infantry regiment that caused a great deal of interest when it arrived in Washington in the late spring of 1861 wearing kilts. It was also the regiment that became so famous in August of that same year, when a number of its members mutinied and were sent by McClellan to the Dry Tortugas. James Reid had not been among them, however; he had been captured during the First Battle of Bull Run and spent six months in a Confederate prison camp near Richmond. When he was released in January 1862, he rejoined his regiment, and spent the first nine months of the year in the Carolinas under General Burnside. When Burnside was given command of the Army of the Potomac in November, the Seventy-ninth New York was brigaded with the Second Michigan, under the command of Colonel Poe, as part of the Ninth Army Corps, and Reid was promoted to assistant adjutant general.

Frustratingly little is known about Reid, either before or after the war, and Emma never mentioned him in any written record, except in one letter to Robbins. There is, therefore, no record of how or when Emma and Reid struck up their friendship. Most likely it began while the army was at Falmouth before the battle of Fredericksburg. As mail carrier, and as orderly to Colonel (and acting Brigadier General) Poe, Emma was often at headquarters, and would have had frequent contact with the six-foot-three-inch, blue-eyed adjutant. Reid may in fact have been the officer of the Seventy-ninth New York whom Emma helped off the field during the second day of the battle. What is clear is that by the time Robbins returned to the regiment, Reid and Emma were, as Robbins put it, "particular friends," a fact that he noted with a certain amount of pique. "Have not had a very long chat with Frank and I feel quite lonely without him," Robbins wrote in his journal on the twenty-second, "but I suppose he enjoys his tentmate. . . . General's Aide Ass't Adj't Gen'l Reed [sic] seems a fine fellow & is very fond of Frank."

It was not that Robbins wanted anything more from his relationship with Emma than he already had—he was still very much enamored of the delicate Anna Corey. But he apparently did not want less than he had come to expect from Emma, either. Whether or not Emma had mentioned Reid to Robbins in her letters, he clearly did not expect to find her quite so devoted to the young officer.

As Christmas Day dawned bleak and cold, the soldiers of the Army of the Potomac were in a very different state of mind than they had been the year before, during their first Christmas of the war. Then, the memories of the one engagement at Bull Run were well behind them, they had boundless confidence in their new commander, and were certain that come spring, the war would be won quickly. Now their beloved McClellan was gone for good, not one of them had the slightest degree of confidence in Burnside, including Burnside himself, and nobody thought the war would be over anytime soon. To make matters worse, they were still camped on the northern bank of the Rappahannock in full sight of the rebel army. As Emma recalled, the "unnecessary slaughter of our men at Fredericksburg had a sad effect upon our troops, and the tone of the Northern press was truly depressing. The wailing for the noble dead seemed wafted on every breeze."[2]

After a cheerless holiday "soldier's dinner" of hardtack, beef soup, and coffee, Robbins retired to his tent to write in his journal, and once again, his thoughts turned to Emma's relationship with Reid. "Quite recently I have become acquainted with Mr. Jas Reid of the 79th NY Vo. With my limited acquaintance, and my ever reliable Frank, I can pronounce him one of nature's noblemen and if I should choose to ever publish any of these scribblings he and his 'pet' [Frank] will figure somewhat as individuals who repose in the pleasantest arbor of friendship." It is hard to know what to make of Robbins's entry. What did he mean by calling Emma Reid's pet? Did he think that the married Reid and Emma were more than just friends? And what did he mean by "the pleasantest arbor" of friendship. It is hard to imagine that Robbins, such a devout Christian, could have believed that anything immoral was going on in Emma and Reid's tent, and still regard both Reid and Emma so highly. But his tone seems to imply that, at the very least, something unusual was happening between the two of them.

Whatever his suspicions, he continued to seek out Emma's company. The next day, Reid was taken ill with a stomach flu, and Robbins and Emma took the opportunity to spend the day together. Borrowing Reid's horse for Robbins, they rode around all day, he accompanying her on her mail duties, and she accompanying him when he visited various friends from his days at Camp Parole.[4]

On December 28, Emma visited Robbins again, this time to show him a copy of a novel she had recently acquired. Robbins noted that he "had quite a lengthy call from Frank but all his social qualities were given to a new work entitled *Pauline of the Potomac, or General McClellan's Spy*, he pronounced it a "low quality work of fiction" and from a very brief examination I agree with my *literary friend*."[5] The book, by Charles W. Alexander, writing under the alias Wesley Brewster, told the dramatic story of a young French girl, Pauline

D'Esay, who became a daring spy for General McClellan. Robbins was dismissive of the work—it was a piece of highly melodramatic pulp fiction—but like Fanny Campbell, the book seemed to capture Emma's imagination. On January 2, Robbins wrote in his journal that "my spirits were rather enlivened in a stroll with Frank through and past some of the camps about us. Both the conversation, upon past experiences and associations, and walk were enjoyed as the day has been very beautiful with its warm sunlight."

At the same time, Robbins was preoccupied with his own personal life. On January 9, he wrote that he was anxiously awaiting a letter from home, one which he had expected should have arrived by then; two days later he noted that he "received a letter from a dear friend," which, from his correspondence log, appeared to be from Anna Corey. Apparently, this was the letter he had been hoping for. On the twelfth, he started his entry coyly, writing that "nothing of unusual importance today . . . unless it be that which also interests my private and sensitive feelings," without risking to record what those sensitive feelings were. But it may have been that the news he received from Anna Corey was the subject of his discussion with Emma the following day, when "Frank returned from Alexandria." Robbins noted that Frank brought "no news of importance. Had a long chat with him as is usual for friends after a few days' separation."[6] But apparently Robbins had some "news of importance" for Emma. Something, at least, must have prompted Emma to take the unusual step, three days later, of writing Robbins her own, heartfelt letter, and to take the even more unusual step of signing her real name.

> *Camp at Falmouth Va*
> *Jan. 16/63*
>
> *Dear Jerome,*
> *In the first place, I will say that I am happy to know that you are prospering so well in matters of the heart. In spite of the ridicule which sentiment meets with everywhere, I am free to state that*

upon the success of our love schemes depends very much of our happiness in this world. . . . Dear Jerome, I am in earnest in my congratulations & daily realize that had I met you some years ago I might have been much happier now. But Providence has ordered it otherwise & I must be content. I would not change now if I could—if my life's happiness depended upon it. I do not love you less because you love another, but rather more, for your nobleness of character displayed in your love for her—may God make her worthy of so good a husband.

Your loving friend,
Emma[7]

Robbins must have appreciated her sentiments; apparently her letter brought them closer than ever. On the eighteenth, he wrote that the evening was "the pleasantest of the day, chatting with Frank."[8]

By now, winter weather was solidly upon them. Emma recalled later, "A severe winter I thought it was; for in riding a distance of two miles, in two instances I had my feet frozen." Some soldiers went to great lengths to weatherize their tents, building stockades, laying wood floors. Robbins was now sharing a tent with Dr. Clelland, and the two of them spent many hours first collecting stones and bricks and then building a proper fireplace, hearth, and chimney. To pass the time, Robbins also began to use his free time to study anatomy and other medical subjects under the tutelage of the surgeons in preparation for the medical career he now dreamed of having after the war. Emma, still bunking with Reid, presumably also found ways to keep her tent warm, but she left no record of what they were.

About this time, Emma, and the rest of her regiment, learned some rather startling news that confirmed for Emma that she was not the only female member of the Army of the Potomac: A baby had been born to a corporal in a New Jersey regiment camped not far from Emma's own. The woman, whose name has been lost to history, had successfully concealed her sex, as well as her pregnancy, under the protection of an oversized overcoat, until she went into labor while on picket duty. An officer on duty at the time wrote about the incident in a letter home, saying that the soldier "complained of being unwell, but little notice was given his complaints at first. His pain and other symptoms of severe indisposition increased, so evident that his officers carried him to a nearby farmhouse. There the worthy corporal was delivered of a fine, fat little recruit!" The news spread from camp to camp, greeted with amazement, amusement, and a great deal of speculation about the paternity of the child, and most of the gossip, if not the evidence, pointed to her tent mate. Strangely, there was little condemnation of the woman herself among the rank and file, most of whom seemed to have nothing but admiration for a woman who could handle the stress of being a soldier and an expectant mother at the same time, and in fact a number of her comrades collected contributions for the mother and child, who were both soon sent home to the new mother's parents.[9]

But if Emma was secretly pleased to see that the men expressed more admiration than condemnation for a female comrade, the astonishing news must have also caused her some amount of consternation, if only because it alerted the men to the possibility that other women were in their ranks, and therefore might make them more likely to be suspicious of characteristics like small feet and smooth cheeks. Although Emma did not seem to realize it yet, there were already those who were beginning to have doubts about their mail carrier; doubts that would soon turn into malicious gossip.

On January 20, Burnside made one last attempt at rescuing his reputation by planning and initiating another halfhearted attempt to cross the Rappahannock, but it failed miserably, with the lead regiments becoming literally stuck in the knee-deep mud caused by days of heavy rainfall and near gale-force winds that began just as Burnside put his plan into motion. Neither Emma nor Robbins was a part of the disaster that became known as Burnside's Mud March, but they both witnessed the bedraggled and frozen men as they returned from the abortive mission two days after it had begun. On the twenty-third, Robbins recorded, "I scarcely know what to write this evening for it is now very clear that Burnside has been prevented by a higher power than earth to strike the fatal blow to the rebellion. All day [General] Franklin's grand division has been wearily plodding their way back to old quarters."[10] The sun came out again just as soon as the march was over, but it was too late for Burnside, who was unceremoniously relieved of command of the Army of the Potomac. This time, however, there was no triumphant return for the still-beloved McClellan, as many of the men openly hoped. Instead, command of the Army of the Potomac now went to the brash Joseph Hooker, whose headquarters were so infamously immoral that his name was to become synonymous with the world's oldest profession.

Burnside did, however, at least temporarily retain command of the Ninth Army Corps, to which the Second had been transferred before Fredericksburg. When Hooker took over, the Ninth was all but banished to Fort Monroe for several months, ostensibly to force Robert E. Lee to keep a significant force to defend Richmond from the southeast. They left for the Peninsula on February 13, again traveling by steamers from Aquia Wharf, just as they had nearly a year before. On that trip, Emma and Jerome were barely speaking; this time, they kept each other company. Robbins recorded, "Sometime during the night a fist fight occurred among some of the roughs which created quite an uproar for a time; otherwise I rested very well having a pretty warm berth with Frank and Sargt. Shakespeare for bedfellows on the cabin floor."[11]

Returning to the Peninsula must have brought back many memories for both of them. This time, however, the Second did not venture farther than the immediate vicinity of Fort Monroe. Robbins was still assigned to the regimental hospital, while Emma continued to serve as mail carrier. Still, they occasionally saw each other, and Robbins's entries about Emma suggest that their friendship was once again warm and playful. On March 3, Robbins noted that Emma had come by to visit while he had been out on hospital business. "While away I notice by a note left between these two leaves that Frank was over and he says from spite read my journal and carried away some of my . . . magazines. And now just for 'spite' I shan't say any more about it. Though I didn't think him fair for carrying away *all* my magazines."[12] There is no mention of Reid in Robbins's journals during this time, although his regiment was also on the Peninsula.

The Second Michigan's return to Fort Monroe did not last long. In mid-March, they were brought back up to Washington and then sent out to Kentucky as part of the Army of the Cumberland, presumably in anticipation of a renewed effort by General U. S. Grant to capture Vicksburg in the spring. When Emma arrived in Lebanon, Kentucky, she claimed that she received orders to penetrate enemy lines dressed as a rebel soldier. Wearing a uniform "borrowed" from a captured Confederate prisoner, she crossed the picket lines and into rebel territory on foot. Soon she came to a town that was occupied by Confederate cavalry, where a party seemed to be taking place in the town square. She soon learned that a rebel cavalry captain, named Logan, had just married a young widow.

The captain noticed Emma. "I was questioned pretty sharply by the handsome captain in regard to the nature of my business in that locality, but finding me to be an innocent, straightforward Kentuckian, he came to the conclusion that I was all right." But he also wanted to know why the boy was not with his regiment. Emma replied that she had been injured, and was now lost. The captain seemed to believe this as well, but was also convinced that the boy was now well enough to return to active duty. He demanded that Emma, whom he called "my lad," re-enlist with his company. He told her that she could do so freely, in which case she would receive a bounty, or she could be conscripted at gunpoint. Either way, he told her, if she tried to leave, she would be shot as a deserter.[14]

The captain gave Emma two hours to decide, but ordered that she be kept under guard. When the allotted time had passed, the captain returned, and demanded to know her answer. Emma, who was fearful of having to swear loyalty to the Confederate cause, refused. Nonetheless, the captain ordered her to join his company. "I was glad to find it was a company of cavalry that was being organized, for if I could once get on a good horse there would be some hope of my escape." As they rode out of town, the captain told her that she would thank him for his persuasiveness someday, as he was saving her from her own cowardice.

They did not get far before they came across a party of Federal cavalry, and an intense skirmish broke out. Luckily for Emma, a Union officer recognized "Frank Thompson" and subtly motioned for her to ride around behind him. When Captain Logan noticed her movement, and rode to block it, Emma raised her pistol, and shot the handsome newlywed in the face. In the midst of the confusion that followed, Emma claimed, she was able to ride to safety. Although she seemed to believe that the wound she inflicted on Captain Logan was not fatal, she had some pangs of guilt, if not sympathy for his new wife. "I was sorry, for the graceful curve of his mustache was sadly spoiled, and the happy bride of the previous morning would no longer rejoice in the beauty of that manly face and exquisite mustache of which she seemed so proud, and which had captivated her heart ere she had been three months a widow." [15]

This, according to Emma, was her last exploit behind enemy lines. In some respects it is the least believable, if only because if in fact the Federal officer did recognize Emma, or Frank Thompson, in the company of the company of enemy cavalry, his first thought would likely have been not that she was a Union spy but a Confederate double agent. But Emma claimed that, without any further questioning, she was "highly commended by the commanding general for my coolness throughout the whole affair, and was told kindly and candidly that I would not be permitted to go out again in that vicinity, in the capacity of spy, as I would most assuredly meet with some of those who had seen me desert their ranks, and I would consequently be hung up to the nearest tree." [16]

If this escapade occurred, it had to have happened as soon as the Second arrived in Kentucky in late March; on April 4, Robbins recorded that he had spent most of the day with "Frank who has been and is unwell." Then, sometime between April 11 and April 17, Emma rather abruptly left her regiment, and the army, forever. By April 19, Frank Thompson was officially listed as a deserter on his regimental muster rolls, a crime punishable by death. The simplest way to avoid Frank Thompson's arrest was to make him disappear, something Emma could do as easily as she had conjured him in the first place. After leaving camp, she made her way to Cairo, the near-est large town—presumably on foot, and there resumed the "proper clothing of my gender, never to put on another disguise." [17]

Emma later explained that she left her regiment only to avoid de-tection; that she was ill, suffering a relapse of the malaria she had contracted in the swamps of the Chickahominy, and that she believed that her true gender would be discovered if she stayed in the army any longer. According to Emma, she requested a medical furlough, but it was denied, so she felt she had no choice but to leave before being discovered. This was the single explanation that she proffered in later years, and one supported by Robbins's journal entry on April 4 when he mentioned that "Frank" was "unwell." [18]

But she herself indicated that she was not just physically sick, but emotionally fragile as well. One day during this time, when she was convalescing in her tent, a shell exploded in camp. Several soldiers, who had been relaxing and talking together, were killed instantly. The unexpected tragedy seemed to cause something in Emma to snap. In her own words, all her "soldierly qualities fled," and she was "once again a poor, cowardly, nervous, whining woman, and as if to make up for lost time, and to give vent to my long-pent-up feelings, I could do nothing but weep hour after hour, until it would seem that my head was literally a fountain of tears and my heart was one great burden of sorrow." [19]

It is hard to believe that it was only an accidental explosion, or even the fear of discovery that was putting Emma, usually so stoic and fearless, in such a fragile state of mind. Perhaps it was the fact that on April 1, James Reid resigned his commission. Writing from Ninth Corps headquarters at Lebanon, Kentucky, to Lieutenant Colonel Lewis Richmond, Assistant Adjutant General, Reid explained. "My wife's health," he wrote, "has been for the last six months very precarious, and lately I have received several intimations from her medical advisers that she cannot recover unless she is conveyed to her native country [Scotland]. This cannot be done without my presence, as neither she nor myself have any relatives in this country." [21]

Reid did not leave until April 20, at least three days after Emma did, but surely it was not a coincidence that Emma's emotional crisis occurred almost simultaneously with his announcement. Robbins's entry on the fourth, when he noted her poor health, went on to suggest that Emma was in effect, lovesick, a fact that made Robbins sad as well as somewhat jealous. "It is unpleasant," Robbins remarked, just after commenting on Emma's health, "to awaken to the conviction that one dear as a friend can be forgets in their selfish interest that others may not be void of the finer sensibilities of the human heart. It is a sad reality to which we awaken when we learn that others are receiving the *devotion* of one from whom we only claim friendship's attention." [22]

In addition to Reid's impending departure, Colonel Poe, Emma's friend and mentor, also announced that he would soon be leaving the regiment. He had resigned as colonel in order to accept his expected appointment as brigadier general, but, perhaps due to questions about his conduct at Fredericksburg, that appointment had never been confirmed. In the meantime, command of the regiment had been given to William Humphrey. Not only would Emma miss Poe personally, but she could not be certain that Humphrey would allow her to continue as mail carrier, a position that gave her the uncommon freedom that helped her maintain her ruse. Although Reid announced his resignation before Poe, Poe left first, on April 11. Robbins recorded the scene of his departure, which Emma, no doubt, also witnessed:

> One of the most affecting incidents occurred today in the farewell of Co. Poe from the officers and privates of our reg. A thorough soldier and disciplinarian beloved by all. Many were the tears shed and heart pangs experienced. . . . In the farewell address of the Co. he spoke of us in the highest terms and spoke with the deepest feelings. Several times he was compelled to stop in his remarks to suppress the tears which involuntarily started.[23]

Five days later, Emma was gone. Robbins first noted her absence on the seventeenth. "I was surprised this evening upon making inquiry after Frank Thompson to hear he had not been seen since yesterday noon. The present and first thought being he must have gone out of the picket line and found getting back a difficulty."[24] But even if he did not admit it in his journal that night, Robbins clearly suspected that that was not the case, and the next day, his suspicions were borne out. "Frank's desertion is pretty fully confirmed. I learn today that he had a slight difficulty at the Brigade Headquarters which caused his sudden departure. The difficulty being his being stopped by the sentinel from passing and his appeal to Col. Morrisson producing a verdict against."[25]

It is not clear from this entry whether Emma was trying to approach or leave headquarters; what is clear is that, in Poe's absence, Emma's freedom had been curtailed, possibly due to suspicions about her real identity, or even the nature of her relationship with James Reid. Something that Reid said to Robbins about Emma as he was leaving two days later sent Robbins into an uncharacteristic rage.

Dr. Bonine with several other officers started from here on the one o'clock train, among them Lt. Reid, Frank's particular friend.

By the by do you know I have learned another lesson in the great book of human nature? Frank has deserted for which I do not blame him. His was a strange history. He prepared me for his departure in part . . . yet I did not think it would be so premature. Yet he did not prepare me for his ingratitude and utter disregard for the finer sensibilities of others. Of all others whom I trusted as friends he was the last I deemed capable of the petty baseness which was betrayed by his friend R at the last moment.

A misanthrope would write a chapter in detestation of the human race did he have my experiences in this circumstance of life and while I own a slight disgust to such a character I am excited to pity that poor humanity can be so weak as to repay the kindest interest and warmest sympathy with deception.[26]

But what was it that Reid said to Robbins to make him so disgusted with Emma? Robbins said no more about it, but perhaps the journal entry of another soldier who was in the vicinity at the time sheds a clue. On April 22, William Boston of Company H of the 20th Michigan Infantry, wrote in his own journal, with a fair amount of salacious glee:

We are having quite a time at the expense of our brigade postmaster. He turns out to be a girl and has deserted when her lover, Inspector Read [sic], and General Poe, resigned. She went by the name of Frank . . . and was a pretty girl. She came out with Co. F of the Second Michigan Regiment and has been with them ever since.[27]

William Boston's entry seems to confirm what Robbins hinted at, that Reid and Emma were lovers, and that Reid let this be known to Robbins, and apparently to others, before he left. Or, perhaps, Reid and Emma were discovered, and the word got out. Either way, it seems to explain what Robbins was so angry about. By the middle of May, however, Robbins's anger seems to have dissipated. On May 16, he noted in his journal that he had received a letter "from my friend 'Emma E. Edmundson' whose history has been given in part and which would make a very interesting volume. Of a truth, it is stranger than fiction." The letter he referred to was probably one that Emma addressed on May 10, from Washington, D.C., one of the few that was found with Robbins's journal when he died.

Washington D.C.
May 10, 1863

Dear Jerome,
This is Sabbath afternoon and I am sitting in the parlor of a private boardinghouse . . . and anxious to drop you a line before going to visit some of the hospitals where so many of Hooker's poor wounded soldiers are. Mrs. Campbell and I are going (the lady of the house) to carry them some oranges and see what we can do for them. . . .

"Reid" wrote me that he had a long conversation with you about me. I want you to write me the import of it. Will you please do so. . . . If tomorrow is fine I shall have some photographs taken and will send you one. I want you to send me one of yours without fail.

Oh Jerome, I do miss you so much. There is no person living whose presence would be so agreeable to me this afternoon as yours.
How is "Anna"? I hope you have received a favorable answer to

your letter sent just before I came away. I always remember you, and sometimes her, at the Throne of Grace. May God bless you both and make you faithful to him and to each other.

My intention is to go at once into the missionary work not withstanding the protestations of my friends to the contrary. I will write you from New York as soon as I make arrangements there. . . .

Goodbye my dear boy.

E. Edmonds

Above: Emma after the war. (State Archives of Michigan.)

Below: Linus H. Seelye was one of the few men in Emma's life who accepted and loved her unconditionally. (From *The Seelys of New Brunswick*.)

CHAPTER TEN

Flint Michigan
March 1882

THE BELL on the door of Damon Stewart's dry-goods store jingled. Stewart glanced up to see a neatly dressed matron, her face shielded by a light veil, enter the shop, then returned to his work at his desk. Moments later, he looked up again as his clerk approached to tell him that the woman wanted to speak to him in person. Putting down his papers, Stewart crossed over to Emma with a bit of annoyance; he was quite busy. Nonetheless, he introduced himself politely, and asked how he could be of service. As the woman raised her veil, Stewart felt a vague flicker of recognition, but could not place her weathered face.

"Are you Damon Stewart?" the woman asked, not sure that the mature middle-aged man was in fact her old friend. But the man nodded that he was.

"Can you by chance give me the present address of Franklin Thompson?" she responded, in a hushed voice.

The name clearly took Stewart by surprise. He had not seen his former comrade and tent mate in almost twenty years, when Thompson helped carry a wounded Stewart off the field at Williamsburg. Stewart's injuries had been serious enough that he had been sent home for a time. He later re-enlisted with another Michigan regiment, and had heard through the grapevine about Thompson's mysterious desertion in Kentucky in the spring of 1863. But while the fate of young Thompson, of whom Stewart had been quite fond, was a subject of much discussion among Michigan veterans, no one knew what had become of him. Now, hearing the name from this stranger's lips, he was suddenly struck by her resemblance to his former comrade.

"Are you his mother?" Stewart asked, peering intently at the woman.

"No, I am not his mother," she answered, suppressing a slight smile.

"His sister, perhaps?" Stewart suggested. Then, as the woman heard someone approaching, she startled Stewart by reaching out for the pencil he still held in his hand, and grabbed a card on the counter. She scribbled something on it, then handed it to Stewart. "Be quiet!" it read. "I am Frank Thompson."

Stewart looked at the card, then at the woman, then at the card again. Taking it in, he slumped down on a stool in shock, but Emma, smiling broadly now, stood calmly, waiting for the news to sink in. When it did, and Stewart recovered his bearings, he smiled, too, and greeted Emma as warmly as she had hoped. He was full of questions; as Emma began to explain her story, and her reason for appearing on his doorstep, Stewart took his visitor by the arm, and waved to the clerk that he and his guest were leaving. Stewart escorted Emma to his house, where his wife also greeted her husband's former comrade graciously, once she, too, had recovered from the surprise of learning that her husband's first bunkmate had been a female.[1]

Emma was gratified, and relieved, by the Stewarts' warm reaction, and after a hearty lunch, she told them everything—well, almost everything—about her past, her decision to enlist, and what she had been doing in the intervening years.

* * *

Things had not gone as Emma had expected when she wrote to Jerome Robbins from Washington in May of 1863. She did not become a missionary, as she had once told Robbins she might. There is also no record of what became of James Reid; presumably he did take his wife back to Scotland, and from there, the trail grows cold.

Sometime after she wrote to Robbins from Washington in May, she went to Harpers Ferry, and dropping the last syllable of her proper surname, now went by the name Emma Edmonds. As such, she volunteered as a nurse at a hospital run by the U.S. Sanitary Commission. Presumably she did not discuss her time in the army under the alias Frank Thompson, but her experience would have nonetheless made her a valuable asset to the medical staff.

Emma used what free time she had to write a book about her experiences during the first two years of the war. Part fact, part fiction, the memoir, as she called it, included things she had experienced, or witnessed, or heard about, as well as some stories that were likely the work of her fertile and dramatic imagination. From her years as a book salesman, Emma had a keen sense of what people wanted to read about; at a time when the outcome of the war was far from certain, the book above all paid homage to the bravery, sacrifice, and nobility of the Union soldier, to whom it was dedicated. It also paid homage to the bravery, sacrifice, and nobility of the author. In the popular, highly melodramatic tone of much Victorian literature, she recounted her decision to enlist in the army, which she says was directly inspired by "the Throne of Grace," her experiences in camp, on the Peninsula, at Fredericksburg and beyond. But it is coyly written to camouflage her identity, and that of her regiment, and she generally referred to people either by aliases or by their initials. She was also purposely vague about her gender identity; for much of the book the reader could safely assume that the author was one of the many women who attached themselves to regiments as nurses or "daughters of the regiment."

There is one mention of Jerome Robbins by name, but even then, she pretended as though he was only a passing acquaintance. Writing about the day on the Peninsula, during the Seven Days battles, when she was directed to warn the various hospitals in the rear to evacuate, she noted that, at one hospital:

> One of the noble-hearted nurses refused to leave those helpless men, whom he had taken care of so long, and was taken prisoner. I marked that noble boy's countenance, dress, and general appearance, and, by making inquiry afterwards, I found out that his name was J. Robbins, of the Second Michigan Regiment, and after he had undergone the hardships of imprisonment and been exchanged, I had the honor of meeting and congratulating him; I felt that it was a greater honor than to converse with many of our major generals.[2]

Apparently Emma could not resist including him in the book, but she was careful to do so in a way that would protect him from any possible charge that he had known her secret.

The most dramatic parts of the book were her stories of espionage: the first trip behind enemy lines at Yorktown, her exploits while dressed as an Irish peddler woman, her successful reconnaissance while disguised as a female slave during the Second Battle of Bull Run, and her dramatic escape from the Confederate cavalry in Kentucky. These stories were—and are—impossible to verify, but, true or not, they added a great deal of drama to the book, and are the source of the enduring popular belief that Emma was in fact a spy.

There are also events that could not have happened to her because she was documented to be somewhere else at the time. For example, Emma's regiment was not at Antietam, yet she wrote about being there, and even included the melodramatic story of the dying woman soldier, so similar to Clara Barton's experience, which Emma may have heard or read about at the time. Emma also wrote about the siege at Vicksburg, which occurred several months after she left the army, as though she had been present. It is possible, however, that her source for that material was Jerome Robbins, who had been there and may have written to Emma about it.

The book made much of the heroics of her fellow soldiers, she also took every chance she got to castigate able-bodied men of the North who did not do their part, even quoting the famous taunt written by Oliver Wendell Holmes, then a young soldier, to the "Stay-at-Home Brigade." (Emma did not credit him as the author by name; perhaps she did not know who the author was.)

> Now, while our soldiers are fighting our battles
> Each at his post to do all that he can,
> Down among rebels and contraband chattels,
> What are *you* doing, my sweet little man?
>
> All the brave boys under canvas are sleeping
> All of them pressing to march with the van,
> Far from their homes where their sweethearts are weeping;
> What are *you* waiting for, sweet little man?
>
> You with the terrible warlike mustaches,
> Fit for a colonel or chief of a clan,
> You with the waist made for sword-belts and sashes,
> Where are your shoulder-straps, sweet little man?
>
> We send you the buttonless garments of woman!
> Cover your face lest it freckle or tan;
> Muster the apron-string guards on the common—
> That is the corps for the sweet little man.

It was an interesting choice for Emma to include in her book, with its emphasis on "de-sexing" male noncombatants, when she herself was the exact opposite, but she seems to take great pride that unlike most women, and apparently a fair number of men, she could not be counted among the apron-string guards.

When her manuscript was completed, Emma packed it carefully in a valise and boarded a train for Hartford, where she went to see her old friend Mr. Hurlbert. Emma left no account of their reunion, but it is safe to assume that he was dumbfounded to learn that the boy he had hired five years earlier was in fact a woman. Apparently, he recovered from his shock with the same good-natured aplomb with which he originally greeted her, and agreed to publish her work. The first, short-lived edition of Emma's book debuted in 1864 under the title *Unsexed, or the Female Soldier,* but when the title proved to be too racy for contemporary audiences, it was reissued a year later with the softer title *Memoirs of a Soldier, Nurse and Spy: A Woman's Adventures in the Union Army.* The 1865 edition also contained a rather defensive publisher's note, presumably written by Mr. Hurlbert, or possibly by Emma herself, with his approval, which presented the story as the factual account of a dedicated patriot.

> The "Nurse and Spy" is simply a record of events which have transpired in the experience and under the observation of one who has been on the field and participated in numerous battles . . . serving in the capacity of "Spy" and "Nurse" for over two years. While in the "Secret Service" as a "Spy" which is one of the most hazardous positions in the army—she penetrated the enemy's lines, in various disguises, no less than eleven times, always with complete success and without detection. . . . Should any of her readers object to some of her disguises, it may be sufficient to remind them it was from the purest motives and most praiseworthy patriotism, that she laid aside, for a time, her own costume, and assumed that of the opposite sex, enduring hardships, suffering untold privations, and hazarding her life for her adopted country, in its hour of need. . . . In the opinion of many it is the privilege of woman to minister to the sick and soothe the sorrowing—and in the present crisis of our country's history, to aid our brothers to the extent of her capacity. . . . Perhaps she should have the privilege of choosing for herself whatever may be the surest protec-

tion from insult and inconvenience in her blessed, self-sacrificing work.[3]

If indeed Hurlbert was the author of the note, he seems to conveniently overlook the fact that there was no patriotism involved when Emma first showed up on his doorstep, advertising herself as a boy "who was hard to beat at selling books."

Nurse and Spy was an enormous success, selling 175,000 copies, making it a best seller for its day; by way of comparison, the first edition of Harriet Beecher Stowe's *Uncle Tom's Cabin,* a publishing phenomenon, sold 300,000 copies when it came out in 1852. Characteristically, Emma was not interested in hoarding her sudden wealth. By then, she had returned to her nursing duties in Harpers Ferry, and when she learned of the soaring sales, she wrote to Mr. Hurlbert directing him to send her share of the profits directly to the Christian Commission, with instructions that it should be used exclusively for the care of wounded soldiers and veterans.

If Emma expected to be a missionary rather than a best-selling author by the time the war was over, Jerome Robbins's future did not go exactly according to plan, either. There is no evidence that Emma ever saw her "dear boy" again, or whether she ever knew that he did not marry Anna Corey after all. Several weeks after Emma's letter to Robbins in May 1863, he went home on furlough. On his way there, he believed himself to be "promised" to Anna, and vice versa; on the way back, he believed neither. He never explained in his journal what happened, but shortly after that visit, Anna Corey married Aaron Sunderlin, a prosperous farmer from Ionia County, whom Robbins must have known. From then on, there are no more tally marks indicating letters to or from Anna; but he did begin a steady correspondence with Hattie Farnum, the younger sister of a friend he had known for years. Shortly after Robbins was mustered out of the army at the end of the war—having served for the entire duration, and been promoted to assistant surgeon—he and Hattie were married.

Robbins entered the University of Michigan Medical School, where he studied under his old friends Alonzo Palmer and Henry Lyster, and went on to have a distinguished medical career in Hubbardton, Michigan. Oddly, the 1870 census shows that among Jerome and Hattie Robbins's neighbors were Anna and Aaron Sunderlin.

Emma's life took another unexpected turn in the late winter of 1864. While she was working in Harpers Ferry, she met, or perhaps was reacquainted with, a young man from New Brunswick, who had come to the United States seeking work as a carpenter. Like Jerome Robbins, he was thoughtful and gentle; like James Reid, he was tall and blond, and married. Emma said many years later, in passing, that she had known Linus in New Brunswick before the war, and that in fact it was he who had helped her obtain a set of men's clothing when she first became Frank Thompson. That may have been one of her embellishments—in other accounts she was vague as to how she acquired her disguise—but Emma and Linus did come to know each other in Harpers Ferry. Emma reveled in the company of someone from "home," and, if he did not already know it, she soon told him the truth about the past few years. There was something about Linus, who was nine years her senior, that made Emma feel safe; he did not judge her, did not seem intimidated by her strong character or her outrageous exploits. Many men would have judged harshly a woman who had lived in such intimate contact with other men as Emma had during the war; even if they did not question her morals, they would have judged her at the least as unladylike. But Linus always seemed amused by Emma.

In April of 1865, word came that the war was finally over. Almost exactly four years after it had begun, General Lee surrendered to General U. S. Grant at Appomattox Court House. Emma shared in the sense of elation and relief that swept over the entire country, North and South. But after the initial joy at seeing, as Emma put it, "victory perched upon national banner, and the dear old Stars and Stripes" floating "over every city, town, and hamlet," she found herself, like the rest of her adopted country, somewhat unsure of what to do next. She was now twenty-three years old, a single woman whose nursing skills were no longer needed. For Emma, not being needed was the worst possible situation to be in, and she was suddenly at a complete loss, made more bitter by the departure of her friend Linus, who went home to New Brunswick to be present for the birth of his first child.

Not sure what else to do, Emma returned to Oberlin, Ohio, home to Oberlin College, where she had recuperated for a time after leaving the army, "with the intention of resuming my studies." Founded in 1833 by Methodist ministers, Oberlin was one of the first fully coeducational and racially integrated colleges in the country. That same year, Mary Patterson graduated from Oberlin—the first black woman in the United States to receive a college degree. It was also a hotbed of the nascent women's suffrage and temperance movements, causes that Emma believed in. But despite the free and open atmosphere, Emma found school "too monotonous, after so much excitement." In the early spring of 1866, she packed her bags once again, this time bound for home for the first time in seven years. When she finally arrived in Magaguadavic, she found much had changed. Her sister Frances still lived with her husband on the farm next to the Edmondsons', where Thomas now resided alone. Both Betsy and Isaac had died not ever knowing what had become of their youngest child. Family legend has it that after Emma left home, Isaac became increasingly withdrawn, and after Betsy died, he spent his last few years sitting and staring out the window, watching the road for the return of his long-absent child.[4]

Emma spent the summer in New Brunswick, once again hunting and canoeing with Thomas, and walking for hours alone in the thick green woods. But she grew restless again, and in the fall, she decided to return to Oberlin. On her way, she passed through Saint John, the hometown of her friend Linus Seelye. The Seelyes were a prominent family there; Linus's grandfather was among the British Loyalists who fled the American colonies during the Revolutionary War to seek the haven of the crown on the New Brunswick seacoast, and the province was now dotted with evidence of his progeny—Seelye Cove, Seelye Beach, Seelye Spire. Perhaps she heard the name, and decided to seek him out; perhaps they met by chance. But Emma did see him, and learned that he was now a widower; that his baby daughter died in infancy, and that his wife, Hannah, had followed her six months later.[5]

Emma surely paid her condolences, and continued her journey, but from then on she and Linus began to correspond regularly. For him, the vibrant, reckless Emma helped ease the pain of his loss, while for Emma, Linus was a comforting link to home, and, more important, one of the few people, with the exception of the ever faithful Thomas, who accepted her the way she was. During their long correspondence, Linus managed to convince the woman who had said she would never marry to become his wife. She did so on April 27, 1867, at the Weddell House Hotel in Cleveland, a fashionable establishment where President Lincoln had stayed on his trip to Washington for his inauguration six years earlier. Emma tried to sum up what came next in an interview years later: "Well, you know how the census takers sum up all our employments with the too easily written words, 'married woman.' That is what I became; and of course that tells the entire story."[6] Despite her cynicism, though, by all accounts her marriage was, perhaps as much to her surprise as to anyone's, a strong and happy one, which she considered to be one of her most cherished blessings.

Postwar America was a place of enormous growth and modernization, with plenty of opportunities for an enterprising carpenter and his young wife. The transcontinental railroad was completed in 1869; a cross-country trip that once took weeks or months now took five days. The rapid expansion, and the manpower shortage caused by the war, meant endless opportunities for those who could take advantage of them. For the next few years, Emma and Linus moved from town to town throughout the American Midwest, capitalizing on the postwar construction boom. They spent the first year of their marriage in Kansas City, then moved to Charlevoix, Michigan, where Linus Seelye had a number of relatives. There, on April 14, 1869, Emma gave birth to a son, whom they named Linus, but, to her horror but perhaps not her surprise—despite many rapid advancements in the field of medicine, the infant mortality rate was still nearly 40 percent—the boy died the same day.[7]

As soon as Emma was well enough to travel, they moved again, this time, to Evanston Illinois, where they stayed for two years. Linus's business was thriving, and Emma once again became pregnant, but also once again, the boy, named Homer, lived less than a day. Both Emma and Linus were devastated—the nurturing, compassionate side of Emma, the side that needed to be needed, had come full circle from her own childhood, and now she desperately wanted to be mother hen to a large flock of children. Linus, too, reeled from the pain of losing three children in infancy. Seeking a change of scenery again, they returned to Oberlin, the closest thing Emma had to a home in the United States.[8]

April 1873 marked the tenth anniversary of Emma's desertion from the army. She had been married for six years, had given birth to two children and lost as many, and, now, at thirty-two, she despaired of her chances for having more. But in the fall, she became pregnant for a third time, much to her surprise and delight. Alice Louise Seelye was born the following August. Not long afterward, Emma learned through her church of two recently orphaned brothers, a two-year-old and an infant, whose mother had presumably died in childbirth. Perhaps because Emma was nursing her own baby, perhaps to help take the place of the two boys she had lost, Emma persuaded Linus to allow her to take the boys, Charles and Freddy, in and raise them as their own.

The family stayed in Oberlin another two years. But as the winter of 1875 approached, an opportunity presented itself that caught Emma's imagination. In the years following the war, the United

Methodist Church, under the auspices of the Freedmen's Aid Society, sponsored a number of orphanages for black children throughout the South. One such institution, in St. Mary Parish, Louisiana, was run by a Methodist minister from Ohio named William Godman, in partnership with the Reverend J. C. Hartzell, one of the first black Methodist ministers in Louisiana. The orphanage was home to sixty-seven children, including many whose fathers had died while serving in the "colored" regiments of the Union army. The orphanage had originally been housed in New Orleans, but in 1875, a benefactor donated a large plantation on the banks of Bayou Teche.

Mr. Godman began planning to expand the orphanage's capacity, hire more teachers, and build a seminary school on the newly acquired property. In his annual report to the church elders in Ohio, Godman reported, "We have built on the banks of the Teche a home to which they can come, and where they can be clothed, fed, instructed, and fitted for the activities and responsibilities of the present life and for the enjoyments of that higher life which is to come." Now, he continued, he and Hartzell "suggest that a good man and his wife from the North, whether minister or layman, be secured as superintendent of the home and the plantation, with the chance to make his living out of one third of the crops and the boardinghouse, on condition of keeping everything in repair, having oversight of all the farmers, teaching and directing them in all practical matters, keeping the orphans that may be here to a certain number, receiving and caring for any others that may be otherwise provided for, and giving necessary rooms to the teachers and their families."[9]

As soon as Emma heard about the position, she persuaded Linus that they should apply for the job. Linus, with his skills as a carpenter, would be in charge of keeping the buildings and improvements in good repair, while Emma would oversee the orphanage. When they arrived, they found what was, in many respects, an idyllic situation. As Godman described it:

Down along the banks of the Teche are massive live oaks whose branches are covered with moss and which cast a grateful shade, and at intervals are lofty pecan trees laden with nuts. Here is to be the home of our orphans; here their schoolhouse, their workshop, and their playgrounds. On the opposite side of the parish road is a field of seven hundred acres, rich sugar land, enclosed with an osage-orange hedge on three sides, while beyond are more than nine hundred acres of woodland, on which is much valuable timber. Amid the oaks and cypresses of this swamp flows a small bayou, wherein the garfish floats lazily along and the alligator basks in the scant gleams of the sun.[10]

The new school, La Teche Seminary, opened its doors in 1875; in addition to housing orphans and providing a basic education, it could prepare the older students for higher education as well. A few years later, the seminary was renamed Gilbert Academy, in honor of its principal benefactor, William Gilbert, of Ohio. Gilbert Academy became one of the leading secondary schools for black students in the New South, and a feeder school for the prestigious New Orleans University. The orphanage was later renamed Sager Brown in honor of two New York benefactors. Sager Brown is no longer an orphanage, but remains an active humanitarian organization under the auspices of the United Methodist Church.

The years at La Teche were pleasant ones for Emma, perhaps the most enjoyable of her life. There, she had finally found a place where she could put her prodigious energy and compassion to full use, doing what she believed to be God's will, feeling needed and loved. And caring for so many children, in addition to Alice, Freddy, and Charlie helped her to live with the loss of her own infant sons. But it was not to last. The sultry Louisiana climate was not good for Emma's health, and eventually, she suffered another bout of the malaria she first contracted on the banks of the Chickahominy so many years before. Reluctantly Emma and Linus concluded that they would have to leave the orphanage they had worked so hard to expand. In the fall of 1880, Linus took his ailing family north to California, Missouri, a tiny town west of St. Louis. Emma slowly regained her health, but not before the children were all stricken with measles. The boys recovered, but six-year-old Alice died on Christmas morning.[11]

The loss of bright, sunny Alice was shattering for the entire family. Again, they moved on, perhaps to try to leave behind the painful memories. This time, they headed for Fort Scott, Kansas, a thriving frontier military base in the early stages of domestication. Once again, there was plenty of work for carpenters, and soon the family was able to move into a small frame house in one of the nicest parts of town. But after Alice's death, Emma's mood darkened, and her health deteriorated again. In addition to the lingering effects of malaria, her left leg, which she had so badly injured during the war, was troubling her more and more. Some days, she was barely able, or willing, to dress and come downstairs. Often she lay for days in her darkened room, grieving for her daughter.[12]

As time went by, the pain of Alice's loss eased into a dull ache, but her left leg got worse rather than better. As a former army post, Fort Scott was teeming with veterans. For some reason, the sight of so many men who were, Emma knew, receiving pensions for their service, and compensation for their wartime injuries, began to irritate her. Had she not also served and suffered for the same cause? Was she not also entitled to a pension? Whether it was a desire for the income, or the recognition, or simply a distraction from her grief, Emma gradually came to think of little else.

There were two rather serious hurdles in her way. The War Department had never knowingly awarded a soldier's pension to a woman for military service, although some female veterans, like Alfred Cashiers, retained their male identities after the war and had successfully applied for pensions under their alias. And a few women who served in other capacities had been honored after the war, including a woman named Mary Porch, who was given a pension for espionage activities, although not as a soldier.[13] But even though various stories of women who had served in combat had been slowly coming to light in the nearly two decades since the war ended, the War Department officially denied that women had successfully served in the Union army as men, and none had formally asked for, let alone received, a pension as women. Even more seriously, the War Department most definitely did not award pensions to deserters, as Franklin Thompson was listed on the service rolls.

Emma was not deterred. She felt that she was owed a pension, and she made up her mind to get one. The first step would be to establish that Franklin Thompson had in fact served with the Second Michigan. Not wanting to show her hand too soon, however, she enlisted Linus's help. On February 16, 1882, Linus wrote a letter to the Michigan Adjutant General's Office, requesting "a certificate of the Service of Franklin Thompson of Company F, 2nd Reg. Mich. Volunteers. Have it show full data as shown by the records."

A week later came the following reply:

Respectfully returned with the information that a certificate of the service of Franklin Thompson, Co. "F." 2nd Mich. Inf. will be furnished him on his own application.

This left Emma no choice—she would have to ask for her records herself, but how? She realized that whatever she said would carry more weight if she had it notarized. The following Monday, she went to the Bourbon County Court House and, presumably to the surprise and confusion of the county clerk, swore out the following affidavit, which she promptly mailed back to the Michigan adjutant general.

S.E.E. Seeley [sic] being duly sworn on oath says that Franklin Thompson late of Co. "F" Second Mich Vol Inf and applicant were one and the same person. That applicant enlisted as Franklin

Thompson which was an assumed name. That applicant left the command before the expiration of term of service and makes this statement under oath for a certificate of service.

S.E.E. Seelye

Even this was not enough for John Robertson, the adjutant general, who must have been perplexed by the communication. He again pressed for more detail. On March 8, he wrote back to Emma the following:

It is requested that S.E.E. Seeley give first name in full.

Jno. Robertson

Adjutant General

Her attempt to preserve her anonymity having failed, Emma had to decide whether to put the truth in writing or not. Within days, she replied, spelling it out for Robertson as clearly as she could, and not bothering to hide her exasperation at the runaround she clearly felt she was being given.

To that Adjutant Genl. State of Michigan my full name is Sarah Emma Evelyn Seelye. I enlisted and served as Franklin Thompson in Co "F" 2d Mich Vols. And refer you to Capt Damon Stewart of Flint Mich, Lieut Wm Turner of same, Capt Wm R Morse, Lawrence Kansas of Flint Mich, Gen O. M. Poe of Sherman's staff. I would say if you don't want to give me the certificate of service just say so.

Sarah Emma E. Seelye

One can only imagine Robertson's reaction as he took in the import of Emma's letter. It is fair to guess, however, that once he did, he wished that the letter had arrived before he wrote *Michigan in the War,* the official history of Michigan's role in the war. In describing the Second Michigan, Robertson ended with a note about the brigade postmaster who went AWOL.

In Company F, 2d Michigan, there enlisted at Flint Franklin Thompson (or Frank, as usually called) aged twenty, ascertained afterward and about the time he left the regiment to have been a female, and a good looking one at that. She succeeded in concealing her sex most admirably, serving in various campaigns and battles of the regiment as a soldier; often employed as a spy, going within the enemy's lines, sometimes absent for weeks, and is said to have furnished much valuable information. She remained with the regiment until April, 1863, when it supposed she apprehended a disclosure of her sex and deserted at Lebanon, Kentucky, but where she went remains a mystery.[14]

Now the answer to the riddle had landed on his desk, too late for him to include it in his book. But whatever his personal reaction, there was no hint of it in the letter he sent back to Emma on March 13, in which he noted, dryly:

It appears from official records on file in the office that Franklin Thompson, Company F, Second Regiment Michigan Infantry enlisted on the 25th day May, 1861 at Detroit Mich and was duly mustered into the service of the United States for the term of three years. Deserted at Lebanon, Ky. April 22 1863.

Meanwhile, Emma set about garnering support from other quarters. She wrote at once to her old friend Mr. Hurlbert—one of the few people who knew her both as Frank Thompson, book salesman, and as Emma Edmonds, author of *Nurse and Spy*—asking him to provide a statement on her behalf. She also realized that she would need corroboration of her claim that she, Emma Seelye, was in fact Frank Thompson, as well as confirmation that Frank Thompson had been an exemplary soldier. For that, she would need the help of her former comrades.

Jerome Robbins might have seemed a natural place to start—he, too, knew her as both Frank Thompson and as Emma—but Emma did not write to him. Perhaps she did not know where he was, but more likely, she realized that she needed the help of men who had not known the truth about her during the war. She needed men who could honestly state that they had not known, or even suspected, that Frank Thompson was a woman, both for their sake, and for hers. In order for her plan to work, the Victorian sensibility of the day required that her morals be above reproach, and if it became known that Robbins knew the truth during the war, it would be assumed, or at least alleged, that they had been lovers.

No, she needed someone who had known her well, but never suspected that she was a woman, someone who knew her well and could attest to her good character, someone who was gone by the time the ugly rumors recorded by William Boston got started. Someone like Damon Stewart. It was a great risk, showing up on his doorstep unannounced; after all, she had no way of knowing how he would react, no way of knowing whether he had heard rumors about her after the war. She did know this was something she had to do in person; that a letter, out of the blue, would not be enough to convince him that she was in fact Frank Thompson.

* * *

That is how she came to be sitting in the Stewarts' living room that day in March 1882. Emma did not explain to Damon Stewart why she had chosen to appeal to him first. To him, she simply explained that she had deserted out of a fear of discovery, due to her serious illness; that now, these twenty years later, she had decided to petition the government for relief; and that she had come to ask for his help.

CHAPTER ELEVEN

———◆◆◆———

March 1882

EMMA was relieved to discover she had made the right choice. Stewart enthusiastically promised to help Emma in any way that he could. He also made two suggestions. First, he asked permission to contact a friend of his who was a reporter for the local newspaper, arguing that Emma needed to publicize her story to garner widespread support for her cause. The second was that he be allowed to send word to several of her former comrades living in Flint, and ask them to come over and get reacquainted with the long-lost "Frank." Emma agreed to both suggestions, and soon a reporter, identified to history only as A.M.G., appeared. Stewart explained the story, his surprise at seeing his old friend again, and together, he and Emma patiently answered her many questions.

"I believe none knew him more intimately than I did," Stewart told the reporter. "We not only camped together . . . but I, being much the elder, acted as guide, philosopher, and friend to the young warrior. What did I think of him as a soldier? Well, he stood guard, police duty, and fatigue work with us all, and drilled, still he was never an expert with a gun—didn't seem to take naturally to firearms." (To this last, Emma objected strenuously when the article was published; apparently he said this to A.M.G. out of Emma's earshot, or she would likely have objected then and there. She did not hold it too much against him, though, even though she thought he was dead wrong; she considered herself to have been any man's equal in the handling of a gun.) But, Stewart continued, Frank "was faithful and brave, however, and gained all hearts by his cheerful, obliging activity, and strong good sense. . . . In the Battle of Williamsburg, I was wounded, left the regiment soon after, and did not see Frank again until the other day."[1]

When asked if he ever suspected that Frank was a woman, Stewart was adamant that he had not.

> Never! We jested about the ridiculous little boots and called Frank "our woman" but he took it all in good part, and well, Mrs. Seelye would hardly be our guest now if I remembered anything of Frank that was not straight. I never heard a coarse word from his lips, or saw an unsoldierly act committed by him during my comrading with Frank. I remember his calling our chaplain an old whited sepulcher and adding with concise bravery that he was not the possessor of one grain of true manhood, to say nothing of Christianity, but we were many of us much of the same mind; so we never set it down against him.[2]

In the ensuing article, the reporter rather delicately described Emma as having "black hair and eyes" and a "quick, intelligent expression," and rather delicately summarized her "general appearance" as "suggesting the idea that she might have made her toilette with scrupulous care as to neatness, but possibly without a mirror."

Several weeks later, the reporter wrote to Emma asking several follow-up questions. One was whether Emma's book, *Nurse and Spy,* was "authentic." Emma answered "Not strictly so," explaining that "most of the experiences recorded there were either my own or came under my own observation." She also explained that "I wrote it almost immediately after leaving the army, and it was published mainly

in the interests of the Sanitary Commission . . . it was the hastily written work of a novice." [3]

Emma stayed with the Stewarts for nearly a week, during which
time several of her former friends in Flint came by to see her, among
them William McCreery, Milton Benjamin, and Sumner Howard,
who was now Speaker of the Michigan House of Representatives.
Each reunion was like that with Damon Stewart—shock, followed by
curiosity, followed by enthusiastic pledges of support. And each
readily agreed to provide affidavits attesting to her identity, and her
good character. Stewart's averred that: "Emma E. Seelye is the iden-
tical person who enlisted under the name of Franklin Thompson, as
a private in Company 'F.,' Second Regiment, Michigan Infantry,
Volunteers at Detroit, Michigan, on or about the first day of May,
A.D. 1861."

From that time until Stewart was injured, in May 1862:

> Franklin Thompson, (Emma E. Seelye) remained with said company
> and regiment, and performed cheerfully and fully and at all times any
> duty which was assigned her, and this deponent further says, that so
> far as he can remember, said duty consisted chiefly of either acting as
> nurse or carrying mail. And deponent further says, that during all of
> said time, said Franklin Thompson (S. Emma E. Seelye), bore a
> good reputation, always behaved as a person of good moral charac-
> ter and a consistent Christian, and was always ready for duty.

McCreery's was similar:

> This is to certify, that in the month of May, 1861, I enlisted in Com-
> pany "F," Second Regiment, Michigan Volunteers Infantry, and that
> during the same month, one Franklin Thompson, enlisted as a pri-
> vate soldier in the same company. He proceeded with the regiment
> to Washington and was present at the first battle of Bull Run, and in

the several engagements on the peninsula, Virginia. He was for some time Regimental Mail Carrier, and was especially attentive to the sick in hospital. A few days since I met this same Frank Thompson (whom I immediately recognized) in the person of Mrs. S. Emma E. Seelye, now a resident of Kansas.

Recognizing the potential damage to the reputation of a woman who spent so much time in such an unladylike activity, each made a point of Emma's good character, and her compassion for the wounded. Howard noted that Frank Thompson "developed a peculiar talent as a nurse. More than one member of the company can attest to the care, kindness, and self-sacrificing devotion of 'Frank' to the sick soldiers of the regiment. 'Frank's' manly bearing, soldiering qualities kindness and devotion to the sick deserve to be recognized in a liberal and substantial manner." William Turner made a point of saying that the soldier known as Frank "bore a good reputation, behaved as a person of good moral character, and was always ready for duty." Emma was thrilled with this testimony—it was more than she had dared hope for. Her spirits rose even further when she arrived home to find a supportive letter from Mr. Hurlbert waiting for her: Dated March 8, 1882, it read, in part:

Madam:
Your letter of the 23rd February is received and contents noted. I am willing to state all I know in regard to your services in the army and among the sick soldiers. I suppose you did enlist in a Michigan regiment as Frank Thompson; heard nothing from you until you left the army. When you returned, you wrote a book, Nurse and Spy. *We as publishers gave the Sanitary Commission and other causes hundreds of dollars from the profits of the book; also gave you, I think, two $500 bonds . . . which you used among the sick and wounded at Harpers Ferry.*
You ask me if S.E.E. Seelye and Frank Thompson are one and

the same. I answer yes. I know they are the same person. I knew of Frank Thompson in Nova Scotia and knew of Miss S. Emma Edmonds here; can state that she was a good Christian lady, honest and true as far as my knowledge extends. When Frank Thompson left the army in Michigan, he returned the books and wrote us that he had enlisted, and that it was his duty to do so if he knew he would be killed. You, Mrs. Seelye, have done everything in your power for the sick and wounded soldiers and for the Union cause. You deserve a pension from the government.

Soon after Emma left Flint, the article about her visit was published in the local paper. The dramatic story of the Second Michigan's long-lost mail carrier created a minor sensation, and was soon reprinted in papers throughout the state. Among those who saw it was Albert Cowles, who, like Jerome Robbins, had been a hospital steward in the Second Michigan. After the war, Cowles became a lawyer, and was now a judge in Lansing. Cowles, who had been a particular friend of Frank Thompson's, sent the article to Emma in Fort Scott, along with a nice letter and a photograph of himself taken during the war. Emma, extremely pleased to hear from him, and gratified by his kindness and encouragement, wrote back immediately:[4]

[Y]our favors are received; many thanks for them and the enclosed newspaper article. Thanks, many thanks for the picture. I would gladly send you mine in return but have none on hand, but will get some copied and send you one of "Frank" alias Miss E. before she was married. I think I can never be persuaded to sit for another picture. I have been sort of an invalid for years—don't go out scarcely at all, but try to do my own work, and play mother to two small boys.

A few weeks later, Emma received another letter from Cowles, this time enclosing a formal invitation from Colonel Frederick Schneider to attend the reunion of the Second Michigan in Lansing in October. Schneider, who had been in Company A, was now the commander of the Second's post of the Grand Army of the Republic, a nationwide organization for Civil War veterans. Emma was deeply flattered by the invitation, and spent an agonizing week deciding whether or not to accept it. Finally, she declined, explaining that she was too ill to go, but asked that Cowles convey a message to her former comrades on her behalf.

> *I cannot express to you how much I feel moved by the invitation to be present at the reunion of the noble survivors of the Second Michigan Infantry—every one of whom I love as if they were my own brothers, and will go much farther than Lansing for the pleasure of shaking hands with them—God bless them! I should be delighted to attend the reunion but unfortunately, I am quite out of health, much more so than usual, for I am writing this in bed, not being able to sit up. Please express my thanks to Colonel Schneider for his kind letter, also my regrets that I cannot accept the invitation. Tell him I shall reply to his letter as soon as I am well enough to do so. . . . My brief message to the boys is this: Frank's heart beats just as warm and true as when it beat under a regulation blouse.*

As a postscript, Emma asked that the men, "each and every one of them," send her a picture of themselves for her scrapbook.[5]

Despite her absence, the fate of Frank Thompson was the talk of the reunion that fall. Soon afterward, Judge Cowles sent Emma a group picture of the regiment taken on the steps of the Michigan capitol building, and informed her that a committee had been formed to help Emma's campaign for a pension in any way it could. Again, Emma was deeply moved by the unexpectedly positive reaction she received from the men who contacted her.[6] At a time when the idea of women at war was so alien, it would have been understandable if they had reacted with anger and humiliation upon learning that a young woman had been among them in such intimate proximity. The fact that they embraced her cause so warmly is a testament to the affection and respect they felt for Frank Thompson, and their appreciation for the compassion and commitment "he" had shown to the sick and wounded during the war. Still, as tolerant as their reaction was, it may also have been due at least in part to Victorian notions of gallantry: it is unlikely that they would have forgiven a man who both deceived and deserted them as readily as they apparently forgave Mrs. Seelye.

The first thing the committee of Emma's former comrades did was to enlist the support of two members of Congress: Byron Cutcheon, a former major with the Twentieth Michigan, who now sat on the Committee on Military Affairs, and E. B. Winans, who served on the Committee on Invalid Pensions. Byron Cutcheon remembered "Frank Thompson" vividly. His regiment, like the Second, was part of the brigade commanded by Orlando Poe at Fredericksburg, when Emma served as Poe's orderly, and Cutcheon had been impressed by "Frank's" bravery under fire. He immediately offered to sponsor legislation to remove the charge of desertion from Franklin Thompson's service record. Winans, too, agreed to help, by sponsoring a bill to award Emma a soldier's pension. He wrote personally to Emma, telling her that she would need to obtain a physician's report detailing the disabilities she attributed to her time in the army. Fortunately, Emma's doctor, Thomas Barnett, was a member of the Board of Examining Surgeons for Pensions. In February 1884, Barnett submitted a sworn statement to the Committee on Invalid Pensions stating that, in addition to her lame leg, Emma suffered from symptoms of heart disease and inflammatory rheumatism, which he attributed to her frequent bouts with the malaria she originally contracted during the Peninsula campaign.[7]

One early spring afternoon, as the legislative process was grinding slowly forward, Emma was surprised to find an unexpected, but most welcome, visitor at her door—William R. Morse, the first captain of Company F, and her friend from her days as a boarder with the Joslins. Like Stewart, Morse had been injured at the Battle of Williamsburg; he, too, had finished the war with another regiment. Morse, who was then living in Cincinnati, had heard about Emma, and when he found himself in Fort Scott on other business, decided to go see the former Frank Thompson for himself.[8]

In an interview that Morse gave to the Kansas City *Star* afterward, he said that upon his arrival at the Seelye residence, "I was shown into a neat but plain little parlor. In a few minutes, the lady made her appearance and recognized me. I spent a very pleasant hour in talking over old times and in listening to the story of her life" which, he added, was the "most peculiar incident that ever came under my notice." Explaining Emma's decision to adopt a male alias, Morse said that "having conceived the idea that the world shed its favors unequally, favoring the male more than the female, she adopted the costume of the former" and became a Bible salesman. Morse accepted Emma's explanation that she left the army due to her health, and told the *Star* that "Franklin was known by every man in the regiment, and her desertion was the topic of every campfire. The beardless boy was a universal favorite, and much anxiety was expressed over her safety. We never heard of her again during the war, and could never account for her desertion."[9]

Interestingly, Morse's recollection that there was much "anxiety" about Frank's whereabouts, and that they could not account for her sudden departure, is slightly at odds with William Boston's diary, which stated that "quite a time" was had over the fact that the AWOL postmaster was in fact a girl, and had deserted when her "lover," Inspector Reid, resigned his commission. Perhaps Morse was unaware of the rumors; more probably, he was deliberately being delicate for Emma's sake. Morse ended the interview by noting that Emma was seeking a pension from the government, and remarking "she certainly deserves it and I hope she may get it."[10]

Shortly after his visit, Morse swore out an affidavit on Emma's behalf, which stressed Emma's good conduct during the war, saying in part that "by her uniform faithfulness, bravery, and efficiency, and by her pure morals and Christian character, she won the respect, admiration, and confidence of both officers and men in [the] company and regiment." Around the same time, Colonel Schneider also submitted an affidavit, jointly with James Brown and Sylvester Larned, in which they, too, stressed her more traditionally womanly attributes. "[I]n view of [Emma's] many ministrations of tenderness and mercy," they wrote, "thousands of soldiers who were the recipients of her timely attention and nursing must remember her with the most filial regard. She is now the same true, loyal woman that she was in those eventful, stormy days of 1861 to 1865, when the country was passing the agonizing throes of civil war." [11]

On March 18, 1884, Byron Cutcheon introduced a bill, H.R. 5334, to "remove the charge of desertion from the record of Franklin Thompson, alias S.E.E. Seelye," accompanied by a report from the Committee on Military Affairs. The report stated, "This is a case of a female soldier who served for about two years as a private soldier in Company F, Second Michigan Volunteers, rendering good service in the ranks, in the hospital, and as mail carrier for the regiment and brigade." The report attributed Emma's decision to enlist in the army to a "strange impulse," but said that she "served faithfully until April, 1863, when she was taken sick at Lebanon, Ky., and being unable to obtain a furlough, and fearing the discovery of her sex, she absented herself without leave, and from that time was borne upon the rolls as a deserter." Attached to the report were the numerous affidavits and letters Emma had collected from her comrades, as well as the letter from Mr. Hurlbert explaining what Emma had done with the proceeds of her book, which the report described as proof of the "sterling qualities of her character." [12]

Also attached was a sworn statement from Emma herself, describing her service, and sidestepping the issue of espionage raised, presumably, by the exploits described in *Nurse and Spy,* as well as the entry about Frank Thompson in *Michigan in the War.* "I make no statement of any secret services. In my mind there is almost as much odium attached to the word 'spy' as there is to the word 'deserter.' There is so much mean deception necessarily practiced by a spy that I much prefer everyone should believe that I never was beyond the enemy's lines rather than to fasten upon me by oath a thing that I despise so much. It may do in wartime, but it is not pleasant to think upon in time of peace." [13]

It is an odd statement, neither a confirmation nor a denial. It may be that Emma was in fact not a spy, and therefore could not say so under oath, but that she wanted to preserve the mystery to make herself more interesting, or simply because she did not want to admit that she had lied in her book. It is also possible that Emma was in fact a spy, and, likewise, could not lie under oath, but did not want to admit to espionage for some reason, perhaps because she honestly was not proud of what she had done. Whichever it was, her statement was a clever solution to a dicey problem.

The report, which was personally authored by Cutcheon, concluded by saying:

From all this mass of testimony it is established beyond a doubt that "Frank Thompson" private, of Company F, Second Michigan Infantry, and Mrs. S. E. E. Seelye are one and the same; that she served honestly, and faithfully for two years as a private soldier, in the ranks, in the hospital, as mail carrier and as orderly to General O. M. Poe; that during her term of service she bore an unblemished character as a soldier, and promptness and cheerfulness in the discharge of every duty. . . . The writer of this report was at the time she was mail carrier and orderly to General O. M. Poe a field officer in Poe's brigade, and knew "Frank Thompson" well, and can bear witness to the fact that he (she) was a general favorite in the brigade, and without reproach on her character. [14]

On the same day that Cutcheon introduced his bill to remove the deserter charge from Emma's record, Winans introduced a companion bill that would grant her a pension of $12 a month. The report accompanying that bill summed up Emma's situation by saying, "Truth is ofttimes stranger than fiction. . . . Though by the rules of war a deserter, yet her course of conduct after shows that same zeal in the service of her country in her proper character as actuated her when she first dedicated herself to the cause which she felt to be the highest and noblest that can actuate man or woman." [15]

The pension bill sailed through and was signed by President Chester A. Arthur on July 5, 1884. But oddly, Cutcheon's bill to remove the deserter charge moved more slowly. For now, Emma remained in the odd position of being a deserter with a pension.

The extra $12 a month was not as much as Emma had hoped, but, in combination with Linus's thriving construction business, it was enough for Emma to be able to convince Linus to help her pursue a new dream. The rousing support of her former comrades had done much to erase Emma's depression, and she now wanted to repay the kindness, if not directly to them, then to the veteran community at large, by building and managing a home for disabled or destitute veterans in Fort Scott. In May, even before the pension bill was signed into law, Emma and Linus bought a ten-acre property on the outskirts of Fort Scott that is still known as Seelye Hill, and began planning for construction. [16]

Later that summer, Emma received an invitation to attend that year's regimental reunion, to be held in Flint in October. Again her reaction was mixed. Emma was still self-conscious about her appearance—she always asked her friends to send pictures of themselves, but always refused to send one of herself. She was also in poor health. Both the physical and the emotional journeys she would be required to make in order to accept the invitation seemed daunting. But this time, whatever trepidation she may have felt was overshadowed by her desire to see and thank her many supporters in person, and she agreed to attend. She went alone, without Linus, who stayed to care for the boys.[17] The reunion was held at the Casino Hotel in downtown Flint. There is no record of Emma's feelings as she slipped into the hall, or who first noticed and approached her. Approximately ninety of the seven hundred surviving members of the regiment were present, many of them accompanied by their wives. The hotel ballroom was bustling; patriotic poems were read, patriotic songs were sung, patriotic speeches were given.

If Emma was older and grayer than she had been twenty-odd years earlier, so, too, were the men, many of whom sported bushy gray whiskers over what had once been rosy, adolescent cheeks. Many of the men who had rallied to her aid over the past year and a half were there: Damon Stewart, Sylvester Larned, William Turner, William Morse. At the sight of each old friend, Emma's eyes welled with tears. But even as she greeted them with gratitude and excitement, her eyes must have scanned the room for Jerome Robbins's familiar face. There is no record of whether or not Robbins was there, however, although he and Hattie still lived in nearby Hubbardton, and among his papers when he died was a transcript of the keynote address given that day by Colonel W. J. Handy.

Orlando Poe, Emma's old commanding officer, was there, as handsome as ever. He had returned to engineering after the war, designing and overseeing construction of various projects around the Great Lakes, and was a prominent figure in the state. Poe and his old mail carrier shared a warm reunion. Poe was accompanied by his wife, Nellie, whom Emma had met during the war, when Nellie had occasionally visited her husband when the regiment was camped near Washington. One wonders whether Nellie greeted Emma with quite as much enthusiasm; she may have been less than pleased to learn that her husband's orderly and frequent companion during the fall and winter of 1862 had in fact been a young woman.[18]

The reunion program included a number of speakers, including Captain Morse and Sgt. Shakespeare. Colonel Handy's address was witty and irreverent, and above all deeply moving: He spoke of "the fraternity in army, the community of dangers, hardships, enjoyments, the participation in battles and victories and the companionship in adventures" that "bind the members of a regiment strongly together. To them, the regiment is both family and home." Like many of her comrades, Emma must have felt at home that day in a way she had not felt for two decades. And she must have joined in the cheers for Handy's last wish for them, that "when your call does come, and you are discharged from Life's hospital, as you cross the river to the other shores, you may find all our boys in line, to welcome and conduct you to a perpetual camp, where there shall be no duty more arduous than dress parade, and where the rations shall be unlimited."

Nobody garnered more attention from the crowd than Emma herself. All day long, the hall buzzed with her name, and when word spread that she was in fact present, those who had not yet had the chance to see her began to clamor for her to come up to the stage, where they could get a good look. Partly thrilled, partly mortified, but very moved, Emma made her way through the throng to the stage, where she waved, and then gave a brief address:

> My dear comrades, my heart is so full I cannot say what I would to you. Tears are in my eyes, but I shall never, never forget your love and kindness to Frank Thompson. All that I can say is, that I am deeply grateful, and may God bless you.[19]

Her remarks were greeted with thunderous applause, and for the rest of the afternoon, and throughout the banquet that evening, Emma was the star attraction. But even as Emma basked in the company of the men she loved so dearly, tongues were apparently wagging, and some time before the night was out, Emma heard something that hurt her deeply. Several months after she returned from Flint, she wrote to Richard Halstead, a member of the Second who had helped her immensely after her accident during the Second Battle of Bull Run, and whose acquaintance she renewed at the reunion.

> *I have been sick ever since I met you in Flint—not always sick in bed, but sick at heart. . . . Who was the lady who volunteered the information? I was properly punished for going to the reunion— God forgive me for going. It has always been the pride of my life that I had been a member of the 2nd Mich, but I discovered while at Flint that the honor of membership has cost me more than I am willing to pay—that of slurs upon my character. [I] shall be sorry all my life that the government ever granted me a pension. But I shall give it back with interest in the shape of a Hospital if the Lord grants me a few more years.*[20]

There is no record of what "information" caused Emma so much pain—or who "volunteered" it. Perhaps it was Nellie Poe, or Nellie's sister, who was married to Dr. Lyster of the Second Michigan, or perhaps even Hattie Farnum Robbins, if she and her husband were in fact there. Or it could have been any of the wives present, who were not as tolerant of Emma's deception as their husbands apparently were.[21]

The fact that the men received her so gladly, while their wives were less enthusiastic, was not limited to Emma's experience. Despite the general intolerance for women who step beyond the social norms prescribed for them, Civil War soldiers tended to judge their comrades, male and female, by a different standard. There was the case of the New Jersey corporal who went into labor on picket duty, whose comrades rallied around her and her child. And there were other cases during and after the war when soldiers kept quiet about females in their ranks, as Jerome Robbins had so faithfully done. As one historian has pointed out, "just as they showed remarkable tolerance and respect for women soldiers during the war, [many veterans] continued to honor them long after the conflict." [22]

Civilians, particularly female civilians, did not tend to share this view. If veterans valued courage in themselves and in others, their wives judged female soldiers by the same standards of social conduct by which the wives judged themselves and each other, and they generally found their husbands' female comrades lacking in every important characteristic. At a minimum, mucking about in war camps was unladylike. At worst, it was immoral.

Once back in Flint, though, Emma did not let the gossip get in the way of her plans for a home for veterans, which were going full steam ahead. There was no progress on Cutcheon's bill to remove the deserter charge from her record, something that weighed on her heavily. Emma concluded that more support was necessary, so she turned to Orlando Poe, the highest-ranking officer who knew both Emma and Frank Thompson. After the reunion, Emma wrote to Poe and asked him to send a letter to Cutcheon in support of the legislation. In response, Poe sent a letter to Cutcheon, dated January 4, 1885, which read in part:

> I am this moment in receipt of a letter from Mrs. S.E.E. Seelye of Fort Scott, Kansas, requesting me to write you and testify to her identity with one Frank Thompson, who served as an enlisted man in the Second Michigan Volunteer Infantry. . . . I cannot recall when "Frank Thompson" first came under my personal notice, but I distinctly remember that "Frank" was on duty as brigade mail carrier just preceding the Battle of Fredericksburg, in December 1862, and was my orderly in that battle. Frank continued on such duty until after we arrived at Lebanon, Ky., early in April 1863. I have no personal knowledge of her movements after [that] until I met her at a reunion of my regiment at Flint, Michigan, in the autumn of 1884, where there was no difficulty

about her identification with "Frank Thompson." I think I would have recognized her anywhere. My wife, who knew her in the army, and was with me at Flint, recognized her equally with myself. I would be perfectly willing to go on the stand and swear that the soldier known as "Frank Thompson" and the woman now known as Mrs. S. E. E. Seelye are one and the same person. I know my wife, as well as many officers of the regiment, would give the same testimony.[23]

Poe made a point of saying that he had not known or even suspected that Frank was a female, although he apparently recognized that that was hard to believe. "As a soldier, Frank Thompson was effeminate looking, and for that reason was detailed as mail carrier, to avoid taking an efficient soldier from the ranks. . . . A single glance at her in her proper character caused me to wonder how I ever could have mistaken her for a man, and I readily recall many things which ought to have betrayed her, except no one thought of finding a woman in soldier's dress." But, perhaps because Poe was still in the army, he added, "I don't think I could be deceived that way again."[24]

Poe's letter was added to Emma's file, but Cutcheon's bill continued to languish. There were, apparently, some objections to removing the deserter charge on the grounds of self-proclaimed poor health, particularly when a medical furlough had been requested and denied. On the other hand, as Cutcheon pointed out whenever he could, "this remarkable case can hardly be objected to on the ground that it is likely to set a dangerous precedent."[25] Still, the year came and went with no progress for him to report to Emma.

While she waited to hear from Washington, Emma and Linus began construction on the veterans home. The spacious white frame house was designed with eight large rooms, one of which was intended to serve as a hospital. The other bedrooms would be for destitute or invalid veterans. Linus, with the help of Freddy and Charlie, who were now fourteen and twelve, did most of the work himself.[26]

In July 1886, two years after the pension bill was passed, Emma received word from Cutcheon that his bill had finally passed as well, and was signed into law by President Grover Cleveland. She was thrilled to be officially in good standing with the veteran community, the only one that really mattered to her.[27]

There was, however, still one more step, Cutcheon informed her: She must now make an application for all back pay and any balance of bounty that would have been due her had she never been charged with desertion. Emma did so immediately, hoping that she would be entitled to several hundred dollars, which she planned to use to open her veterans home for business. But again the wheels of Washington ground slowly, and it was not until the spring of 1889 that Emma received a check from the War Department. When it did come, the check was for less than half what she had hoped.[28]

In the meantime, the new house on Seelye Hill was finished, and she, Linus, and the boys moved in. By now, Emma was something of a celebrity in Fort Scott. The local paper had run several articles on her over the past few years, including reprinting the article that was written about her visit to Damon Stewart, as well as periodic updates about the legislation sponsored on her behalf. The notoriety gave Emma a certain amount of freedom. She liked to go about in men's trousers from time to time when she was working out of doors, and was often seen chopping wood or toting a shotgun in search of small game—behavior that in any other woman would have been scandalous, but that, in Emma's case, was simply attributed to her "unusual" background.[29]

Generally, her new neighbors viewed her with a combination of curiosity and respect, and, in the case of some of the children, with a fair amount of fear. True or not, the word had gotten around that Mrs. Seelye was a former spy, and "spying on the spy" became a favorite game of boys and girls, who would dare one another to sneak close to Seelye house to get a look at their eccentric, and possibly heroic, neighbor. One little girl recalled years later that her father, who was also a veteran of the war, told her that Emma "was a soldier, and a Union spy. She may have been the means of saving the lives of many soldiers. A spy does save many lives; she may even have saved mine." Part of the fun of the game was the fear that she might catch you—it must have been somewhat anticlimactic, therefore, that when Emma finally did discover the game, she did not shoot at them, but invited them over for cookies. From then on, the children in the neighborhood took great pride in their association with the famous Mrs. Seelye, even if their mothers could never quite get used to the way their odd neighbor wore heavy boots underneath her dresses.[30]

Linus, too, was proud of his wife, and was amused by her clothing and demeanor. He was often heard to brag about her marksmanship, which he freely admitted was better than his own. He also did not seem to mind that most of her close friends were former soldiers, who would often stop by to reminisce about the war. One of her neighbors was a veteran of an Ohio regiment, and his children remembered that he would often go next door in the evenings to "discuss something about the Civil War with Mrs. Seelye." Family lore remembers that Linus was content to defer to Emma about matters large and small; as one put it, "If Emma wanted a fence to go up and Linus didn't, the fence went up." But by all accounts, Linus's tolerance came from strength rather than weakness; he was a quiet but confident man who was not the least bit threatened by Emma's strong will. Nor did her lack of interest in clothes stop him from caring about them himself; neighbors of the Seelyes remembered that often, Emma would be wearing pants, or the simplest of skirts with boots underneath, while Linus would head to church in a tall hat and tails.[31]

In the winter of 1891, eighteen-year-old Fred married a pretty sixteen-year-old neighbor named Lucy Sterling, whom he had met and fallen in love with two years earlier. Lucy's parents worried that she was too young to get married, but surprisingly, given her own feelings about marriage when she was Lucy's age, Emma approved of the match. After the wedding, Lucy came to live with the Seelyes in the house on Seelye Hill, and, over time, Emma and Lucy became constant companions. Lucy was eager to please her formidable mother-in-law, and quickly offered to take over many of the domestic chores that Emma did not like to do. It was more than the extra pair of hands that Emma came to love about the shy, quiet Lucy, who may have filled the void created by Alice's death. Or maybe it was the fact that Emma had not had many close female friends since she left her sisters in New Brunswick. In any event, the fifty-year-old woman and the sixteen-year-old girl would remain close for the rest of Emma's life. However, Emma rarely talked to Lucy about her past, other than to mention, once, that her father had desperately wanted her to be a boy, a fact that still nagged at Emma. She did not openly discuss the war with anyone who was not also a veteran, and, despite being warm and casual about most things, seemed pointedly closed to questions about it.[32]

For the first few years of his marriage, Fred worked for Linus in the construction business, but by the end of 1892, the building boom in Fort Scott was slowing down, and Fred decided he needed to look for work elsewhere. Emma was stoic when Lucy and Fred moved to La Porte, Texas, a new boomtown near Houston, but she must have missed them terribly.[33]

A year later, the Panic of 1893 caused banks all over the country to close their doors, some never to reopen. The Seelyes' bank, First National Bank of Fort Scott, did reopen in August, but so many people had been ruined that Linus's business failed. Charlie, taking after his mother, joined the army around the same time, and there was now nothing to keep them in Fort Scott. They had never had the money to open the veterans home Emma dreamed of, and now it was clear that they never would. Sadly, they sold the house they had built with such high hopes, and followed Lucy and Fred to La Porte.[34]

With the proceeds from the Seelye Hill house, Emma and Linus bought a small cattle farm on San Jacinto Bay. Although they had come south reluctantly, their first few years in Texas, like the time on Bayou Teche, were marked by a degree of peace and satisfaction. Lucy had given birth to a baby boy, and, since the new farmhouse had plenty of room, Lucy, Fred, and baby Harry moved in with Linus and Emma. It was a happy time for Emma. She loved working in the garden, tending to her small orchard of fruit trees, and watching over Harry on the long front porch overlooking the bay. Occasionally she would take a small rowboat into the bay, alone, recalling, perhaps, the many hours she spent alone in a canoe on Magaguadavic Lake.[35]

But there were still shadows. At fifty-two, Emma looked and felt much older. Her once thick, shiny black hair was now gray; her left leg grew steadily worse. When Lucy became pregnant with another baby, and decided that they needed a place of their own, Linus and Emma realized they could not keep up the farm alone, and moved into a small house, which Linus built himself, in La Porte.[36]

As stubborn as ever, Emma continued to correspond with the War Department, badgering it for an increase in her pension. She felt in particular that she had not been adequately compensated for the injury to her leg that she received in the accident during the Second Battle of Bull Run. The War Department was insisting on more proof, a demand that struck Emma as unreasonable. In one letter, dated September 24, 1896, she pulled out all of the stops, chastising, pleading, playing for sympathy, instilling guilt. *"Dear Sir,"* she wrote,

I can but reiterate my former statement; as it is simply impossible for me to obtain testimony from "eye witnesses" to the injuries which I received when thrown from the mule, as formerly stated. I was entirely alone, there was not a soul within miles of me as far as I know, when the accident occurred. . . . [B]eing miles away from any Company and Regiment neither surgeons nor comrades could give testimony as "eye witnesses" nor to the extent of the injuries which I received, especially as I took the utmost pains to conceal *the facts in the case. Had I been what I represented myself to be, I would have gone to the hospital and had the surgeon make an examination of my injuries, and placed myself in his hands for medical treatment and saved years of suffering. But being a* woman *I felt compelled to suffer in silence and endure it the best I could, in order to escape detection of my sex.* I would rather have been shot dead, *than to have been known as a woman and sent away from the army under guard as a* criminal. *I had received* severe internal *injuries in the accident above referred to, which caused frequent hemorrhage of the lungs, had I reported that fact alone and applied for medical treatment, the very first step would have been an examination of my lungs, which to me, simply meant* dismissal *from the service.*

Now, Mr. Meddonburn, how can I have the cheek to ask men to swear *to that which they knew so little about? And after a lapse of thirty-five years, they no doubt, have forgotten what little they did know about it.* I can not do it! . . . *I am almost sixty years of age, am not able to work, a part of my left side is becoming paralyzed. My left lower limb is most of the time so swollen and painful that I have to keep it bandaged from the ankle to the knee, and I have not worn a shoe, proper, on my left foot for over two years. I am* never *free from rheumatism, sometimes in bed for weeks, not able to turn over.*

The pension which I receive is not sufficient to pay my doctor bills, and a person to wait on me. . . . I enclose a true copy of a letter from the Publisher of Nurse and Spy *to show you how freely I spent my money for the government in its time of need—should I expect less liberality in my time of need?*

Very respectfully,
S. Emma E. Seelye

N.B. I believe you can do much *for me, if you and your Colleagues*

*will do as Congress did, viz, Consider this an extraordinary case,
and waive a few of the technicalities of the pension laws. I know
you consider me deserving of something better than a starvation
pension. Remember, I am the only woman in the United States
whom the Government ever pensioned as a Soldier! Why not make
an extra effort before I get to the poor house?*[37]

Although it is tinged with suffering, the letter captured so much of
Emma's essence—dramatic, stubborn, clever, proud. But despite her
emotional plea, Emma did not receive an increase in her pension, nor
did she end up in the poorhouse. Now that they were in town, Linus,
who was still remarkably fit, was able to find relatively steady work,
and Fred and Lucy were a constant source of support.[38]

In La Porte, Emma became reacquainted with a former member
of the Second Michigan, a merchant named Isaac Hagler. It was
Hagler who urged her to apply for membership in the local chapter
of the Grand Army of the Republic, the nationwide Civil War veterans group. Emma was initially reluctant—membership was reserved
for veterans who had been honorably discharged, and she was somewhat afraid to reopen her record for public scrutiny. Moreover, there
were no known female members of the G.A.R. But Hagler was insis-
tent, and finally, in the winter of 1897, Emma submitted the necessary paperwork.[39]

Several months later, Emma received a written invitation from the
commanders of G.A.R. Post No. 9 in Houston—which was named,
appropriately, after Emma's beloved General McClellan—to attend
their annual encampment in April. Emma was frail, but was nonetheless determined to go. The third week in April, Emma, apparently in
the company of Isaac Hagler, boarded a train for the short ride to
Houston. It was to be her last extended trip.[40]

The topic of Emma's application for membership was one of the
main items on the agenda. Speaking on her behalf, A. G. Weissert,
the former national G.A.R. commander, said in part, "Every now

and then a woman has appeared who has claimed membership in the Grand Army of the Republic . . . and they have always proven to be frauds. You know our order says only such as have an honorable discharge from the army or the navy can be received into membership. Sarah Emma Edmonds Seelye has such a discharge. The Commander of this Post, of which she desires to become a member, submitted the papers to me. I have found the discharge regular in all respects." With Emma brimming with pride, the membership voted her in, and the next day, she was mustered into the G.A.R. in a lavish ceremony. It was the highlight of her life, she said afterward, the greatest honor she ever received or could imagine.[41]

She returned to La Porte with a glow that her family had not seen in a long time, but it was to be short-lived. Linus was ill much of that summer, and rarely able to work for more than a short stretch at a time. Emma, too, fell ill the following fall with another bout of malaria. Fred and Lucy, with their children, came to spend the winter, taking care of the two near-invalids. Emma seemed to recover somewhat in the spring, as did Linus, but toward the end of the summer, she was stricken with sudden and severe paralysis, most probably the result of a stroke. Emma Seelye, alias Frank Thompson, died on September 5, 1898, at the age of fifty-six. She was buried in La Porte, but at the urging of G.A.R comrades, on Memorial Day, 1901, her remains were moved to the G.A.R. burial ground in Houston's Washington Cemetery after a lovely and elegant military funeral, of which, her relatives felt sure, she would have been extremely proud.[42]

Several years after Emma's death, Linus Seelye returned to New Brunswick, where he died in 1917 at the age of eighty-five. Jerome Robbins outlived them both. When he died in 1921, at the age of eighty, Emma's letters were among his private papers, and a copy of her obituary from a Kansas newspaper was neatly folded inside his wartime journal. A "remarkable character," it said, "has passed away."[43]

AFTERWORD

Was Emma Edmonds a spy? The belief that she was, based on the exploits she described in *Nurse and Spy,* is certainly firmly entrenched in popular culture. But some historians have cast doubts on her claims, pointing out that, among other things, there is nothing in official military records to support her claim; that some of her stories are contradicted by known facts; and that some of her claims are simply too audacious to be believed.

These doubts alone might be enough to put to bed forever the idea that Emma went behind enemy lines if we did not know, without a shadow of a doubt, that Emma was clever and daring enough to successfully pose as a man for more than four years. That fact alone must make us wonder whether she was not also clever and audacious enough to go behind enemy lines in various guises, even if she did not produce the kind of actionable intelligence that she sometimes claimed. And she certainly had the opportunity to go behind enemy lines. As mail carrier, she had uncommon freedom and mobility, and the muster rolls reflect that she was frequently "absent on duty" at times that correspond to the events she describes. There is also Michigan adjutant general John Robertson's entry about Frank Thompson in his official history of the regiment in *Michigan in the War,* written before he had the evidence to connect the author of *Nurse and Spy* with Thompson, in which he noted that "Thompson" was "often employed as a spy, going within the enemy's lines, sometimes absent for weeks, and is said to have furnished much valuable information."

Still, one could make much of the fact that Robbins, who left in some ways the most reliable account of Emma's experiences in the war, never mentioned or even suggested that she engaged in espionage activities in his journal.

Or did he?

On April 17, the day Robbins first noticed that "Frank" was missing, he wrote that he thought that "he must have gone outside the picket lines and found getting back in a difficulty." But what would Emma have been doing "out of the picket lines"?

It is a tantalizing clue, but only that. History shares some secrets, keeps others. The fact is that while there is just enough evidence to believe that Emma was in fact a spy to prevent us from dismissing her claims altogether, there is not enough to prove it conclusively. We are left with a mystery.

But it is what we do know about Emma Edmonds's life that interests me far more than what we do not know about her espionage activities. We know that she was a girl who had the daring and imagination to circumvent the social restrictions of her time by inventing and becoming Frank Thompson; who had the courage to put herself in harm's way when it was not at all necessary that she do so; and who ultimately had the stubborn fortitude to publicly reunite her adolescent alias with her adult self, and claim her rightful due. It was not enough for her to be just Emma Edmonds, or Franklin Thompson, or even Mrs. Linus B. Seelye. It was not until she was able to publicly admit to being—and to be accepted and even celebrated as—all three at once, that the girl, the warrior, and the woman could become whole, and finally find some semblance of peace.

NOTES

Chapter One

Much of the information about Emma's early life is drawn from the first full biography of Emma, by Sylvia G. L. Dannett, *She Rode With the Generals*. Dannett, in turn, based much of her account on Emma's memoirs, as well as an interview of Emma published in the Fort Scott (Kansas) *Monitor* on January 17, 1884. Dannett also relied on other newspaper articles, as well as on interviews of Emma's descendants, who are since deceased. Other scholarship regarding Emma's life includes Elizabeth D. Leonard's *All the Daring of a Soldier: Women of the Civil War Armies;* Professor Leonard's introduction to the reprint of Emma's memoirs, Sarah Emma Edmonds, *Memoirs of a Soldier, Nurse and Spy: A Woman's Adventures in the Union Army;* and Betty Fladeland's "New Light on Sarah Emma Edmonds Alias Frank Thompson."

1. Dannett, *She Rode With the Generals,* 15.
2. Ibid., 18.
3. Ibid., 16–17.
4. Fort Scott *Monitor,* January 17, 1884.
5. Dannett, *She Rode With the Generals,* 19–22.
6. Ibid., 19–20.
7. Ibid., 21.
8. Edmonds, *Nurse and Spy,* 129.
9. Dannett, *She Rode With the Generals,* 23.
10. Fort Scott *Monitor,* January 27, 1884.
11. Ibid.
12. Ibid.
13. Ibid.

14. Ibid.

15. Ibid.

16. Ibid.

17. Dannett, *She Rode With the Generals*, 27.

18. Ibid., 27–29.

19. Nancy Cook, "Mark Twain—The Complex World of the Successful Author," 244–252.

20. *The Morning News*, St. John, N.B., April 5, 1854, as quoted in Dannett, *She Rode With the Generals*, 29.

21. Fort Scott *Monitor*, January 17, 1884.

22. Emily Thornwell, *The Lady's Guide to Perfect Gentility.*

23. "Rights and Wrongs of Women," *Harper's New Monthly Magazine*, vol. 9 (June 1854), 76–78.

24. Fort Scott *Monitor*, January 17, 1884.

25. Ibid.

26. Ibid.

27. Dannett, *She Rode With the Generals*, 37–40, based on Fort Scott *Monitor*, January 17, 1884.

28. Fort Scott *Monitor*, January 17, 1884.

29. Dannett, *She Rode With the Generals*, 41.

30. Fort Scott *Monitor*, January 17, 1884.

31. Ibid.

32. Ibid.

33. Ibid.

34. Ibid.

Chapter Two

The description of the political situation that led to the outbreak of the Civil War, and the discussion of the events leading up to the attack on Fort Sumter, are drawn from several works, including Bruce Catton's *The Civil War;* James McPherson's *Battle Cry of Freedom: The Civil War Era;* and David J. Eicher's *The Longest Night: A Military History of the Civil War.*

Information about the formation of the 2nd Michigan Infantry Regiment comes from several sources as well, including *Michigan in the War,* compiled by John Robertson, Adjutant General, and Frank B. Woodford's *Father Abraham's Children: Michigan Episodes in the Civil War,* as well as three excellent Web sites, Don Harvey's Michigan in the Civil War, the 2nd Regiment Infantry Michigan Volunteers Reactivated's site, which includes a link to the article in the May 16, 1861, *Wolverine Citizen* cited below, and 2nd Michigan Volunteer Infantry, Company A. All three sites contain a wealth of information that was helpful not only in the writing about the formation of the regiment, but about the regiment's activities throughout the time that Emma served.

For information about the phenomenon of women soldiers in the war, I have primarily relied on two recent studies on the subject: Elizabeth Leonard's *All the Daring of a Soldier: Women of the Civil War Armies* and DeAnne Blanton and Lauren M. Cook's *They Fought Like Demons: Women Soldiers in the American Civil War.*

1. Dannett, *She Rode With the Generals,* 47, quoting from the Detroit *Free Press,* October 6, 1935.

2. Edmonds, *Nurse and Spy.*

3. Woodford, *Father Abraham's Children,* 17–20.

4. Ibid. *See also* Robertson, *Michigan in the War,* 187–188.

5. Robertson, *Michigan in the War,* 188.

6. The *Wolverine Citizen,* May 4, 1861. See also Dannett, 53–34.

7. Edmonds, *Nurse and Spy,* 3; Fort Scott *Monitor* interview.

8. Blanton and Cook, *They Fought Like Demons,* 25 et seq.

9. Ibid., 26.

10. Ibid., 30.

11. Blanton and Cook, *They Fought Like Demons,* 7.

12. Ibid., 25–44, and Leonard, *All the Daring of a Soldier,* 257 et seq., (for two excellent analyses on the various reasons that women went to war).

13. Ibid., 28, 38–39, 170 et seq.; Leonard, *All the Daring of a Soldier,* 185–191.

14. Blanton and Cook, *They Fought Like Demons,* 37–39; Leonard, *All the Daring of a Soldier,* 185–191.

15. Ibid.

16. Fort Scott *Monitor,* January 17, 1884.

17. Woodford, *Father Abraham's Children,* 31–33 (describing 1st Michigan); *see also* Robertson, *Michigan in the War,* 188–189.

18. Dannett, *She Rode With the Generals,* 52.

19. Woodford, *Father Abraham's Children,* 32.

20. Address to reunion of 2nd Michigan, Flint 1884.

21. Billings, *Hardtack & Coffee,* 78.

22. Jerome Robbins Journal.

23. Edmunds, *Nurse and Spy,* 13.

Chapter Three

Much of the general information about military life in Washington in the spring of 1861 comes from Margaret Leech's *Reveille in Washington,* and John D. Billings' *Hard Tack and Coffee.* The latter was the first-hand memoir of a Massachusetts soldier, and is one of the most useful primary sources on day-to-day life in the army. The discussion of Clara Barton is based on Stephen B. Oates's excellent *A Woman of Valor: Clara Barton and the Civil War.*

1. J. Robbins Journal.

2. Ibid.

3. Ibid. *See also* Edmonds, *Nurse and Spy,* 5.

4. Leech, *Reveille in Washington,* 66 et seq.

5. Edmonds, *Nurse and Spy,* 9.

6. J. Robbins Journal.

7. Billings, *Hardtack & Coffee,* 73–89.

8. Ibid.

9. Edmonds, *Nurse and Spy,* 169.

10. Robertson, *Soldiers Blue and Gray,* 152.

11. Ibid.

12. Billings, *Hardtack & Coffee,* 76 et seq.

13. Ibid. 83.

14. Blanton and Cook, *They Fought Like Demons,* 109.

15. Ibid.

16. Ibid., 42, 48 et seq.

17. Billings, *Hardtack & Coffee,* 65.

18. J. Robbins Journal.

19. Edmonds, *Nurse and Spy,* 169.

20. Freemon, *Gangrene and Glory*, 205.

21. Adams, *Doctors in Blue*, 14.

22. Edmonds, *Nurse and Spy*, 7.

23. Billings, *Hard Tack and Coffee*, 50–51.

24. Fort Scott *Monitor*, January 17, 1884.

25. Oates, *A Woman of Valor*, 8–10; Freemon, *Gangrene and Glory*, 52; Bollet, *Civil War Medicine*, 409 et seq.

26. Adams, *Doctors in Blue*, 176.

27. Edmonds, *Nurse and Spy*, 227.

28. Oates, *A Woman of Valor*, 7–8; 25.

29. Ibid., chapter 1.

30. Ibid., 8.

31. Ibid., 18.

32. Ibid., 19.

33. Edmonds, *Nurse and Spy*, 9.

34. Catton, *The Civil War*, 39; McPherson, *Battle Cry of Freedom*, 334–335.

35. Woodford, *Father Abraham's Children*, 43.

36. J. Robbins Journal.

37. Edmonds, *Nurse and Spy*, 12.

38. Ibid.

Chapter Four

1. Catton, *The Civil War*, 42.

2. Edmonds, *Nurse and Spy*, 12–13.

3. Ibid., 12.

4. Ibid., 13.

5. Ibid., 14.

6. Ibid., 13.

7. Ibid., 15.

8. Ibid., 16

9. Ibid., 19.

10. Robertson, *Michigan in the War*, 189.

11. J. Robbins Journal.

12. Edmonds, *Nurse and Spy*, 20.

13. Ibid.

14. Ibid., 21.

15. Ibid., 23.

16. Ibid., 23–24.

17. Leech, *Reveille in Washington*, 103–107.

18. Edmonds, *Nurse and Spy*, 25–26.

19. Catton, *The Civil War*, 51.

20. Beatie, *Army of the Potomac*, 393–414. *See also* Leech, *Reveille in Washington*, 110; McPherson, *Battle Cry of Freedom*, 361.

21. Edmonds, *Nurse and Spy*, 26.

22. Beatie, *Birth of Command*, 435–437.

23. Edmonds, *Nurse and Spy*, 29.

24. Ibid., 26.

25. See Freemon, *Gangrene and Glory*, 47–49.

26. Edmonds, *Nurse and Spy*, 27.

27. Ibid., 28.

28. Leech, *Reveille in Washington*, 109.

29. Ibid. 112.

30. Ibid., 114.

31. J. Robbins Journal.

32. Edmonds, *Nurse and Spy*, 27.

33. J. Robbins Journal.

34. Ibid.

35. Ibid.

36. Ibid.

37. McPherson, *Battle Cry of Freedom*, 361–362.

38. J. Robbins Journal.

39. Ibid.

40. Ibid.

41. Ibid.

42. Ibid.

43. Ibid.

44. Wiley, *The Life of Billy Yank*, 57.

45. Ibid.

Chapter Five

For background information on the Peninsula campaign, I relied on several sources, including Joseph P. Cullen, *The Peninsula Campaign 1862;* Stephen W. Sears, *To the Gates of Richmond: The Peninsula Campaign;* Shelby Foote, *The Civil War: A Narrative—Fort Sumter to Perryville;* Earl C. Hastings, Jr., and David Hastings, *A Pitiless Rain: The Battle of Williamsburg 1862;* and David J. Eicher, *The Longest Night: A Military History of the Civil War.* The accounts of Emma's espionage activities, in this and other chapters, are based almost solely on *Nurse and Spy,* first published in 1864. Despite the widespread acceptance of her claims in popular culture and even among some historians, the credibility of these accounts is the subject of intense debate. For narrative purposes, Emma's claims are presented as she told them. The validity of her claims is analyzed more fully in the Afterword. General information about the evolution of the Federal Secret Service is based primarily on Edwin C. Fishel's *The Secret War of the Union: The Untold Story of Military Intelligence in the Civil War.* It should be noted that Fishel himself is dismissive of Emma's espionage claims, primarily on the grounds that there is no record of Emma having been on the Federal payroll as a spy, and because some of the intelligence she claimed to have produced proved inaccurate.

1. Edmonds Pension File.
2. Edmonds, *Nurse and Spy,* 31.
3. J. Robbins Journal.
4. Earl C. Hastings, Jr., and David Hastings, *A Pitiless Rain,* 10.
5. Cullen, *The Peninsula Campaign 1862,* 15.
6. Edmonds, *Nurse and Spy,* 32.
7. J. Robbins Journal.
8. Edmonds, *Nurse and Spy,* 32.
9. J. Robbins Journal.
10. Edmonds, *Nurse and Spy,* 34.
11. Ibid., 35.
12. Ibid., 37. *See also* J. Robbins Journal.
13. Ibid., 36–37. *See also* J. Robbins Journal.
14. Edmonds, *Nurse and Spy,* 35.

15. Cullen, *The Peninsula Campaign,* 40–42.

16. Fishel, *The Secret War of the Union,* 130 et seq.

17. Edmonds, *Nurse and Spy,* 42.

18. Ibid., 55–56.

19. Ibid.

20. Ibid., 59–66.

21. Ibid.

22. Ibid.

23. Ibid.

24. Ibid.

25. Ibid.

26. Sears, *To the Gates of Richmond,* 61.

27. Edmonds, *Nurse and Spy,* 67.

28. J. Robbins Journal.

29. Sears, *To the Gates of Richmond,* 62, 65.

30. Cullen, *The Peninsula Campaign,* 45.

31. Edmonds, *Nurse and Spy,* 68–69.

32. Ibid., 68.

33. Ibid., 68–69.

34. Ibid., 69.

35. Hastings and Hastings, *A Pitiless Rain,* 117.

36. Edmonds, *Nurse and Spy,* 70.

37. Ibid.

38. J. Robbins Journal.

39. Sears, *To the Gates of Richmond,* 88.

40. Edmonds, *Nurse and Spy,* 72.

Chapter Six

1. Sears, *To the Gates of Richmond,* 103–105; Cullen, *The Peninsula Campaign,* 46.

2. Edmonds, *Nurse and Spy,* 118.

3. Sears, *To the Gates of Richmond,* 107–110; Cullen, *The Peninsula Campaign,* 48–49.

4. Ibid.

5. Edmonds, *Nurse and Spy*, 84.

6. Ibid.

7. Ibid., 87–90.

8. Ibid.

9. Ibid., 93.

10. Ibid., 93–97.

11. Ibid.

12. Edmonds, *Nurse and Spy*, 101; Cullen, *The Peninsula Campaign*, 54.

13. Sears, *To the Gates of Richmond*, 120.

14. Cullen, *The Peninsula Campaign*, 54–55.

15. Edmonds, *Nurse and Spy*, 103–105.

16. Ibid., 105–107.

17. Ibid., 108.

18. J. Robbins Journal.

19. Edmonds, *Nurse and Spy*, 108–109.

20. Sears, *To the Gates of Richmond*, 147.

21. Edmonds, *Nurse and Spy*, 109.

22. Ibid., 111.

23. Sears, *To the Gates of Richmond*, 148.

24. Edmonds, *Nurse and Spy*, 109.

25. Sears, *To the Gates of Richmond*, 145.

26. Edmonds, *Nurse and Spy*, 145.

27. Moe, *The Last Full Measure*, 143.

28. Cullen, *The Peninsula Campaign*, 70.

29. Edmonds, *Nurse and Spy*, 149.

30. Fort Scott *Monitor*, January 17, 1884.

31. J. Robbins Journal.

32. Sears, *To the Gates of Richmond*, 168–169; Foote, *The Civil War*, 471–472.

33. Ibid. *See also* Cullen, *The Peninsula Campaign*, 64–66.

34. Edmonds, *Nurse and Spy*, 118.

35. J. Robbins Journal.

36. Edmonds, *Nurse and Spy*, 120.

37. Cullen, *The Peninsula Campaign*, 78. *See also* Eicher, *The Longest Night*, 280–281.

38. Sears, *To the Gates of Richmond*, 183.

39. Ibid., 185–189.

40. Ibid., 195.

41. Ibid., 191.

42. Ibid., 207–211; *see also* Cullen, *The Peninsula Campaign*, 98–99.

43. Message from General Van Vliet to Colonel Ingalls, as quoted in Edmonds, *Nurse and Spy*, 122.

44. Edmonds, *Nurse and Spy*, 125.

45. Ibid., 126.

Chapter Seven

1. Edmonds, *Nurse and Spy*, 129.

2. Cullen, *The Peninsula Campaign*, 125.

3. Edmonds, *Nurse and Spy*, 122.

4. Ibid., 130.

5. Ibid., 133.

6. Ibid., 136.

7. Ibid., 134.

8. Ibid.

9. J. Robbins Journal.

10. J. Robbins Journal.

11. Ibid.

12. Ibid.

13. OR, Series 2, Vol. 4, Part 1..

14. J. Robbins Journal.

15. Edmonds, *Nurse and Spy*, 141.

16. Ibid., 143.

17. Ibid., 149.

18. J. Robbins Journal.

19. McPherson, *Battle Cry of Freedom*, 505.

20. Foote, *The Civil War*, 596.

21. Edmonds, *Nurse and Spy*, 151.

22. Ibid., 155–157.

23. Fishel, *The Secret War for the Union*, 191–193.

24. Ibid.

25. Fort Scott *Monitor,* January 17, 1884.

26. Edmonds, *Nurse and Spy,* 167.

27. J. Robbins Journal.

28. Ibid.

29. Ibid.

30. Edmonds, *Nurse and Spy,* 160; J. Robbins Journal.

31. Edmonds, *Nurse and Spy,* 162.

32. Oates, *A Woman of Valor,* 91–93.

33. J. Robbins Journal.

34. Edmonds, *Nurse and Spy,* 174.

35. Ibid., 174–176.

36. Ibid.

37. Ibid.

38. Ibid.

39. Ibid.

40. Ibid.

41. Ibid.

Chapter Eight

The general description of the Battle of Fredericksburg is based on several sources, including: James M. McPherson, *Battle Cry of Freedom: The Civil War Era;* David J. Eicher, *The Longest Night: A Military History of the Civil War;* Francis Augustin O'Reilly, *The Fredericksburg Campaign: Winter War on the Rappahannock.* The information about Clara Barton's role at Fredericksburg, as well as much of the description of Lacy House, is from Stephen B. Oates, *A Woman of Valor: Clara Barton and the Civil War.*

1. McPherson, *Battle Cry of Freedom,* 570.

2. McClellan's farewell address as quoted in Edmonds, *Nurse and Spy,* 179.

3. Foote, *The Civil War,* 757.

4. Ibid.

5. J. Robbins Journal.

6. Catton, *The Civil War,* 111.

7. McPherson, *Battle Cry of Freedom*, 570.

8. Ibid. *See also* Foote, *The Civil War*, 765; Eicher, *The Longest Night*, 396–397.

9. Foote, *The Civil War*, 766.

10. Ibid., 766–767.

11. Edmonds, *Nurse and Spy*, 180.

12. Eicher, *The Longest Night*, 397–398.

13. Ibid.; *See also* McPherson, *Battle Cry of Freedom*, 570.

14. Ibid.

15. Edmonds, *Nurse and Spy*, 181.

16. Dannett, *She Rode With the Generals*, 208.

17. Edmonds, *Nurse and Spy*, 181.

18. Oates, *A Woman of Valor*, 110–111.

19. J. Robbins Journal.

20. Eicher, *The Longest Night*, 397–399; McPherson, *Battle Cry of Freedom*, 570–571; Oates, *A Woman of Valor*, 105; O'Reilly, *The Fredericksburg Campaign*, 57 et seq.

21. Oates, *A Woman of Valor*, 102–105.

22. Ibid., 105–106.

23. Eicher, *The Longest Night*, 398–399; Oates, *A Woman of Valor*, 106.

24. Oates, *A Woman of Valor*, 106–107.

25. Edmonds, *Nurse and Spy*, 181.

26. Dannett, *She Rode With the Generals*, 210.

27. Ibid. *See also* Edmonds, *Nurse and Spy*, 181.

28. J. Robbins Journal.

29. Edmonds, *Nurse and Spy*, 182.

30. Moe, *The Last Full Measure*, 207.

31. Eicher, *The Longest Night*, 401.

32. Stackpole, *The Fredericksburg Campaign*, 209.

33. Edmonds, *Nurse and Spy*, 182–183.

34. See Dannett, *She Rode With the Generals*, 213.

35. Edmonds, *Nurse and Spy*, 183.

36. O'Reilly, *The Fredericksburg Campaign*, 274.

37. Ibid.

38. Woodford, *Father Abraham's Children*, 76.

39. Stackpole, *The Fredericksburg Campaign*, 226.

40. Edmonds, *Nurse and Spy*, 184.

41. Oates, *A Woman of Valor*, 114–115.

42. Letter of A. J. Juckett, December 19, 1862, Fredericksburg, Virginia.

43. Edmonds, *Nurse and Spy*, 182.

44. J. Robbins Journal.

45. Ibid.

46. Ibid.

47. Ibid.

48. Ibid.

49. Ibid.

Chapter Nine

1. J. Robbins Journal.

2. Edmonds, *Nurse and Spy*, 187.

3. J. Robbins Journal.

4. Ibid.

5. Ibid.

6. Ibid.

7. J. Robbins Papers.

8. J. Robbins Journal.

9. Blanton and Cook, *They Fought Like Demons*, 103–104.

10. J. Robbins Journal.

11. Ibid.

12. Ibid.

13. Edmonds, *Nurse and Spy*, 188–189.

14. Ibid.

15. Ibid.

16. Ibid., 191.

17. Ibid., 192.

18. J. Robbins Journal.

19. Fort Scott *Monitor*, January 17, 1884.

20. Edmonds, *Nurse and Spy*, 219.

21. See Dannett, *She Rode With the Generals,* 226.

22. J. Robbins Journals.

23. Ibid.

24. Ibid.

25. Ibid.

26. Ibid.

27. William Boston Diary, 00.

28. Letter from Emma Edmonds to Jerome Robbins, J. Robbins Papers.

Chapter Ten

1. Dannett, *She Rode With the Generals,* 246–248.

2. Edmonds, *Nurse and Spy,* 126.

3. Ibid., Publisher's Note.

4. Dannett, *She Rode With the Generals,* 237–238.

5. The Seelyes of New Brunswick.

6. Detroit *Post and Tribune,* May 30, 1915, as quoted in Dannett, *She Rode With the Generals,* 239.

7. Dannett, *She Rode With the Generals,* 241.

8. Ibid., 242.

9. William Godman, *Gilbert Academy and Agricultural College* .

10. Ibid.

11. Dannett, *She Rode With the Generals,* 242.

12. Ibid., 243–244.

13. Leonard, *All the Daring of a Soldier,* 184; 235–237.

14. Robertson, *Michigan in the War,* 205.

Chapter Eleven

Like much of the information about Emma's early life, much of what is known about Emma's last years comes from Dannett's *She Rode With the Generals.* Dannett researched her book in the late 1950s, and had the opportunity to interview several of Emma's family members and acquaintances, including her daughter-in-law, Lucy Seelye, and various neighbors from her days in Fort Scott, who have since passed away. Other sources include newspaper articles, and documents contained in the Edmonds Pension File at the National Archives.

1. Dannett, *She Rode With the Generals,* 246–249.

2. Ibid.

3. Ibid.

4. Ibid., 254–256.

5. Ibid.

6. Ibid.

7. Edmonds Pension File.

8. Ibid.

9. Ibid.

10. Ibid.

11. Ibid.

12. Ibid.

13. Fort Scott *Monitor,* January 17, 1884.

14. Edmonds Pension File.

15. Ibid.

16. Dannett, *She Rode With the Generals,* 262.

17. Ibid., 263.

18. Ibid., 264.

19. Ibid.

20. Letter from Emma Edmonds to Richard Halstead, January 27, 1885, as quoted in Dannett, *She Rode With the Generals,* 265.

21. Dannett, *She Rode With the Generals,* 265.

22. Blanton and Cook, *They Fought Like Demons,* 187.

23. Edmonds Pension File.

24. Ibid.

25. Ibid.

26. Dannett, *She Rode With the Generals,* 274–275.

27. Ibid.

28. Ibid.

29. Ibid., 275–278.

30. Ibid.

31. Ibid., 279–282.

32. Ibid., 280–283.

33. Ibid.
34. Ibid., 285.
35. Ibid., 286–288.
36. Ibid.
37. Edmonds Pension File.
38. Dannett, *She Rode With the Generals*, 288–291.
39. Ibid., 289.
40. Ibid., 289–290.
41. Ibid.
42. Ibid., 291–295.
43. J. Robbins Papers.

BIBLIOGRAPHY

Unpublished Sources

Jerome John Robbins Papers, Michigan Historical Collections, Bentley Historical Library, University of Michigan, Ann Arbor.

RG 15. Record of the Veterans Administration, Sarah Emma Edmonds Pension File, Application #526889, Certificate #232136, National Archives, Washington, D.C.

RG 94. Records of the Adjutant General's Office, Compiled Military Service Records, National Archives, Washington, D.C.

Published Sources

Adams, George Worthington. *Doctors in Blue: The Medical History of the Union Army in the Civil War.* Baton Rouge: Louisiana State University Press, 1952.

Beatie, Russel H. *Army of the Potomac: Birth of Command November 1860–September 1861.* Da Capo Press, 2002.

Billings, John D. *Hardtack and Coffee: The Unwritten Story of Army Life.* Lincoln, Nebraska: University of Nebraska Press, 1993.

Blanton, DeAnne, and Lauren M. Cook. *They Fought Like Demons: Women Soldiers in the American Civil War.* Baton Rouge: Louisiana State University Press, 2002.

Bollett, Alfred Jay, M.D. *Civil War Medicine: Challenges and Triumphs.* Tucson, Arizona: Galen Press, Ltd., 2002.

Casper, Scott E., and Joanne D. Chaison and Jeffrey D. Groves, eds., *Perspectives on American Book History: Artifacts and Commentary.* Amherst: University of Massachusetts Press, 2002.

Catton, Bruce. *The Civil War*. Boston: Houghton Mifflin Company, 1960.

Catton, Bruce. *Mr. Lincoln's Army*. Garden City, New York: Doubleday & Company, Inc., 1951.

Cullen, Joseph P. *The Peninsula Campaign 1862: McClellan and Lee Struggle for Richmond*. New York: Bonanza Books, 1973.

Dannett, Sylvia G.L. *She Rode with the Generals: The True and Incredible Story of Sarah Emma Seelye, Alias Frank Thompson*. New York: Thomas Nelson & Sons, 1960.

Fanjoy, Harold N. and C. G. Ward. *The Seelys of New Brunswick*. Saint John New Brunswick: Ronalds Printing, 1992.

Fishel, Edwin C. *The Secret War for the Union: The Untold Story of Military Intelligence in the Civil War*. Boston: Houghton Mifflin Company, 1996.

Fladeland, Betty L. "New Light on Sarah Emma Edmonds Alias Frank Thompson." Michigan History 47 (1963): 357–62.

Foote, Shelby. *The Civil War: A Narrative. Fort Sumter to Perryville*. New York: Vintage Books, 1958.

Freeman, Douglas Southall. *Lee's Lieutenants: A Study in Command*. 3 vols. New York: Scribner's, 1942–44.

Freemon, Frank R. *Gangrene and Glory: Medical Care during the Civil War*. Madison, New Jersey: Farleigh Dickinson University Press, 1998.

Hasting, Earl, Jr., and David Hastings. *A Pitiless Rain: The Battle of Williamsburg, 1862*. Shippensburg, Pennsylvania: White Mane Publishing Company, 1997.

Johnston, Terry A., ed. *Him on One Side and Me on the Other: The Civil War Letters of Alexander Campbell and James Campbell*. Columbia, South Carolina: The University of South Carolina Press, 1999.

Leech, Margaret. *Reveille in Washington 1860–1865*. New York: Harper & Brothers, 1941.

Leonard, Elizabeth D. *All the Daring of a Soldier: Women in the Civil War Armies*. New York: W.W. Norton & Co., 1999.

Leonard, Elizabeth D. *Yankee Women: Gender Battles in the Civil War*. New York: W.W. Norton & Company, 1994.

Markle, Donald E. *Spies and Spymasters of the Civil War*. New York: Hippocrene Books, rev. ed. 2000.

McPherson, James M. *Battle Cry of Freedom: The Civil War Era*. New York: Ballantine Books, 1988.

Mitchell, Patricia B. *Home Front Regiment 1861–1865*. Chatham, Virginia, 1999.

Moe, Richard. *The Last Full Measure: The Life and Death of the First Minnesota Volunteers*. New York: Henry Holt and Company, 1993.

Oates, Stephen B. *A Woman of Valor: Clara Barton and the Civil War*. New York: The Free Press, 1994.

O'Reilly, Francis Augustin. *The Fredericksburg Campaign: Winter War on the Rappahannock*. Baton Rouge: Louisiana State University Press, 2003.

Pratt, Fletcher. *A Short History of the Civil War: Ordeal by Fire*. Mineola, New York: Dover Publications, Inc., 1948.

Robertson, James I. Jr. *Soldiers Blue and Gray,* Columbia, South Carolina: University of South Carolina Press, 1998.

Robertson, John. *Michigan in the War,* Lansing, Michigan: W.S. George, 1882.

Salmon, Marylnn. *Women and the Law of Property in Early America*. Chapel Hill: The University of North Carolina Press, 1986.

Sears, Stephen W. *To the Gates of Richmond: The Peninsula Campaign*. Boston: Houghton Mifflin Company, 1992.

Shep, R.L. *Civil War Era Etiquette*. Mendocino: R.L. Shep, 1988.

Stackpole, Edward J. *The Fredericksburg Campaign*. Mechanicsville, Virginia: Stackpole Books, 1957.

Stern, Philip Van Doren. *Secret Missions of the Civil War*. New York: Wing Books, 1959.

Tsui, Bonnie. *She Went to the Field: Women Soldiers of the Civil War,* Guilford, Connecticut: TwoDot, 2003.

Varhola, Michael J. *Everyday Life During the Civil War*. Cincinnati, Ohio: Writer's Digest Books, 1999.

Wiley, Bell Irvin. *The Life of Billy Yank: The Common Soldier of the Union*. Baton Rouge: Louisiana State University Press, 1952.

Woodford, Frank B. *Father Abraham's Children: Michigan Episodes in the Civil War*. Detroit: Wayne State University Press, 1961.

Bibliography

Woodworth, Steven E. *While God is Marching On: The Religious World of Civil War Soldiers*. Lawrence, Kansas: The University of Kansas Press, 2001.

Woolsey, Jane Stuart. *Hospital Days: Reminiscence of a Civil War Nurse*. Roseville, Minnesota: Edinborough Press, 1996.

ACKNOWLEDGMENTS

Maybe it is not a coincidence that I have a number of smart, amazing women to thank for helping me tell this story about one of their own. Stephanie Cabot is certainly all that and so much more, including, incidentally, my agent. Whether talking to grates or to God, I am blessed to call her friend. I am also deeply indebted to the incomparable Suzanne Gluck for taking me on in the beginning and making this book possible.

At Free Press, I was beyond lucky to be under the wing of my wonderful editor, Liz Stein, whose talent, insight and commitment made the book not just a reality, but so much better than it otherwise would have been. Thanks also to Maris Kreizman for all of her hard work and enthusiasm; the wonderful copyeditors at Free Press, who repeatedly saved me from myself; and to Rachel Klayman for first believing in this project. I am also deeply grateful to Clara Bingham, who introduced me to the writer's life, and whose fearlessness and honesty I admire beyond words.

Like anyone interested in Emma, I am indebted to the late Sylvia Dannett, who was among the first to recognize the importance of Emma's story. Without her primary research, done when people who knew Emma were still alive and able to share their recollections, this book would not have been possible. Thanks also to the staff at the Bentley Historical Library at the University of Michigan; Don Cooper of Nova Scotia, Canada, who generously helped a stranger navigate the genealogical records of York County, New Brunswick; and Harold Fanjoy, for sending me the Seely family history, The Seelys of New Brunswick.

I also owe an enormous debt of gratitude to my colleagues at NASD for supporting this project in innumerable ways and for being the best people to work with that I can imagine, particularly Elisse Walter, who proves it is possible to be both brilliant and genuinely kind; Marc Menchel, whose own

Acknowledgments

book I am looking so forward to reading, when he finally decides to write it; and Eric Moss, for being so supportive and fun to work with, besides.

And then there is the home front. Many thanks to my boys, Sam and Will, for their patience and understanding; to my sister, Milly Armao, for her steady encouragement; and to my parents, Jean and Bill Leedy, for everything, of course, but in particular, to my dad for giving me the history bug and sharing his expertise, and to my mom for passing along her love of the written word, if not her proofreading skills. And, finally, to Douglas, who, like Emma, believes in charting his own course. Thank you for your unflagging support; your ridiculously generous spirit, and most of all, for showing me and our boys that life is most interesting not just when you dream big, but when you have the courage to try to make those dreams come true.

INDEX

Abolitionist movement, 18, 140

Alabama, 20

Alexander, Charles W., 165–166

Alexandria, Virginia, 32, 73, 133, 138

Alexandria and Orange railroad line, 145, 147

Anderson, Robert, 22

Anesthetics, 61

Antietam, Battle of, 138–139, 141, 160, 182

Appomattox Court House, 186

Aquia Creek Wharf, Virginia, 150, 161, 169

Arlington, Virginia, 56, 62

Arlington National Cemetery, 58

Army Medical Corps, 44

Arthur, Chester A., 207

Balloon reconnaissance, 82–83

Ballou, Maturin, 5

Baltimore, Maryland, 35

Barnett, Thomas, 203

Barton, Clara, 45–46, 139–140, 153, 159, 182

Battle Creek Artillery, 29

Beauregard, P.G.T., 21, 22, 47, 48, 54

Belle Island, 140

Belvedere (transport), 161

Benjamin, Milton, 199

Blackburn's Ford, Virginia, 53, 62, 65, 89

Blackwell, Elizabeth, 43

Blair, Austin, 24

Blockade, 48, 132

Bonine, E.J., 79–80, 104, 162, 175

Boston, William, 175–176, 196, 204

Bottom's Bridge, Virginia, 117, 119

Bounties, 28

Brown, James, 205

Brown, John, 18

Brownell, Katy, 26–27

Buchanan, James, 21

Bull Run, First Battle of, 53–63, 65, 67, 89, 133, 148, 163, 199

Bull Run, Second Battle of, 133–134, 136–139, 143, 148, 182, 210, 216

Bull Run creek, 47, 52–54, 133

Burnside, Ambrose, 146–149, 151, 152, 154–156, 158, 159, 163, 164, 168–169

Burnside's Mud March, 168–169

California, Missouri, 192

Cameron, Scott, 44

Campbell, Fanny (fictional character), 5–6, 8, 27, 39, 166

Camp Curtis, Pennsylvania, 34

Camp Parole, Annapolis, 128–129, 137, 138, 151, 155, 160, 162

Centreville, Virginia, 52–54, 56, 89, 133, 148

Chantilly, Virginia, 133

Charlevoix, Michigan, 189

Chesapeake Bay, 128–129

Chickahominy River, 96, 97, 102, 104, 106, 107, 109–111, 114, 117, 119, 172

Christian Commission, 185

Christianity, 63–64

Clelland, Dr., 162, 167

Cleveland, Grover, 213

Cleveland, Ohio, 33, 188

Cold Harbor, Virginia, 98

Committee on Invalid Pensions, 203

Committee on Military Affairs, 203, 205

Confederate States of America, formation of, 20

Constitution of the United States, 25

Corey, Anna. See Sunderlin, Anna Corey

Couch, Darius, 158, 159

Court Street Methodist Episcopal Church, Flint, 20, 24

Cowles, Albert, 201–202

Crimean War, 44

Culpeper, Virginia, 145, 147, 148

Cutcheon, Byron M., 157, 203, 205–207, 211–213

Davis, Jefferson, 20–22

D'Esay, Pauline, 165–166

Detroit, Michigan, 17, 19, 25, 32

Diarrhea, 41

Disease, 41–42, 68, 98, 108, 172, 191, 192, 203, 219

Divers, Bridget, 26–27

Dix, Dorothea, 43–45

Dix, John, 78, 128

Domestic skills, 38–39

Douglas, Stephen, 19

Draft, 28

Dred Scott Decision of 1857, 18

Dysentery, 68

Edmonds, Sarah Emma (Frank Thompson)

antagonism toward men, 2, 4

at Antietam, 139, 182

birth of, 1, 2

birth of children, 189

book written by, 181–185, 198–200

brother Thomas, relationship with, 4, 12, 13, 69, 188

burial of, 219

caught behind enemy lines, 118, 119

childhood of, 3–4

compared to Clara Barton, 45–46

confidence in disguise, 39

dating by, 15–16
death of, 219
death of horse of, 142, 143
deserter status of, 94, 172, 174, 175, 180, 193, 195, 196, 203–207, 211–213
dying men, comfort to, 56–58, 62, 92–93, 99
education of, 3, 28, 63, 187
enlistment of, 25–29, 181
at Fair Oaks, 74
finances of, 12, 13, 15, 16, 185
under fire, 53, 89–91, 103, 118, 119
first disguise of, 8–10
at Fort Monroe, 76–79
at Fort Wayne, 29–32
at Fredericksburg, 153–155, 157, 159, 160
gossip about, 168, 175–176, 209–211
health of, 98, 172–173, 191–192, 202, 203, 205, 207, 216, 219
injuries of, 135–136, 142, 143, 203, 216–217
intelligence activities of, 84–88, 97–100, 134–135, 170–172, 182, 195, 205–206, 213–214, 221–222
at La Teche Seminary, 190–191
leaves home, 6–7
as mail carrier, 75–76, 83, 84, 96, 108–109, 129, 135, 141, 143, 148, 150, 153, 164, 169, 195, 200, 206, 211, 212, 221
at Malvern Hill, 123–124
marksmanship of, 13, 197–198, 214
marriage of, 188
married life of, 188–193
McClellan and, 60, 61, 94, 104, 121, 133, 146
medical examinations and, 30–31, 85, 136, 217
membership in Grand Army of the Republic, 218–219
as nurse, 42–43, 46–47, 56–57, 61–62, 66, 73, 75, 98–99, 103, 105, 130, 181, 185, 200, 205
parents of, 1–4
peddlar woman disguise of, 98, 100, 101, 182
pension, campaign for, 192–205, 216–218
physical appearance of, 9, 30, 37, 198, 216
Poe as mentor to, 75, 94
as Poe's orderly, 155, 157, 159, 162, 164, 173, 174, 203, 206, 208, 211
portrait of, iv
privacy for, 31–32, 37–38
reaction to outbreak of war, 23
reading by, 3, 5–6
rebel soldier disguise of, 170–171
at regimental reunion, 207–210

Edmonds, Sarah Emma *(cont.)*
  Reid, relationship with,
    163–165, 167, 173, 175–176
  religion and, 3, 7, 20, 40, 63, 64,
    67, 103
  Robbins, relationship with,
    63–73, 79, 117, 130,
    137–138, 151, 162, 164–167,
    169–170, 172–177, 210, 222
  at Second Bull Run, 134, 143,
    182, 210, 216
  with Second Michigan, 33–42,
    49–55, 57, 58, 63, 75–79,
    89–91, 102, 113, 114, 122,
    132–133, 138–139, 141, 143,
    148, 157, 199, 202–203, 205,
    207–210
  Seelye, relationship with,
    186–189
  slave disguise of, 85–87, 97–98,
    134, 182
  slavery and, 79–80
  Stewart, relationship with, 37,
    91, 133, 179–180, 197–199
  as traveling book salesman, 7–10,
    12–17, 19, 20, 181
  uniform, boots and weapons of,
    30
  veterans' home, plans for, 207,
    211–213, 215
Edmondson, Betsy, 1–4, 6–7, 12–13,
    187
Edmondson, Frances, 12, 187
Edmondson, Isaac, 1–4, 6–9, 13, 70,
    187

Edmondson, Thomas, 2–4, 12, 13,
    69, 187, 188
Edward's Ferry, Virginia, 141
Emancipation Proclamation, 140
England, 48, 68, 132
Ether, 61
Etheridge, Annie, 26–27
Evanston, Illinois, 189
Ewell, Richard, 99

Fairfax, Virginia, 51, 133
Fairfax Station, Virginia, 139
Fair Oaks, Battle of, 74, 102–105,
    107, 109
Fair Oaks, Virginia, 97
Falmouth, Virginia, 147–150, 161,
    164
*Fanny Campbell, the Female Pirate
    Captain* (Ballou), 5, 70, 166
Farnum, Hattie. *See* Robbins, Hattie
    Farnum
Feminine ideal, 11
Fenton, Judge, 25
Fiftieth New York, 153
First Indiana Cavalry, 134
First Massachusetts, 35, 49
First Michigan, 24–25, 32
Flint, Michigan, 19–20, 22,
    179–180, 197, 208
Flint Union Grays, 24–26, 29
Florida, 20
Fort Monroe, Virginia, 76–81, 83,
    108, 128, 169–170
Fort Scott, Kansas, 192, 204, 207,
    213–215

Fort Sumter, South Carolina, 21–22, 34, 47

Fort Wayne, Michigan, 29–32, 37, 63

Fourth Cavalry, 127

Fourth Massachusetts, 27

France, 48, 68, 132

Franklin, Benjamin, 40

Franklin, William, 154, 156, 158–159, 169

Frederick, Maryland, 138, 139

Frederick, Richmond and Potomac railroad line, 147

Fredericksburg, Virginia, 76, 97, 147–150
   Battle of, 150–161, 164–165, 203

Freedmen's Aid Society, 190

Free slaves, 129–130

Gaines' Mill, Virginia, 116, 117, 119, 121, 123

Galloway, Mary, 139–140

Geneva Medical College, 43

Georgetown, Virginia, 61

Georgia, 20

Gilbert, William, 191

Gilbert Academy, 191

Glendale, Virginia, 121

Godman, William, 190–191

Goode, Thomas, 128

Grand Army of the Republic, 202, 218–219

Grand Reviews, 63

Grant, Ulysses S., 170, 186

Great Awakening, 63

Greeley, Horace, 17, 48

Hagler, Isaac, 218

Halifax, Nova Scotia, 15

Hall, Alan, 98–101

Halstead, Richard, 209–210

Hampton, Virginia, 79, 82, 83

Handy, W.J., 208–209

Hardtack, 37

Harpers Ferry, Virginia, 47, 48, 54, 141, 145, 149, 181, 185, 186
   John Brown's raid on, 18

Harper's New Monthly, 11

Harrisburg, Pennsylvania, 34

Harrison's Landing, Virginia, 114, 116, 120, 122, 125, 126, 129, 131, 138

Harter, Thomas, 134–135

Hartford, Connecticut, 13–14, 17, 184

Hartzell, J.C., 190

Heintzelman, Samuel P., 102, 114, 134, 135

Hodgers, Jennie (alias Alfred Cashiers), 28, 192

Holmes, Oliver Wendell, 183

Hooker, Joseph, 169

Howard, Sumner, 199, 200

Humphrey, William, 174

Hurlbert, A.M., 14, 17, 184, 185, 195, 200–201, 205

Infant mortality rate, 189

Ingalls, Rufus, 116

Intelligence activities, 82–88,
97–100, 134–135, 166,
170–172, 182, 195, 205–206,
213–214, 221–222

Jackson, Thomas "Stonewall," 55,
101, 110, 113, 115, 116,
126–127, 133, 137
James River, 76, 77, 80, 81, 97, 111,
114, 116, 117, 120, 122, 125,
127, 128, 140
Joan of Arc, 27, 39
Johnston, Joe, 47, 48, 102, 109
Joslin, T.J., 20, 25, 204

Kansas, 18
Kansas City, 189
Kansas-Nebraska Act of 1854, 18
Kearney, Philip, 103
Kentucky, 170–173, 182, 195, 205
Keyes, Erasmus, 97

Lacy, James Horace, 151, 159
*Ladies' Guide to Perfect Gentility in
Manners, Dress, and Conversa-
tion,* 10
La Porte, Texas, 215, 217–219
Larned, Sylvester, 205, 208
La Teche Seminary, 190–191
Lebanon, Kentucky, 170, 195, 205
Lee, Fitzhugh, 110, 126
Lee, Robert E., 58, 95, 131, 135,
137, 169
at Fredericksburg, 150–152,
154–156

in Maryland, 138, 140
Peninsula campaign and,
109–110, 113, 115–117, 121,
123, 133, 141, 145, 147, 148
surrender by, 186
Lee, William "Rooney," 95, 110
Lincoln, Abraham, 34, 36, 44, 49,
68, 88, 188
Burnside and, 147
call to arms by, 22–24, 26
election of 1860 and, 17–19
emancipation of slaves and,
131–132, 140
Fort Sumter and, 21–22
McClellan and, 67, 76, 96–97,
106, 107, 120–121, 130–131,
137, 140–141, 145–146
Scott and, 48, 59
slavery and, 17, 19
Literacy rate, 19
Logan, Captain, 170–171
Longstreet, James, 145, 147
Louisiana, 20
Lovettsville, Virginia, 141
Lowe, Thaddeus, 82–83
Lyster, Henry B., 42, 186, 210

Magaguadavic Lake, 1–4, 7, 9, 73,
187, 216
Magruder, John B., 79, 82, 83, 88,
89
Malaria, 98, 108, 172, 191, 192,
203, 219
Malvern Hill, Battle of, 122–125,
127

Manassas, Battles of. *See* Bull Run,
    First and Second Battle of
Manassas Junction, 47–49, 51–53,
    76, 131, 133
Mansion House hospital, Alexandria,
    73, 75
Marcy, Robert, 88
Marye's Heights, Fredericksburg,
    155–158
Maryland, 34–35, 62, 131, 138–140
McCall, General, 106
McClellan, George, 68, 75, 160,
    164, 218
    Emma's (Frank's) loyalty to, 60,
        61, 94, 104, 121, 133, 146
    intelligence sources of, 82–85,
        88, 97, 134, 166
    Lincoln and, 67, 76, 96–97, 106,
        107, 120–121, 130–131, 137,
        140–141, 145–146
    organization of army by, 60, 62,
        63
    Peninsula campaign and, 76–77,
        81–83, 86, 89, 92, 95–97,
        101, 102, 105–107, 109,
        113–117, 119–127, 130, 131
    physical appearance of, 59, 77
    popularity of and loyalty to,
        59–61, 137, 146
    portrait of, 94
    reaction to battlefield suffering,
        105–107
    relieved of command, 145–146
    removal and reinstatement of,
        132, 137

Yorktown and, 82, 88, 96, 107,
    140
McCreery, William, 199–200
McDowell, Irwin, 48–49, 52–55, 97,
    101, 106, 116, 121
McKee, Major, 99, 100
Mechanicsville, Battle of, 115–116
*Memoirs of a Soldier, Nurse and Spy: A
    Woman's Adventures in the
    Union Army* (Edmonds), 74,
    101, 118, 181–185, 198–199,
    200, 206
Mercury poisoning, 61
Merrimac (ironclad), 81
Mexican War, 17, 20, 47, 59, 61, 95
Miasma, 79, 108
Michigan, 17, 19–20, 22, 24–26,
    29–33
Michigan in the War (Robertson),
    194–195, 206, 221
Mississippi, 20
Missouri, 17
Missouri Compromise, 17
Moffit, Annie, 6–7
Morse, William F., 24–26, 29, 90–91,
    133, 194, 204, 208
Munson's Hill, Virginia, 47

Napoleon Bonaparte, 59–60
New Brunswick, Canada, 1–8, 15,
    187
New Orleans University, 191
Nightingale, Florence, 41, 44
Ninety-fifth Illinois, 28
Ninth Army Corps, 163, 169

Ninth Virginia Cavalry, 95
Norfolk, Virginia, 114
Notes on Nursing (Nightingale), 41
Nova Scotia, 15, 17, 19
Nursing, 42–47, 56–57, 61–62, 66,
    73, 75, 98–99, 103, 105, 130,
    181, 185, 200, 205

Oak Grove, Battle of, 114–115
Oberlin College, 187
O'Brien, R., 74, 101, 118

Palmer, Alonzo B., 42, 79, 186
Pamunkey River, 81, 95, 111
Panic of 1893, 215
Parolees, 126–128, 133, 137–138, 140
Patterson, Mary, 187
*Pauline of the Potomac, or General Mc-
    Clellan's Spy* (Alexander), 165–166
Peninsula campaign, 76–83, 86, 89,
    92, 95–97, 101, 102, 105–107,
    109–110, 113–117, 119–133,
    140–141, 145, 147, 148, 150,
    181–182
Pennsylvania, 33–34, 131
Perrigo, Henriette, 7
Pinkerton, Allan, 82–84, 88, 134
Pittsburgh, Pennsylvania, 33
Poe, Nellie, 208, 210, 212
Poe, Orlando Metcalf, 75, 76, 78,
    84, 89, 97, 130, 133, 134, 148,
    150, 153–155, 163
    Emma (Frank) as orderly to,
        155, 157, 159, 162, 164, 173,
        174, 203, 206, 208, 211

at Fredericksburg, 158–159, 173
    portrait of, 94
    resignation as colonel, 173–174
    testimonial on Emma's (Frank's)
        wartime conduct, 94,
        211–212
Pope, John, 131–134, 139
Porch, Mary, 192–193
Porter, Fitz-John, 106, 115–117,
    119
Potomac River, 36, 47, 62
Pratt, Charles, 20
Pratt, Lara, 20
Presidential election of 1860, 17–19
Prospect Hill, Fredericksburg, 155,
    156, 158

Quinine, 108

Railroads, 48, 96, 97, 101, 102, 145,
    147, 188
Rappahannock River, 147–150, 154,
    159, 162, 164, 168
Recreation, 40
Reid, James, 170, 181, 186, 204
    Emma (Frank), relationship with,
        163–165, 167, 173, 175–176
    resignation and departure of,
        173–174
Religion, 3, 7, 20, 40, 63, 64, 67, 103
Republican Party, 18–19
Revivalism, 63–64
Revolutionary War, 27, 188
Richardson, Israel B. (Fighting Dick),
    31, 36, 52, 53, 75

Richmond, Lewis, 173

Richmond, Virginia, 53, 76, 77, 81, 83, 84, 88–89, 91, 96, 97, 101, 102, 105–107, 109, 113–117, 120, 121, 125, 126, 130–132, 141, 145, 147

Rich Mountain, Virginia, 59

Robbins, Hattie Farnum, 185, 208, 210

Robbins, Jerome John, 77, 78, 80, 88, 92, 94, 108, 140, 155, 163, 180, 181, 196, 208

death of, 219

Emma (Frank), relationship with, 63–73, 79, 117, 130, 137–138, 151, 162, 164–167, 169–170, 172–177, 210, 222

life after the war, 185–186

marriage of, 186

on McClellan, 146

mentioned in Emma's book, 181–182

as parolee, 126–129, 133, 137–138, 151, 160, 162

portrait of, 112

rejoins regiment, 160–162

at Talleysville hospital, 104, 109, 111–112, 117, 126

at Vicksburg, 182

Robertson, John, 194, 221

Rosecrans, William, 59

Runaway slaves, 79–81, 85

Sager Brown, 191

St. Mary Parish, Louisiana, 190

Salisbury, Westmoreland County, 6, 7

Sampson, Deborah (alias Robert Shurtleff), 27

Sanitation, 32, 38, 41, 68

San Jacinto Bay, 215

Savage's Station, Virginia, 97, 117, 121, 161, 162

Schneider, Frederick, 202, 205

Scott, Winfield, 36, 47–49, 55, 59, 67

Scott Guard, 29

Secession, 19, 20

Second Michigan, 29–42, 49–55, 57, 58, 62, 63, 75–79, 83, 89–91, 102, 113, 114, 122, 132–133, 136, 138–139, 141, 143, 148, 157, 158, 160, 161, 162, 169, 172, 194–195, 202–203, 205, 207–210

Secret Service of the United States, 84

Seelye, Alice Louise, 189, 191, 192, 215

Seelye, Charles, 189, 191, 192, 208, 212, 215

Seelye, Freddy, 189, 191, 192, 208, 212, 214–216, 218

Seelye, Hannah, 188

Seelye, Harry, 216

Seelye, Linus, 207, 208, 212, 214–216, 218

death of, 219

Emma (Frank), relationship with, 186–189

marriage to Emma, 188

married life of, 188–193

Seelye, Lucy Sterling, 214–216,
    218
Seelye, Mrs. Linus. *See* Edmonds,
    Sarah Emma (Frank Thompson)
Seelye Hill, Fort Scott, 207
Seven Days' battles, 115–118,
    181–182
Seventh Michigan, 154
Seventy-ninth New York Volunteers
    (Highlanders), 60, 157,
    163–165
Sharpsburg, Maryland, 138
Shenandoah Valley, 88, 101, 110,
    141, 145
Sick call, 40–41
Silver nitrate solution, 85, 86
Sixteenth Michigan, 161
Sixth Massachusetts, 35
Slavery, 17–19, 64, 79–81, 85–87,
    131–132, 140
South Carolina, 19–22
Southworth, George, 162
Stanton, Edwin, 120
Stewart, Damon, 194, 196, 208,
    213
    Emma (Frank), relationship with,
        37, 91, 133, 179–180,
        197–199
Stowe, Harriet Beecher, 185
Stuart, James Ewell Brown "Jeb,"
    110–114, 121, 126, 127, 135
Subscription publishing industry, 7–8
Sudley Springs, Virginia, 54, 55
Sumner, Edwin, 103, 104, 148–150,
    153, 156, 158

Sunderlin, Aaron, 185, 186
Sunderlin, Anna Corey, 66, 69, 71,
    73, 109, 112, 137, 164, 166,
    167, 176–177, 185
Supreme Court of the United States,
    18
Swamp fever, 108

Talleysville, Virginia, 104, 109, 111,
    117, 126–128, 130
Temperance movement, 64, 187
Texas, 20, 215, 217–219
Third Michigan, 27, 36, 49,
    161–162
Thirty-seventh New York, 78
Thirty-third Virginia, 55
Thompson, Frank. *See* Edmonds,
    Sarah Emma (Frank Thompson)
Tunstall's Station, Virginia, 111
Turner, William, 200, 208
Twelfth New York, 36, 49
Twentieth Michigan, 175, 203
Tyler, Daniel, 52, 53
Typhoid, 41–42, 68, 98

Uncle Tom's Cabin (Stowe), 185
United Methodist Church,
    189–191
U.S. Patent Office, 40, 46
U.S. Sanitary Commission, 41, 181,
    199, 200

Vanderbilt (steamer), 77–78
Vicksburg, Mississippi, 170, 182
Volunteer militias, 23–24

W.S. Williams & Company, 14, 15

Wakeman, Sarah Rosetta (alias Lyons Wakeman), 28

Walker, Mary, 43

War Department, 24, 26, 44, 192, 193, 213, 216

War of 1812, 29, 47, 78

Warrenton Junction, Virginia, 133, 134, 141, 145, 147

Warrenton Turnpike, Virginia, 52, 54, 56

Washington, D.C., 33–36, 40, 47, 55, 58–68, 101, 129, 136–138

Washington, George, 40, 95

Washington, Martha Custis, 95, 126

Webster, Timothy, 84

Weisel, Dr., 111–112, 127

West Point, 95

White House Landing, Virginia, 95, 96, 104, 105, 111, 114, 116, 117, 121, 126, 128

White Oak Swamp, Virginia, 122

Williamsburg, Virginia, 76, 98, 121
    Battle of, 89–92, 103, 179, 204

Winans, E.B., 203, 207

Women's clothing, 10–11

Women's suffrage movement, 187

York River, 76, 81–82, 95, 113, 114, 116, 121

Yorktown, Virginia, 76, 81–83, 88, 96, 107, 114, 140, 182